EAST ANGLIAN ARCHAEOLOGY

Excavations at Billingborough, Lincolnshire, 1975–8: a Bronze–Iron Age Settlement and Salt-working Site

by Peter Chowne,
Rosamund M.J. Cleal and
A.P. Fitzpatrick with
Phil Andrews

with contributions from
Carol S.M. Allen, Joanna K.F. Bacon,
Justine Bayley, Aiden Challis, C.A.I. French,
Guy Grainger, Jill Harden, Hilary Healey,
Mary Iles, M. Laidlaw, Fiona Roe

and illustrations by
Kim Addy, Joanna K.F. Bacon, S.E. James,
Jill Harden, Hilary Healey, Peter Chowne

East Anglian Archaeology
Report No. 94, 2001

Wessex Archaeology

EAST ANGLIAN ARCHAEOLOGY
REPORT NO.94

Published by
The Trust for Wessex Archaeology Ltd
Portway House
Old Sarum Park
Salisbury
Wilts SP4 6EB

in conjunction with
The Scole Archaeological Committee

Editor: David Buckley
Managing Editor: Jenny Glazebrook

Scole Editorial Sub-committee:
Brian Ayers, Archaeology and Environment Officer, Norfolk Museums Service
David Buckley, County Archaeologist, Essex Planning Department
Keith Wade, Archaeological Service Manager, Suffolk County Council
Peter Wade-Martins
Stanley West

Set in Times Roman by Joan Daniells and Jenny Glazebrook using Corel Ventura™
Printed by Witley Press Ltd., Hunstanton, Norfolk

ISBN 1 874350 32 9
ISSN 0307 2460

For details of *East Anglian Archaeology*, see last page

This volume is published with the aid of a grant from English Heritage

Cover photograph:
Excavations in progress in 1978, looking west
Photo: Peter Chowne

Contents

List of Plates vi
List of Figures vi
List of Tables vii
Contributors vii
Acknowledgements viii
Summary/Résumé/Zusammenfassung ix

Chapter 1. Introduction, by Peter Chowne, A.P. Fitzpatrick and Phil Andrews

I.   Summary 1
II. Project background 1
III. Geology and topography 1
IV. Excavation strategy and method 2
V. Site dating and phasing 5

Chapter 2. The Excavations

I.   Pre-Middle Bronze Age activity, by
     Rosamund M.J. Cleal 7
II. Phase 1: Middle–Late Bronze Age, by
     Rosamund M.J. Cleal and Peter Chowne ... 7
     Enclosure 1 7
     Enclosure 1: other features 9
III. Phase 2: Late Bronze Age–Early Iron
     Age, by Rosamund M.J. Cleal and
     Peter Chowne 14
     Pits 14
     Hearths 14
     Other contexts 14
IV. Phase 3: Middle–Late Iron Age, by
     A.P. Fitzpatrick and Peter Chowne ... 16
     Introduction 16
     Enclosure 2 17
     Field system associated with Enclosure 2 ... 19
     Enclosure 3 19
     Features outside Enclosures 2 and 3 ... 20
V. Phase 4: Early Romano-British, by
     A.P. Fitzpatrick and Peter Chowne ... 20
     Dating 20

Chapter 3. The Artefacts

I.   Copper alloy objects, by
     Joanna K.F. Bacon and A.P. Fitzpatrick ... 21
     Phase 1 21
     Phase 3 21
     Phase 4 21
     Unphased 22
     Catalogue 23
II. Iron objects, by A.P. Fitzpatrick and
     Joanna K.F. Bacon 23
     Tools 23
     Objects of personal adornment 24
     Weapons 24
     Catalogue 24
III. Technological finds, by Justine Bayley ... 25
IV. Flint, by Jill Harden 26
     Introduction 26
     Analysis 26

Results 26
Discussion 28
Catalogue 29
V. Jet and other worked stone, by
     Joanna K.F. Bacon and Fiona Roe ... 29
     Jet 29
     Stone axe-hammer 29
     Other stone finds 30
     Catalogue 30
VI. Prehistoric pottery, by
     Rosamund M.J. Cleal 31
     Introduction 31
     Methods 31
     Neolithic pottery 31
     Early Bronze Age pottery 31
     Phase 1 pottery 32
     Discussion 38
     Phase 2 pottery 40
     Discussion 40
     Phase 3 pottery 42
     Discussion 42
     Phase 4 pottery 45
     Fabric analysis, by Carol S.M. Allen ... 45
     Pottery catalogue (compiled by
     Aiden Challis with M. Laidlaw) 47
VII. Post-Iron Age pottery from later features
     and deposits, by Hilary Healey 56
     Romano-British 56
     Medieval 56
     Post-medieval 56
VIII. Briquetage, by Rosamund M.J. Cleal
     and Joanna K.F. Bacon 56
     Introduction 56
     Briquetage containers, by
     Rosamund M.J. Cleal 57
     Phase 2 briquetage containers 57
     Briquetage in grog-tempered fabrics ... 58
     Catalogue 58
     Non-container briquetage, by
     Joanna K.F. Bacon 59
     Catalogue 60
IX. Fired clay, by Joanna K.F. Bacon 67
     Loomweights 67
     Mould 67
     Catalogue 67
X. Worked bone and antler, by
     Joanna K.F. Bacon 68
     Phase 1 68
     Later Phases 68
     Catalogue 68
XI. Human skeletal material, by
     Justine Bayley 73
     Introduction 73
     The articulated burials, by Guy Grainger ... 73
     Catalogue 73
     Description of the skull fragments ... 77
     Discussion 78

Chapter 4. Site Economy and Environment
I.   Animal bone, by Mary Iles   79
        Introduction and methods   79
        Results: general introduction   79
        Major domesticates: results by phase   79
        Element representation for cattle and
        sheep/goat   83
        Other species   84
        Butchery patterns   84
        Discussion and conclusions   84
II.   Molluscs, by C.A.I. French   86
        Introduction   86
        The profile   88
        Results and interpretation   88
        Discussion   88

Chapter 5. Discussion, by
Rosamund M.J. Cleal, A.P. Fitzpatrick and
Phil Andrews
I.   Pre-Mid 2nd Millennium BC   89
II.   Phase 1: Middle–Late Bronze Age
        (Mid–Late 2nd Millennium BC)   89
III.   Phase 2: Late Bronze Age–Early Iron Age
        (Early–Mid 1st Millennium BC)   92
IV.   Phase 3: Middle–Late Iron Age
        (Later 1st Millennium BC)   93
V.   Phase 4: Early Romano-British
        (1st century AD)   95

Bibliography   96
Index, by S. Vaughan   101

List of Plates

Pl. I   1978 excavation from the air, facing
        west   2
Pl. II   Grave *78183*. 1m scale   7
Pl. III Enclosure 1 ditch *78145*, facing
        north. 2m scale   8
Pl. IV Four-post structure F and possible
        fence line, facing west. 2m scale   13
Pl. V   Sunken-feature *752*, facing west.
        2m scales   13
Pl. VI Structure *77102*, facing west. 2m scale   15
Pl. VII 1978 excavation from the air, facing
        south-east   18
Pl. VIII Enclosure 3 ditch *78135*, facing
        north. 2m scale   18
Pl. IX Iron 'poker' in upper fill of ditch
        7710. (Scale = 170mm)   25
Pl. X   Worked human bone: No. 2,
        showing the inner table which was

        not cut and a shallow second cut
        over the right orbit. (Scale = 20mm)   75
Pl. XI Worked human bone: No. 4,
        showing the change in direction of
        the cut and a slight mis-cut below.
        (Scale = 20mm)   75
Pl. XII Worked human bone: No. 5, showing
        saw marks and changes in direction
        on the cut edge. (Scale= 20mm)   76
Pl. XIII Worked human bone: No. 5,
        showing neatly drilled perforations.
        (Scale = 20mm)   76
Pl. XIV Worked human bone: No. 6,
        showing the irregular perforation.
        (Scale = 20mm)   77
Pl. XV Worked human bone: No. 9, showing
        polished bevel edge. (Scale = 50mm)   77

List of Figures

Fig. 1   Location maps   3
Fig. 2   Cropmark evidence and excavated
        area (after Hampton 1983, fig. 81)   4
Fig. 3   Plan all features   6
Fig. 4   Plan pre-Phase 1 and Phase 1
        features   8
Fig. 5   Sections Enclosure 1 ditch   10
Fig. 6   Plan structures and features at east
        end of Enclosure 1   11
Fig.7   Sections post-holes of four-post
        structures A–F   12
Fig. 8   Plan Phase 2 features   15
Fig. 9   Plan Phase 3 features   16
Fig. 10 Sections ditches Enclosures 2 and 3   17
Fig. 11 Plan Phase 4 features   19
Fig. 12 Sections ditches   20

Fig. 13 Copper alloy objects   22
Fig. 14 Iron object: 'poker'   24
Fig. 15 Iron objects   24
Fig. 16 Flint objects   28
Fig. 17 Flint: measurements of non-
        retouched and utilised flakes   29
Fig. 18 Jet objects   30
Fig. 19 Stone object: axe-hammer   30
Fig. 20 Pottery. Late Neolithic and Early
        Bronze Age   47
Fig. 21 Pottery. Middle Bronze Age (Phase 1)   48
Fig. 22 Pottery. Middle Bronze Age (Phase 1)   49
Fig. 23 Pottery. Middle Bronze Age (Phase 1)   50
Fig. 24 Pottery. Middle Bronze Age (Phase 1).
        (Nos 49-54 are possibly briquetage
        in a grog-tempered fabric)   52

Fig. 25	Pottery. Late Bronze Age/Early Iron Age (Phase 2)	52
Fig. 26	Pottery. Middle–Late Iron Age (Phase 3)	53
Fig. 27	Pottery. Middle–Late Iron Age (Phase 3)	54
Fig. 28	Pottery. Middle–Late Iron Age (Phase 3)	55
Fig. 29	Briquetage containers	59
Fig. 30	Fired clay: briquetage	61
Fig. 31	Fired clay: briquetage	62
Fig. 32	Fired clay: briquetage	63
Fig. 33	Fired clay: briquetage	64
Fig. 34	Fired clay: briquetage	65
Fig. 35	Fired clay: loomweights	66
Fig. 36	Fired clay: loomweight, mould	67
Fig. 37	Worked bone and antler (Phases 1 and 2)	69
Fig. 38	Worked bone and antler (Phases 3 and 4)	70
Fig. 39	Worked bone and antler (unphased)	71
Fig. 40	Worked bone and antler (unphased)	72
Fig. 41	Worked human bone: location on skull of fragment Nos 2–15	74
Fig. 42	Animal bone: fragmentation by phase	81
Fig. 43	Animal bone: species by phase	82
Fig. 44	Animal bone: element representation for cattle and sheep/goat	83
Fig. 45	Animal bone: butchery by phase	85
Fig. 46	Mollusc sequence in Enclosure 1 ditch 7710	87
Fig. 47	Billingborough and related sites in the area (after Hayes and Lane 1992, figs 7–10)	90

List of Tables

Table 1	Site phases	5
Table 2	Radiocarbon dates	5
Table 3	Flint totals	27
Table 4	Pottery and other ceramic material from Phase 1 contexts	33
Table 5	Pottery: rim and body forms from Enclosure 1 ditch 7743	36
Table 6	Pottery and other ceramic material from Phase 2 contexts	41
Table 7	Pottery and other ceramic material from Phase 3 contexts	43
Table 8	Pottery and other ceramic material from Phase 4 contexts	46
Table 9	Briquetage and fired clay by phase	57
Table 10	Animal bone: totals from Phases 1–4	80

Contributors

Kim Addy
formerly Illustrator, South Lincolnshire Archaeology Unit

Carol S.M. Allen, BA, MA, PhD, MIFA
Senior Research Officer, Oxford Archaeological Unit

Phil Andrews, BSc, MIFA
Senior Project Officer, Wessex Archaeology

Joanna K.F. Bacon, BA, MAAIS
Archaeological Consultant and Freelance Illustrator

Justine Bayley, BSc, MSc, PhD, FSA
Head of Technology Section, Ancient Monuments Laboratory, English Heritage

Aiden Challis
formerly Pottery Researcher, South Lincolnshire Archaeology Unit

Peter Chowne, PhD, MBA, MIFA
Genius Loci, Cultural Project Consultants Limited

Rosamund M.J. Cleal, BA, PhD, MIFA
Curator, Alexander Keiller Museum, Avebury

A.P. Fitzpatrick, BA, PhD, FSA, MIFA
Project Manager, Wessex Archaeology

C.A.I. French, BA, MA, PhD, MIFA
Department of Archaeology, University of Cambridge

Guy Grainger
formerly Institute of Archaeology, University of Oxford

Jill Harden, BSc, AMA, FSA (Scot.), MIFA
Archaeological Consultant, Inverness-shire

Hilary Healey, NDD, MPhil, FSA
Archaeological Consultant

Mary Iles, BA
formerly Department of Archaeology, University of Southampton

S.E. James, BA, MAIIS
Illustrator, Wessex Archaeology

Moira Laidlaw, BSc
Project Officer, Wessex Archaeology

Fiona Roe, MA, MLitt
Worked Stone Specialist

Acknowledgements

The publication of this report many years after the site was excavated has only been made possible through the help of a large number of people. Some who made contributions to the excavation or early years of post-excavation work may not be mentioned individually but our thanks is recorded to them here.

To begin with, the help of evening class students on the 1975 excavation and various members of successive Manpower Services Commission (MSC) and Special Temporary Employment Programme (STEP) Schemes in 1977 and 1978 is acknowledged. In particular Tom Lane and Jill Harden who supervised various parts of the programme and John Sutton who made an exceptional contribution to the excavation. Brian Simmons, Hilary Healey and Jeffrey May provided much sound advice and encouragement. Jim Pickering enthusiastically photographed the site from the air (see Plates I and VII) and was a regular visitor always keen to show us the results of his work which assisted with interpretation during excavation. Francis Pryor and Charles French were constant sources of inspiration.

Joanna Bacon was responsible for the initial cataloguing and discussion of the small finds which formed the basis of the later post-excavation work on this material. Don Mackreth has kindly commented on the brooches and Aiden Challis prepared an early draft of the pottery catalogue. Peter Hayes provided an initial assessment of the animal bone, and Helen Keeley and Carole Keepax (both of the Ancient Monuments Laboratory, English Heritage) commented on the soil profiles and identified the charcoal respectively.

During the latter stages of post-excavation work various colleagues at Wessex Archaeology have offered help and advice. These include Michael Allen (radiocarbon dating), Julie Gardiner and Phil Harding (flint), Jacqueline McKinley (human bone), and Lorraine Mepham (pottery). Moira Laidlaw prepared the pottery catalogue from an original typescript by Aiden Challis. We are also grateful to various external specialists for their comments: Janet Ambers (British Museum Research Laboratory) and Alex Bayliss (Ancient Monuments Laboratory, English Heritage) on the radiocarbon dating, Vanessa Fell on the iron 'poker', and Fiona Roe on the stone axe-hammer. We are particularly grateful to Justine Bayley (Ancient Monuments Laboratory, English Heritage) for reworking her original reports on the human bone.

Mary Iles would like to thank various members of Southampton University Archaeology Department and the Centre for Human Ecology and Environment for assistance during the compilation of her undergraduate dissertation on the Billingborough animal bone. These include Clive Gamble, Jennifer Bourdillon, Dale Serjeantson, Kate Clark, Kevin Reilley, Pippa Smith, Janet Egerton, and Nick Bradford. Pippa Smith has edited Mary Iles' undergraduate dissertation for publication here and prepared Figures 42–45.

Initial editing and preparation of the text for publication was carried out at Wessex Archaeology by Melanie Gauden and Julie Gardiner with computing expertise provided by Rachel Fletcher. Liz James drew Figures 4, 6, 8, 9, 11, 41 and 47, reworked Figures 1 and 2, and remounted the finds illustrations for publication. Kim Addy drew the 1266 featured pottery sherds (including some briquetage containers), a selection of which are published here (Figs 20–29). Other illustrations were drawn by Joanna Bacon (Figs 3, 7, 10, 12, 13, 15, 18 and 30–40), Jill Harden (Figs 16 and 17), Hilary Healey (Fig. 14) and Peter Chowne (Fig. 19). The authors acknowledge *East Anglian Archaeology* and Tom Lane for permission to use several maps (Hayes and Lane 1992, figs 7–10) which have been redrawn here as Figure 47. Elaine Wakefield prepared Plates I–IX and Justine Bayley provided Plates X–XIV.

The authors are grateful to several individuals who have read an earlier draft of the text and whose advice and constructive criticism have been taken account of in the final report published here. These include Tom Lane, Richard Bradley, Stuart Needham and David Buckley.

Special mention must be made of The Crown Estate Commissioners, the landowners, for permission to carry out the excavation, the tenant, the late Frank Allen for his enthusiastic support and fortitude (when faced with constant interruptions to his agricultural activities), and the various bodies which contributed funds to the excavation and post-excavation work. The bulk of the excavation work was undertaken using resources of successive MSC and STEP job creation schemes. The British Museum made a small grant to assist with the costs of the 1977 excavation and provided a radiocarbon date free of charge. The 1975 excavation was funded by the Department of the Environment, and its successor, The Historic Buildings and Monuments Commission (English Heritage), generously made funds available in 1990–1 and 1996 which enabled post-excavation work to be completed and this volume brought to fruition.

The Archive

The archive is deposited with Lincolnshire Museum Services, 12 Friar Lane, Lincoln under the accession number LCNCC. 173.1996.

A collection of sherds representing the pottery 'type series' from the site has been donated to the British Museum.

Authors Note

The bulk of this report was written in 1990 (by R.M.J.C., A.P.F. and P.C.) at Wessex Archaeology with several of the smaller contributions having been produced some years earlier. Following Peter Chowne's departure to the Museum of London in 1991, various sections have been revised and edited in 1996 (by P.A. with A.P.F.) for publication, and the dates that they were originally submitted appended, where necessary, in the text below. The decision has been taken not to attempt to update the text from its position in 1990. The few references to literature published since then are to work such as the Fenland Survey whose principal conclusions had kindly been made known to us in advance of publication.

Summary

Extensive excavations on the fen margin at Billingborough revealed archaeological remains of considerable regional importance — a Middle Bronze Age enclosure which remains the most extensively and completely excavated enclosure of its type in the area; Late Bronze Age/Early Iron Age salt-making debris which remains one of the earliest and most substantial assemblages of such material in the area; and a pottery sequence for the Bronze Age and Iron Age periods in the region.

The sequence has been extensively used by the Fenland Survey Project, and it is of considerable importance to prehistoric studies in the East Midlands.

Résumé

Des fouilles approfondies menées à la lisière des marais de Billingborough ont révélé des vestiges archéologiques d'une grande importance sur le plan régional. On y a en effet trouvé une enclosure de l'âge du bronze moyen, qui représente l'enclosure ayant fait l'objet des fouilles les plus complètes de la région; des dépôts d'extractions du sel de l'âge du bronze tardif et de l'âge du bronze ancien, et enfin un ensemble de poterie datant de l'âge du bronze et de l'âge du fer.

L'ensemble des poteries a été largement utilisé dans le cadre du Projet de prospection des Fens, et il revêt une importance considérable pour les études préhistoriques de l'est des Midlands.
(Traduction: Didier Don)

Zusammenfassung

Ausgedehnte Grabungen am Rande des Marschgebiets bei Billingborough legten archäologische Überreste von beträchtlicher regionaler Bedeutung frei: eine Einfriedung aus der Mittleren Bronzezeit – die größte und umfassendste Freilegung einer solchen Einfriedung in diesem Gebiet –, auf Salzgewinnung hinweisende Abraumschichten aus der späten Bronze- bzw. frühen Eisenzeit und damit eine der frühesten und größten Anhäufungen ihrer Art in der Region sowie eine Keramiksequenz aus der Bronze- und Eisenzeit.

Die Keramiksequenz, die ausgiebig im 'Fenland Survey Project' benutzt wurde, hat besondere Bedeutung für prähistorische Studien in den East Midlands.
(Übersetzung: Gerlinde Krug)

Chapter 1. Introduction

by Peter Chowne, A.P. Fitzpatrick and Phil Andrews

I. Summary

Extensive excavations of an area of *c.* 5500 m² took place on the fen margin at Billingborough, Lincolnshire (NGR TF 127 332) between 1975 and 1978. This revealed a sequence of occupation spanning approximately 1500 years.

There is slight evidence for Late Neolithic/Early Bronze Age activity but the earliest substantial remains were those of an enclosure dating to the second half of the 2nd millennium BC; a number of four-post structures and other features may also relate to this enclosure. Following a period (or periods) of freshwater flooding and marine transgression, salt production was undertaken on the site during the mid 1st millennium BC. Occupation intensified during the last centuries of the 1st millennium BC, with the construction of two enclosures associated with settlement. In the 1st century AD the enclosures were superseded by a field system. In all phases artefacts, particularly pottery, were well-preserved and found in considerable quantities.

Despite the period which has elapsed since its excavation the site at Billingborough remains of considerable regional importance. The principal reasons for this are:

> the Middle Bronze Age enclosure remains the most extensively and completely excavated enclosure of its type in the area

> the Late Bronze Age/Early Iron Age salt-making debris remains one of the earliest and most substantial assemblages of such material in the area

> the site provides a pottery sequence for the Bronze Age and Iron Age periods in the region. The sequence has been extensively used by the Fenland Survey Project, and it is of considerable importance to prehistoric studies in the East Midlands.

II. Project background
(Fig. 1; Pl. I)

The site at Billingborough (TF127 332) was discovered by B.B. Simmons during fieldwalking as part of a research project on the Car Dyke in Lincolnshire. A dense concentration of Bronze Age pottery was found lying on a slightly raised area bisected by a field boundary ditch and hedge. Cropmark evidence, plotted after the excavation, shows the site to lie in an extensive area of ditches marking fields and enclosures of probable prehistoric and Romano-British date (Fig. 2).

In 1975 an area 40m by 7m was archaeologically investigated in advance of drainage works. The excavation was extended to 60m by 38m in 1977 and then to 100m by 60m in 1978 (Fig. 2) using the resources of a Manpower Services Commission Job Creation Scheme and a Special Temporary Employment Programme.

Like many other excavations substantially financed by the Manpower Services Commission adequate funds were not available for a full programme of post-excavation analysis. This was most unfortunate in the case of Billingborough which has become a type site for Bronze Age settlement in the Eastern Midlands and the primary source of pottery dating for the Fenland Survey Project in Lincolnshire. In view of the limited funds available for the post-excavation analyses it has not been possible follow the guidelines recommended by Frere (1975) and Cunliffe (1983). However, a substantial archive exists. This contains context notebooks and recording forms, site plans and section drawings, photographic negatives, colour transparencies and all of the excavated finds. All of the excavated material from stratified contexts has been examined and is considered in this report. Much of this work has been carried out at little or no direct cost to the project through the generosity of research students and former members of the MSC teams now in employment elsewhere. It is hoped that future researchers will return to the Billingborough material and add to the data and ideas presented below.

Completion of the report in 1996 has been undertaken within these constraints but this, and its subsequent publication, more than two decades after the end of fieldwork, has been made possible through the generous financial support of English Heritage, and has allowed the excavations to be considered within the light of the major programme of archaeological work comprising the Lincolnshire part of the Fenland Project (Hayes and Lane 1992; Lane 1993).

III. Geology and topography
(Fig. 1)

The central part of the western fen edge of Lincolnshire extends from the River Slea/Kyme Eau in the north to the beginning of the peat in the south at Bourne. Between these two points is an extensive tract of clays and silts bounded to the east by the Wash, and thinning out to the west as the land rises up to the Jurassic Limestone ridge which reaches a height of 90m just east of Grantham. Billingborough village is situated 16km south of Sleaford, between the 7m and 15m contours at a point where the limestone dips beneath fen-edge gravels. A series of west/east watercourses, fed from springs, run from the limestone through the gravels, clays and silts, to drain into the 17th-century Forty Foot Drain. East of the Car Dyke these watercourses, known locally as lodes, have been canalised, probably in the Romano-British period (Simmons 1979). The precise origin of the fen-edge gravels is uncertain but they are undoubtedly river terrace gravels, probably from an early course of the River Witham. Billingborough, like all of the fen-edge villages between Bourne and the River Slea, is located on the spring line. The excavated site at Billingborough is situated on the gravels south-east of the modern village and less than 500m to the west of the former fen edge at a

Plate I 1978 excavation from the air, facing west

height of *c*. 5m AOD. The soils overlying the gravels on the site were very acidic, with an average recorded ph of 9.2. In the extreme north-west corner of the site the gravels were sealed by a thin layer of alluvium interpreted as a flood deposit.

IV. Excavation strategy and method
(Fig. 3)

In all seasons of work topsoil and subsoil were stripped by machine down to stratified archaeological deposits or natural gravel, whichever was encountered first. Virtually all of the archaeological deposits were contained within features cutting natural. The comparatively shallow depth of topsoil and subsoil (generally < 0.5m) and the disturbance caused by ploughing and sub-soiling had resulted in the truncation of many features, and only very restricted areas of horizontal stratigraphy survived outside of negative features.

After the topsoil and subsoil had been stripped the surface was hoed, trowelled and planned prior to hand excavation commencing. A 10m grid established across the site was used for planning, with plans normally drawn at 1:20 or 1:50 and sections at 1:10. Levels were taken only on the bottoms of ditches A full colour slide and monochrome photographic record was also maintained.

Excavation initially involved taking out the fills of any modern features (land drains were left *in situ*) and removing the soil contained within the series of substantial medieval plough furrows (up to 3m wide and 0.4m deep) which ran north to south across the site. Virtually all of the remaining post-holes, pits and gullies were fully excavated, and between 25% and 50% of each ditch (the excavated segments of ditches and other features are shown in Fig. 3). Two forms of soil sampling were undertaken: random wheelbarrow loads of spoil were dry-sieved to monitor artefact recovery, and one metre wide 'control sections' across ditches were wet-sieved for small mammal bones, snails, carbonised seed remains etc. The fills of some pits were also wet-sieved.

In each season of excavation the numbering of contexts began at *1*. To differentiate between these, each sequence of numbers was subsequently (during post-excavation) pre-fixed by its year of excavation; thus context *1* excavated in 1975 became *751*, context *1* in 1977 became *771*, and context *1* in 1978 became *781*, and so on. In 1975 and 1977 features were assigned a context number and the layers in that feature differentiated by letter codes; for example, ditch *43* contained layers *43, 43b, 43c* and so on. These letter designations have been retained so that in the case of ditch *7743g*, for example, *77* = 1977, *43* = ditch 43, and *g* = layer g.

2

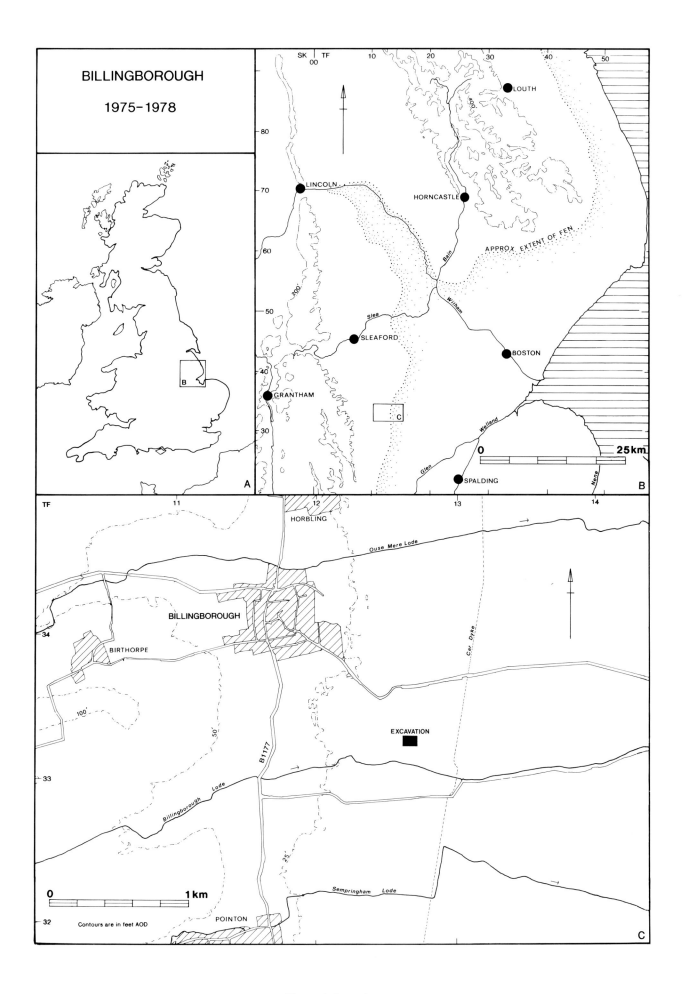

Figure 1 Location maps

3

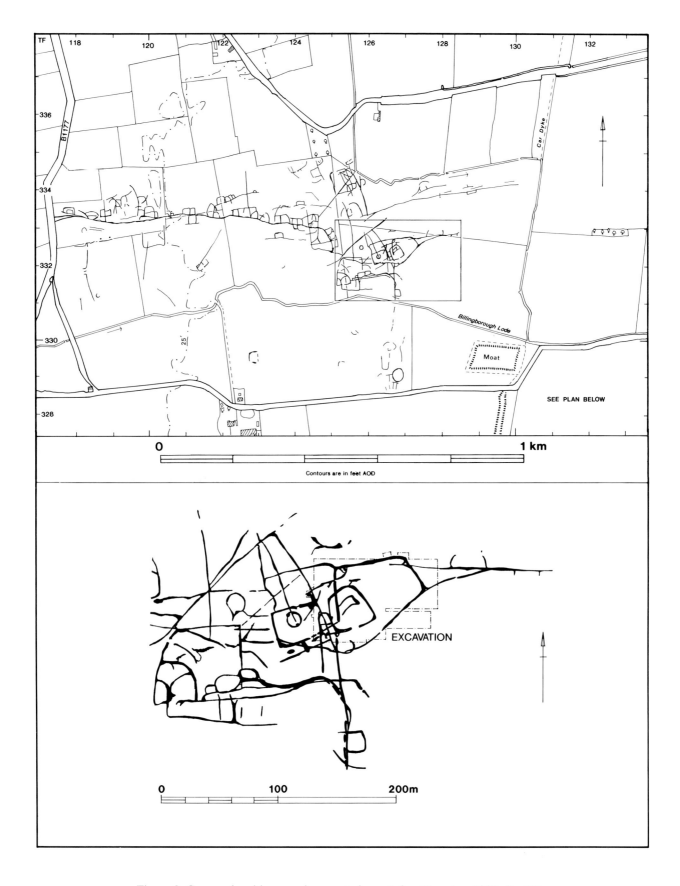

Figure 2 Cropmark evidence and excavated area (after Hampton 1983, fig. 81)

Phase	Period	Date	Description	1978 Phase
1	Middle–Late Bronze Age	15th–?10th century BC	Enclosure 1	1 and 2
2	Late Bronze Age–Early Iron Age	8th–5th century BC	Salt-working	Saltern
3	Middle–Late Iron Age	4th–1st century BC	Enclosures 2 and 3	3a and 3b
4	Early Romano-British	1st century AD	Field system	4

Table 1 Site phases

Laboratory No.	Determination	Material	Context
BM-1410	3148±57 BP **1530-1260 cal BC**	Charcoal	*7510d*; lower fill of enclosure 1 ditch *7510/7710*. Phase 1
HAR-2483	2390±70BP **780-370 cal BC**	Charcoal: *Quercus* sp. from a large timber, 25% identified	Post-hole *7898*. Phase 2
HAR-2523	2410±80 BP **800-370 cal BC**	Charcoal: mainly *Corylus/Alnus* sp. with some Rosaceae, sub-family Pomoideae, both mainly from large timbers	*7743c*; upper fill of Enclosure 1 ditch *7743*. Phase 2
HAR-3101	2500±100 BP **840-390 cal BC**	Charcoal: *Quercus* sp. and *Fraxinus* sp. from large timbers, and sub-family Pomoideae (*e.g.* hawthorn)	Pit *78256*. Phase 2

Radiocarbon dates have been calibrated using the maximum intercept method (Stuiver and Reimer 1986), using data from Stuiver and Pearson (1986), and are expressed at the 95% confidence level with the end points rounded out to 10 years following the form recommended by Mook (1986).

Table 2 Radiocarbon dates

V. Site dating and phasing
(Tables 1 and 2)

The site was in use from the middle part of the 2nd millennium BC until the early years of the 1st millennium AD. During the Middle Ages the area was badly damaged by plough furrows, up to 0.4m deep, resulting from ridge-and-furrow cultivation (see Fig. 3).

Prehistoric occupation of the site has been divided into a series of phases which are summarised in Table 1, these are slightly different to those suggested in the interim report (Chowne 1978). The main changes are that interim phases 1 and 2 are no longer seen as separate entities but as part of a continuous development, and interim phases 3A and 3B are now regarded as near contemporary.

Some problems have been encountered in allocating various features to particular phases. This has largely arisen from the virtual absence of horizontal stratigraphy along with the comparatively small number of stratigraphic relationships between features. In addition, medieval ploughing on the site has done considerable damage and, in particular, has made the identification of structures difficult by the destruction of features in linear swathes. Finally, there is a strong element of residuality in the ceramic assemblages, particularly of Bronze Age pottery in Iron Age features, with many of the smaller features containing little or no pottery. Besides pottery, dating is largely dependent on a limited range of other stratified finds comprising principally a small quantity of metalwork, and on a small number of radiocarbon dates (Table 2) which are presented following Mook (1986). It should be noted that the suggestion that one radiocarbon determination (BM-1410) falls within the group of British Museum radiocarbon determinations which required re-evaluation (Tite *et al.* 1987) and should be discarded (Chowne 1993, 97) is erroneous. The determinations cited by Bowman *et al.* (BM 1629 and 1630) are from a nearby, but different, site at Billingborough Fen next to the Car Dyke (1990, 79, tab. 3).

(Written in 1990/1996)

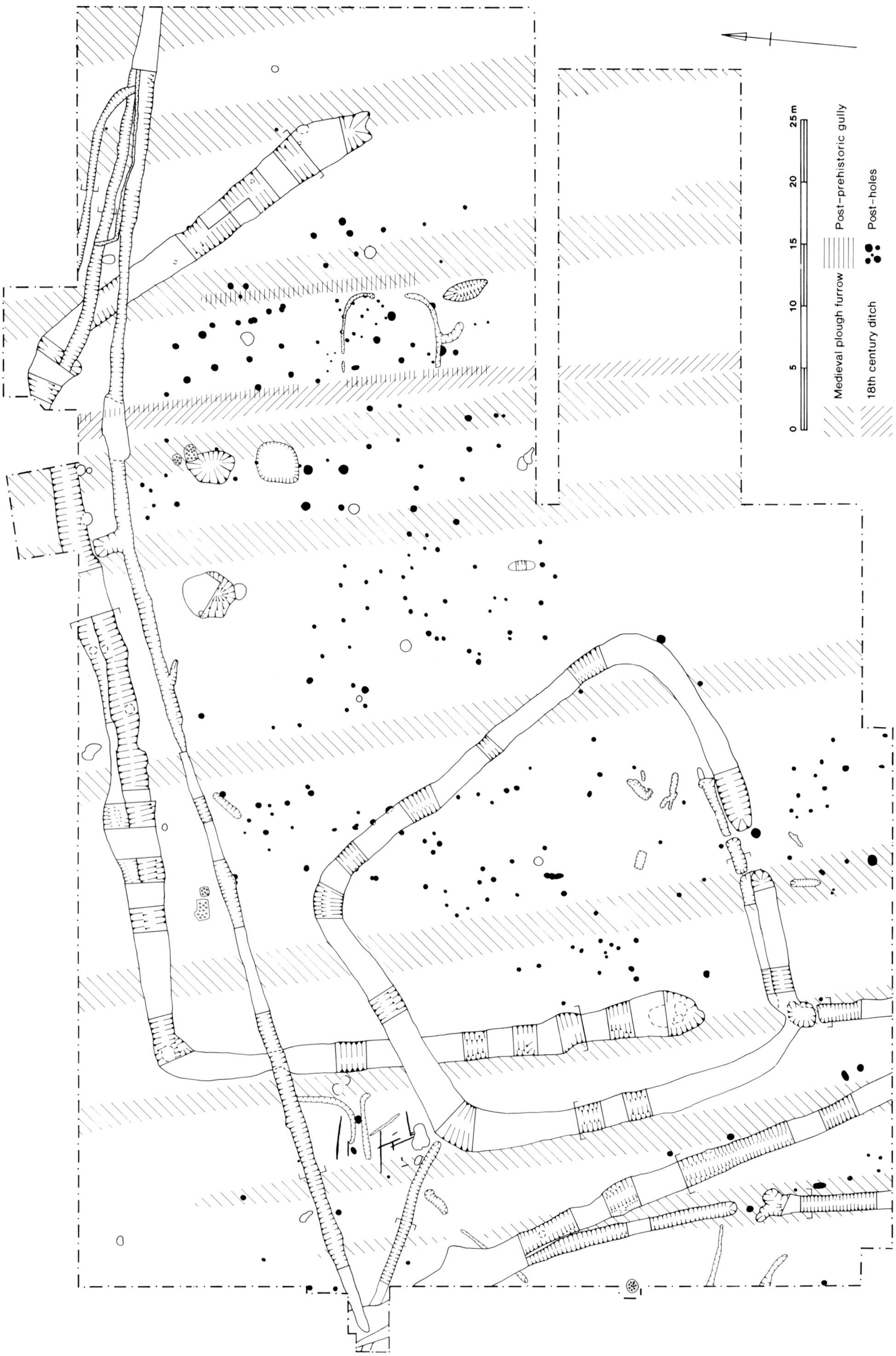

Figure 3 Plan of all features

Legend:

Medieval plough furrow

Post–prehistoric gully

18th century ditch

Post–holes

25m 20 15 10 5 0

Chapter 2. The Excavations

I. Pre-Middle Bronze Age activity
by Rosamund M.J. Cleal (1990)

Pre-Middle Bronze Age activity on the site is attested by the presence of a single sherd assignable to the Peterborough tradition of the later Neolithic. Much of the worked flint may also be of Late Neolithic date, but no features are assignable to this period. Use of the site during the Early Bronze Age is attested by sherds of Food Vessel and Collared Urn, and by stray finds of jet and metalwork. These are not in securely stratified contexts, and the activities they represent are therefore uncertain. However, it is suggested below (see Chapter 5) that grave *78183* may have been a disturbed Early Bronze Age burial (Pl. II), and that some of these finds could have derived from this. The grave fill contained a single sherd of grog-tempered (Phase 1) pottery, possibly intrusive, but is otherwise undated. Grave *78183* lay approximately 10m to the east of the terminal of Phase 1 enclosure ditch *78145* and was aligned east–west (see Fig. 4). The truncated (depth not recorded) sub-rectangular grave contained the remains of an adult female aged over 30 years. This was in an extended supine position, with the left leg apparently drawn up beneath the right leg.

The remains of a second east–west inhumation burial, *77119* (not illustrated), much disturbed by a medieval plough furrow, lay approximately 40m to the north-east of grave *78183*. This was of an adolescent aged about 18 years and is also undated.

II. Phase 1: Middle–Late Bronze Age
by Rosamund M.J. Cleal and Peter Chowne (1990)
(Fig. 4)

The earliest use of the site which has both artefacts and associated structures is the first enclosure, Enclosure 1, which is datable on the grounds of the pottery in its lower layers to around the middle of the 2nd millennium BC, and is likely to be contemporary, in broad terms, with the Deverel-Rimbury complex of southern Britain.

As noted above, the phasing of the site suggested in the interim report (Chowne 1978) was subsequently modified during post-excavation work. Phases 1 and 2 in the interim report were later considered more likely to represent one continuous history of occupation rather than separate episodes, and were therefore both placed within the new Phase 1 for the structural evidence. Although the pottery supports a division of the Bronze Age use of the site into two main ceramic phases, the question of whether this represents re-use of the site or continuous use is unresolved. In view of this the Phase 1 occupation is sub-divided in two: earlier and later. This also implies that the internal features of Enclosure 1 represent either at least two periods of use, or continuous occupation over a period during which the ceramics developed. In the absence of vertical stratigraphy this is difficult to identify. An attempt has been made to separate out those features in which the characteristic Bronze Age grog-tempered wares appear, as

Plate II Grave *78183*. 1m scale

these seem more likely to be contemporary with the lower, rather than with the upper, filling of the enclosure ditch.

Enclosure 1
(Figs 4 and 5)

This enclosure was demarcated on the north, west and east sides by a ditch approximately 1m deep, each side demonstrating a slightly different depositional history. To the south no enclosing feature could be identified, although an extensive area was excavated. The presence of features within the enclosure, and the absence of features to the south suggests that some boundary did exist. The former existence of a hedge or fence, perhaps situated on a bank and therefore leaving no trace, is one possibility, and cropmark evidence shows a possible fourth side despite no evidence for this having been found in the excavation (see Fig. 2. Hampton 1983, 117, figs 80 and 81).

The concentration of numerous features within the enclosure, in contrast to the rarity of them outside, strongly suggests that many if not most of these belonged to the period in which the enclosure was in use. However, several factors, mentioned in Chapter 1, complicate the interpretation of these features. As the site was used again in the 1st millennium BC, at a time when much of the Bronze Age pottery would still have been lying in the topsoil, the presence of Bronze Age pottery alone in a feature cannot be considered an infallible guide to its date, particularly in the case of the features which also lay within the Iron Age enclosure, Enclosure 2, which overlay the south-western corner of Enclosure 1.

Parts of the ditch defining Enclosure 1 were excavated in each of the three seasons of excavation, and the ditch was given a different feature number in each season. These were as follows:

1975: *7530* (northern side)
1977: *7710* (northern side) and *7743* (eastern side)
1978: *78145* (western and northern sides)

In the 1975 and 1977 seasons, each layer within a feature was given the feature number with a letter suffix as described above (see Introduction). In 1978 a running sequence of individual context numbers was used across the entire site.

7

Plate III Enclosure 1 ditch *78145*, facing north. 2m scale

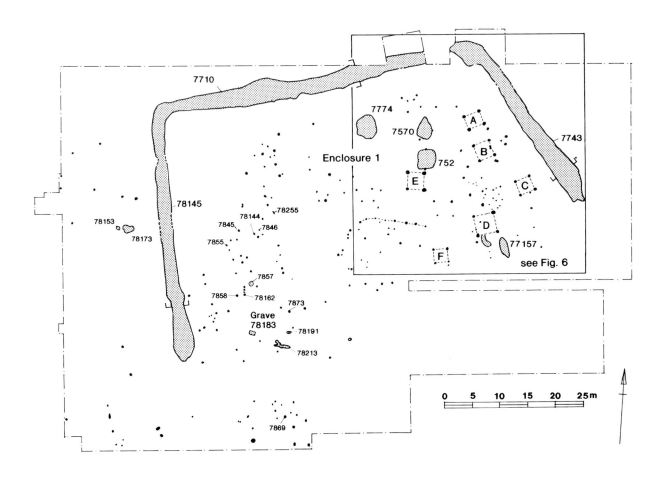

Figure 4 Plan of Phase 1 and earlier features

East side: ditch 7743
(Fig. 5)
The eastern side of the enclosure ditch provides the most complete sequence of ditch filling, which may be divided into lower and upper fillings, on the basis of the stratigraphy and the pottery, and a radiocarbon date of 800–370 cal BC (HAR-2523, 2410± 80 BP) obtained from charcoal in layer *7743c*. Layers *7743*, *7743b* and *7743c* clearly belonged to the upper level, and contained both grog-tempered and shelly pottery as well as some briquetage. Layers *7743e, f, g, h, i, j*, and *k*, assigned to the lower level, contained no briquetage, and only a few sherds of shelly pottery. Layer *7743d* directly precedes *7743c* in all but one of the recorded sections (the longitudinal section — not illustrated), and, like *7743c*, also contained shelly pottery and briquetage.

Along the east side of the enclosure ditch the lower levels consisted of greyish brown clay (*7743f*, *7743g* and *7743h*), layer *7743g* also including chalky fragments and organic stains. Lenses of iron pan also occurred, both at the very bottom of the ditch (*7743k*), and higher up, within *7743h*. The majority of the pottery from the lower ditch deposits of Enclosure 1 came from the east side, with most recovered from layers *7743g* and *7743f*. It is almost entirely grog-tempered, and includes a large part of a single vessel (Fig. 23:40). The fill appears to represent the natural silting of the ditch, with the possible exception of layer *7743e*, which occurred in two sections and the longitudinal section. This layer consisted of a sandy gravel with some iron panning, and was thought on excavation to represent deliberate backfilling of the ditch. It was deposited from the interior of the enclosure, at a time when the ditch had become slightly less than half-filled through natural silting. Where layer *7743e* occurred, it separated the layers designated 'earlier' and 'later' on the grounds of the ceramics.

The upper ditch filling appeared to represent a natural accumulation of silts which were sealed by ashy layer *7743* which can be equated with the Saltern activity (Phase 2). These layers — *7743b*, *7743c*, and *7743d* — consisted of loamy and silty clays containing small stones and chalky flecks. The finds include considerable quantities of both grog-tempered and shelly pottery, briquetage, and fired clay.

North side: ditch 7710
(Fig. 5)
Along this side of the enclosure the upper ditch fill appears to have been disturbed by a possible recut or recuts along at least parts of its length. During excavation layers *7710* and *7710b* were considered to represent a recut of the ditch, running along most of the northern side of Enclosure 1 and dated to the Iron Age on the grounds of the iron 'poker' and scored pottery found within it. However, this feature was shallow, with gently sloping sides, and occupied only the uppermost part of the ditch. At most it would seem likely to repesent the clearing out of what at that time must have appeared as no more than a slight linear hollow.

Beneath this putative recut the lower ditch filling survived undisturbed, and was similar to that on the east side, *7743*, although less rich in artefacts. A very little briquetage was recovered from layer *7710c*. Layer *7710e* represents the primary silting, and was a dark grey clay, while above it layers *7710c* and *7710d* represent the

natural silting up of the ditch, *7710c* including material weathered from the ditch sides. A sample of charcoal from layer *7510d* (=*7710d*) produced a radiocarbon date of 1530–1260 cal BC (BM-1410, 3148±57BP). No molluscs were recovered from the basal layer, nor from the lower secondary fill, but a sample from the upper secondary fill indicates freshwater waterlogged conditions. French (see below, p.88) suggests that at this point in its history the ditch, which would have been approximately three-quarters full of silt, carried slowly-flowing or almost stagnant freshwater, with weedy vegetation growing along the ditch sides.

Apart from the putative Iron Age recut, the north side of the enclosure ditch was cut by later features both at the eastern end, where it was crossed by ditch *7796*, and at the north-western corner, where it was cut by pit *78262*.

West side: ditch 78145
(Fig. 5; Pl. III)
The lower fills in the western side of the enclosure ditch showed a general similarity to the lower levels in the northern and eastern sides. A basal layer of greyish brown sandy clay, *78212*, underlay *78164* which appeared to represent the natural silting of the ditch, filling it to between a half and three-quarters full. These layers were succeeded by a deposit of nearly clean sand and gravel, *78147*, deposited from the west, which bore some resemblance to layer *7743e* in the eastern side of the enclosure ditch. Layer *78147* contained no dating evidence, and is likely to represent the remains of an internal bank which had later been used to partly backfill the ditch. The sterile nature of this layer can be explained by the ditch and bank of Enclosure 1 having been constructed when the settlement was first established. The existence of a bank associated with Enclosure 1 is also suggested by the fact that features rarely occurred within about 3m of the ditch. Those that did all lay within Enclosure 2, an Iron Age feature, and could therefore have belonged to the use of that enclosure. The filling of ditch *78145* is not directly datable but it must pre-date the Phase 2 pit *78256* (see Fig. 8), which was cut through it. A radiocarbon determination from charcoal in this pit of cal BC 840–390 (HAR-3101, 2500±100BP); therefore provides a *terminus ante quem* for this event.

Enclosure 1: other features
(Figs 4 and 6)
The majority of features within Enclosure 1 are sealed only by plough soil, and cannot therefore be assigned to phases on stratigraphic grounds. However, there are exceptions to this, and these exceptions, combined with the ceramic evidence, do suggest that the enclosure was in use for a considerable time. The excavated features probably contemporary with use of Enclosure 1 may be divided into the following classes:

a) Those containing only Phase 1 grog-tempered pottery, with no other evidence for a later date.
b) Features sealed by possible Bronze Age occupation surface *7742*.
c) Other features identifiable as belonging to structures. This is the most tentative class, as it could be argued that structures might be associated with, although situated outside the Phase 3 (Iron Age) Enclosures 2 and 3, or might even occur within the enclosures

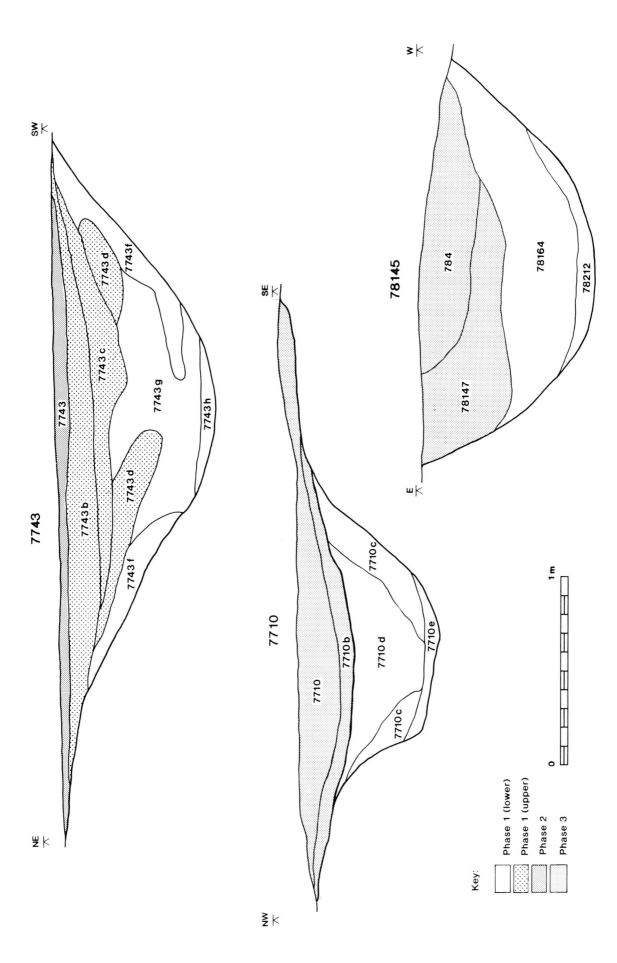

Figure 5 Sections: Enclosure 1 ditch

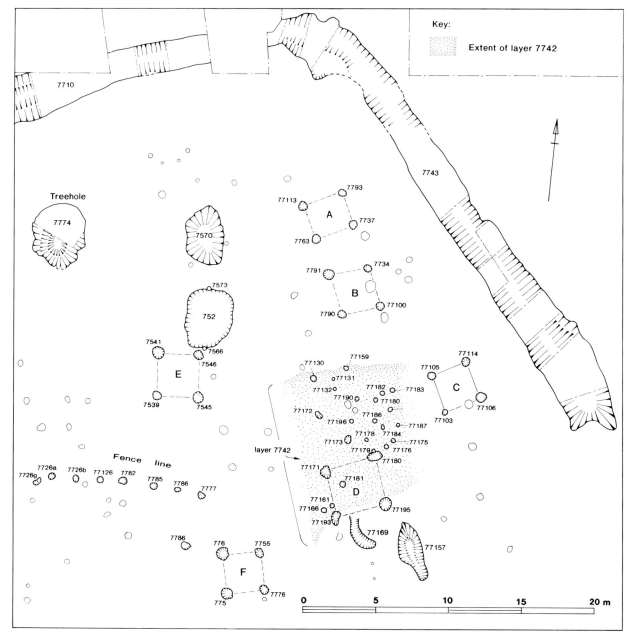

Figure 6 Plan of structures and features at east end of Enclosure 1

bounded by the Phase 4 (Romano-British) ditches. The part of Enclosure 1 also occupied by Enclosure 2 is clearly an even more difficult area with which to deal, although as the features physically enclosed by Enclosure 2 occur almost exclusively in that part of it which also lies within Enclosure 1 it would seem reasonable to assume that most belong with the latter.

d) Features pre-dating salt-making (Phase 2) deposits.

a) Features containing only Bronze Age grog-tempered sherds. This seems a reasonable, although not infallible, criterion to take as an indicator of a Phase 1 date, as the quantity of briquetage and shelly pottery found over large areas of the site suggests that the absence of such material from feature fillings is likely to be the result of the features having filled before those material types appeared. These putatively early features were scattered across the site (see Fig. 4), with three occurring outside the enclosure, one to the south (*7869*), and two to the west (*78153* and *78173*). Several of the features (*7845, 7846, 7857, 7858, 7855,*

7873, 78144, 78162, 78191, and *78213*) are situated within the area of Enclosure 2, and one (*78255*) is cut by Phase 3 ditch *78113,* strengthening the impression that many of the features within Enclosure 2 belong to the Phase 1 occupation. The minor occurrence of one post-hole with grog-tempered pottery (*7869*) and several with no finds at all, outside the apparent boundary of Enclosure 1 on the southern side, might be taken as an indication that there was an entrance into the enclosure at this point, the features therefore representing the remains of fences or other structures associated with the entrance. This is in contrast to the south-eastern part of the excavated area which is entirely blank, as might be expected if an unbroken barrier such as a hedge or bank or both defined the enclosure along the remainder of that side.

b) An occupation layer (*7742*), recognised during excavation as likely to be Bronze Age, was preserved in the area of Phase 2 structure, *77102* (see Figs 6 and 8).

11

This consisted of a very dark greyish brown deposit of silty clay which contained pottery, charcoal and bone. The layer sealed a number of post-holes and was cut by gully *77102* which was interpreted as the foundation trench of a structure. Layer *7742* extended as far south as pit *77157*, which it sealed, and north to post-holes *77130* and *77159*. To the west and east it was truncated by medieval plough furrows. Among the post-holes beneath *7742* were two belonging to a probable four-post structure formed by post-holes *77171*, *77180*, *77193*, and *77195* (see Fig. 6). A copper alloy object, possibly part of a Middle Bronze Age razor (Fig. 13:1), was found in post-hole *77193*.

Layer *7742* was cut by gully *77102*, and must therefore reflect a period of time when the structures represented by the features sealed beneath it had gone out of use and that represented by *77102* not yet built. The date of layer *7742* itself is not clear, as it could on stratigraphic grounds belong to late in Phase 1 or early in Phase 2. Some Iron Age pottery was present (*e.g.* Fig. 27: 96), but this must be due to the difficulties of distinguishing, during excavation, between this layer and the topsoil above it, as the layer is clearly earlier than gully *77102* for which there is convincing evidence of a Phase 2 date.

c) A number of structures may be postulated for the interior of Enclosure 1, although the damage to the Bronze Age deposits caused by the medieval plough furrows has removed some of the evidence. At least six four-post structures, including that sealed beneath layer *7742*, have been identified (Fig. 6), and these are composed of the following post-holes:

A: *77113–7793–7763–7737*
B: *7791–7734–7790–77100*
C: *77105–77114–77103–77106*
D: *77171–77180–77193–77195*
E: *7541–7546–7539–7545*
F: *776–7755–775–7776* (Pl. IV)

The post-holes belonging to each four-post structure were generally of similar size, with the smallest (structure C) being up to 0.5m in diameter and 0.25m deep, and the largest (structure E) being up to 0.6m in diameter and 0.6m deep (Fig. 7). No carbonised grain or other seed remains are recorded from the fills of any of these post-holes and therefore the possibility that the structures were for grain storage cannot be confirmed or denied.

Enclosure 1 may have been sub-divided, on the evidence of at least the alignment of post-holes *7777*, *7786*, *7785*, *7782*, *77126*, *7726b*, *7726a*, and *7726g*. These eight undated post-holes appear to form a line *c.* 12m long (Fig. 6; Pl. IV), though this is at an odd angle to the putative fourth (south) side of the enclosure and may not therefore have been contemporary. The size and depth of the post-holes varies considerably and while this alignment may be fortuitous, the arrangement finds parallels on other Late Bronze Age settlements in eastern England where screens or facades have been identified (see below, p. 91).

It has not been possible to identify any house structures, round or rectangular, among the surviving features of this phase. This is perhaps surprising, but it is conceivable that later damage to the site caused by ploughing has destroyed any evidence for these.

d) Three other features may be assigned to Phase 1 on the basis that they pre-date deposits assignable to the Phase 2 salt-making activity.

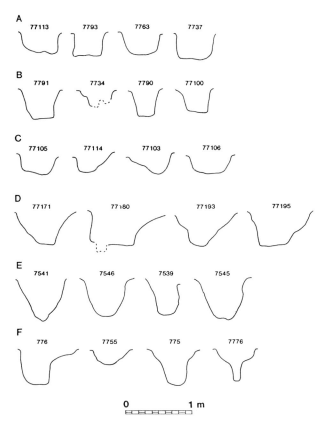

Figure 7 Sections: post-holes of four-post structures A–F

Feature *752* measured approximately 4m by 3m in plan and was 0.5m deep, with a small post-hole at each end, on the long axis (Pl. V). The sides were nearly vertical and showed little sign of extensive weathering, and feature *752* might be interpreted as some form of sunken-floored structure. The bottom fill is recorded as a thin, dark, possibly trampled layer, and this was overlain by layers of brown or yellowish brown soil containing varying amounts of sand and gravel. These fills were sealed by a layer of ash, indicating that *752* was no more than a slight hollow during Phase 2. Pottery vessel Fig. 22: 25 is recorded as coming from the basal fill of pit *752*, although it is conceivable that this vessel (of possible Middle-Late Iron Age date) represents a later insertion into an earlier largely infilled feature (*cf.* the iron 'poker' in Enclosure 1 ditch *7710*, p.20). However, no evidence for a cut which might indicate this was noted at the time of excavation, and there are significant differences in fabric and decoration between this vessel and those undoubtedly of Iron Age date.

Pit *7774* was an irregular, ill-defined feature filled with lenses of gravel, iron pan, and silty clay. It was cut by Phase 2 pit *778* which contained ash and briquetage fragments. The irregular shape and the nature of the fill of pit *7774* suggests that it may have been a tree-hole which held a tree which was, at some stage before the salt-making phase, removed and the hole backfilled. The absence of any contemporaneous features in a radius of approximately 8m around the feature might be taken to support its interpretation as a tree-hole, and to suggest that the tree was not removed when Enclosure 1 was first established.

Plate IV Four-post structure F and possible fence line, facing west. 2m scale

Plate V Sunken feature 752, facing west. 2m scales

Another irregular feature, pit *7570*, 8m to the east of *7774*, may also be assigned to Phase 1 as it was overlain by hearth *7512* which was probably associated with salt making. The sides and base of pit *7570* were clearly defined, and it measured approximately 3m by 5m, and was 0.85m deep. The bottom fill consisted of some clay, possibly the result of flooding, followed by a layer of ash with charcoal. This was succeeded by a layer of yellow gravel with no finds which may represent deliberate back-filling. The feature might be interpreted as a quarry, perhaps for flint, though it could have been dug for a variety of purposes.

III. Phase 2: Late Bronze Age–Early Iron Age
by Rosamund M.J. Cleal and Peter Chowne (1990)
(Fig. 8)

The presence of a salt-making phase was recognised during excavation, and was represented principally by hearths and pits filled with ashy deposits, fired clay and briquetage fragments. Some spreads of similar material also survived. Firebars and other pieces of fired clay probably associated with salt production were found, but none *in situ*. Charcoal from a pit of this phase, *78256*, produced a radiocarbon date of 840–390 cal BC (HAR-3101, 2500±100 BP).

Pits
Four pits (*778, 7795, 7756,* and *78256/78257*) may be assigned to this phase because of the nature of the fillings, and in two cases (*7795* and *78257*) on the basis of the large amounts of briquetage found in them.

Pit *778* was approximately 1.8m in diameter and 0.43m deep, and was cut into the filling of the probable tree-hole *7774*. The fill was a dark greyish to dark reddish brown colour and contained patches of burnt clay. A small amount of briquetage, pottery, and fired clay was recovered; this included a single rim sherd showing the oxidised colour and high frequency of shell inclusions typical of briquetage, but probably belonging to a jar with a simple vertical rim such as also occurred in pit *78257*.

Pit *7756* was a circular feature, approximately 1.4m in diameter and 0.21m deep. It was very similar in shape and size to pit *778*, which lay just over 10m to the north-east, although the fill contained only a small quantity of briquetage.

Pit *7795* was approximately 0.62m in diameter and 0.37m deep, and appeared during excavation to contain an *in situ* clay structure. The clay, which was barely fired and disintegrated on excavation, may have been part of a domed structure. Approximately 1.2kg of briquetage and 0.5kg of fired clay were recovered from this feature.

Pit *78257* cut the western terminal of the Enclosure 1 ditch *78145* in an area in which it was difficult to distinguish features. Layer *784*, which forms the uppermost filling of ditch *78145* elsewhere within the enclosure, was absent from this section and pit *78257* was cut into layer *78147* (see Fig. 5). Pit *78257* contained a large amount of briquetage, fired clay, and shelly pottery, as well as a number of redeposited grog-tempered sherds.

A smaller pit, *78256*, also cut the western terminal of Enclosure 1 ditch *78145* as well as pit *78257*. It was overlain only by layer *781* (plough soil) and produced one sherd of pottery (Fig. 25: 63), similar to that found in pit *78257*.

It could be argued that the single sherd of shelly pottery in pit *78256* was a redeposited piece, and that the radiocarbon date of 840–390 cal BC (HAR-3101, 2500± 100BP) derived from this feature does not date the salt-making activity of this phase. However, it was considered during excavation that pits *78256* and *78257*, although not contemporaneous, probably did form part of a single episode of activity and the date is compatible with others of this phase.

Hearths
Two adjacent, sub-rectangular hearths (*7511* and *7512*), appear to belong to this phase. Both comprised areas of hard white clay with ash, but in neither case was there evidence for a superstructure of any sort. Both contained some pottery and briquetage, but none of the pottery is diagnostic, and may include some residual material. Feature *7512* overlay the fill of hollow *7570*, a Phase 1 feature. A third hearth, *7736*, contained a large quantity of briquetage and overlay post-hole *7763* which belonged to Phase 1 four-post structure A. A pair of heavily truncated unphased hearths, *7816* and *7817* (see Fig. 8), some 40m to the west, may also have belonged to this phase, though this is thought by the excavator (P.C.) to be unlikely as they were not considered to be salt-making hearths. It should be noted, however, that salt-making hearths often occur in pairs.

Other contexts
Salt-making debris was also recognised in spreads of material over some parts of the site, and in particular in the tops of some Phase 1 features, which would have survived as no more than hollows at this time.

A particularly distinctive layer, *7743*, containing much briquetage and fired clay, was present in the top of ditch *7743*, the eastern length of the Enclosure 1 ditch. This was of dark greyish brown silty clay (Munsell 10YR 4/2) which dried to a very distinctive light brownish–grey colour (Munsell 10YR 6/2) and was probably derived from the burning of brackish material, such as dried marine grasses or wood which had absorbed salt water (see below, p.25). These activities appear to have been related to salt production. This distinctive colouration proved a useful indicator of which contexts pre-dated the salt-making phase as it formed the upper layer of many of the features in the enclosure. In addition to briquetage and some residual grog-tempered pottery, layer *7743* also produced a distinctive bevelled rim sherd in a shelly fabric (Fig. 25: 67) which is well-paralleled by a rim sherd (Fig. 25: 66) from pit *78257*.

Elsewhere, the uppermost layer of pit *752* was of a light grey ashy deposit, which possibly included the remains of hearths, and produced a considerable quantity of briquetage, fired clay and some pottery (including Fig. 25: 68 and 70). A spread of dark brown clay with ash, charcoal and briquetage was also recorded close to hearth *7512*, and this layer, *7554*, along with *7524*, to which it could be equated, appear to represent considerable use of this area of the site during this phase.

However, the survival of *in situ* deposits of this phase in the eastern half of the site may only reflect the fact that disturbance from later activity, especially in Phase 3, was concentrated in the western rather than the eastern part of the excavated area. Briquetage was widely scattered across the site, and occurred as far west as gullies *7823*,

Plate VI Structure *77102*, facing west. 2m scale

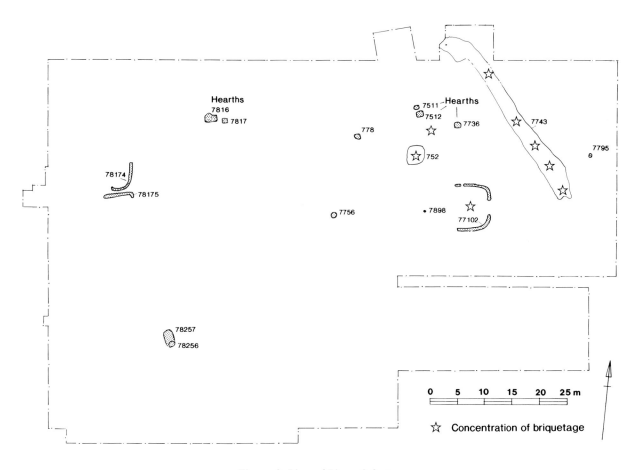

Figure 8 Plan of Phase 2 features

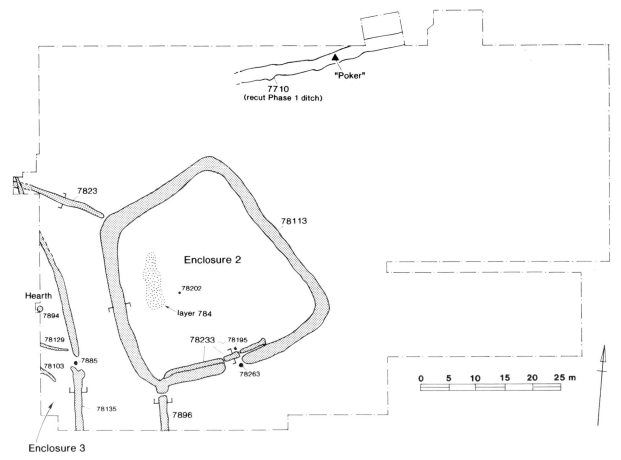

Figure 9 Plan of Phase 3 features

78175, and *7884* along the western edge of the site. The date of these features is uncertain, although they probably belong to Phase 3 and one, *7884*, appeared to be cut by Phase 4 ditch *78138*. Even if the briquetage in them was redeposited this indicates that briquetage was present over the whole of the excavated area.

No structures are certainly assignable to this phase. However, two approximately equal lengths of curvilinear gully, *77102*, which cut layer *7742*, may represent a structure (Fig. 8; Pl. VI) which belongs to this phase. Gully *77102* averaged 0.3m in width, and 0.16m in depth, with a gap, possibly an entrance, between the two lengths at the east end. The area enclosed was 7m wide by at least 5m long; the gullies were truncated at the western end by a medieval plough furrow. The area within the gully was recorded as context *77101*, and this produced grog-tempered pottery, small quantities of shelly pottery, fired clay and briquetage. Much of the pottery is residual from the concentration of Phase 1 activity in this area. The gully itself also contained pottery, briquetage and fired clay, including a large and well-preserved sherd from a briquetage cylindrical vessel (Fig. 29: 1). This is in such good condition, in contrast to the majority of the briquetage from the site, that it would seem unlikely to have lain on the ground surface long before its incorporation into the filling of *77102*. In addition, the appearance of the gully before excavation was not unlike the pale greyish layer in the top of ditch *7743*, and this too indicates that the upper part of the feature at least was filled during the salt-making episode. It is possible that gully *77102* represents a roofed structure, although there are no contemporaneous post-holes within it to support the roof; alternatively, it might

have been no more than a shelter or wind-break and the possible fence line ascribed to Phase 1 may be relevant here (see Fig. 6). There were no surviving hearths in its immediate vicinity, but it lay only 10m from the concentration of briquetage around pits *752* and *7512*, just over 15m from pit *7795*, and 10m from the activity represented by the debris in layer *7743* in the top of ditch *7743*.

Two gullies which lay towards the north-west corner of the site were similar in form to gully *77102*, and may also have been associated with the salt-making activity during Phase 2. Gully *78174* is undated, while *78175*, which contained briquetage, could belong to either Phase 2 or Phase 3. These remains were slight and owed their survival to their lying in a slight depression filled with flood silt which had largely protected them from plough damage, although evidence of (undated) cross-ploughing was clearly visible (see Fig. 3). One otherwise undated post-hole, *7898*, contained a charred oak post which produced a radiocarbon date of 780–370 cal BC (HAR-2483, 2390±70 BP), which is broadly contemporary with the Phase 2 activity; it is possible that some of the other undated post-holes assigned to Phase 1 may have belonged to Phase 2.

IV. Phase 3: Middle–Late Iron Age
by A.P. Fitzpatrick and Peter Chowne (1990)
(Fig. 9)

Introduction
Iron Age activity on the site was represented by Enclosures 2 and 3 (Pl. VII). Both may have contained structures and were part of a broader field system.

16

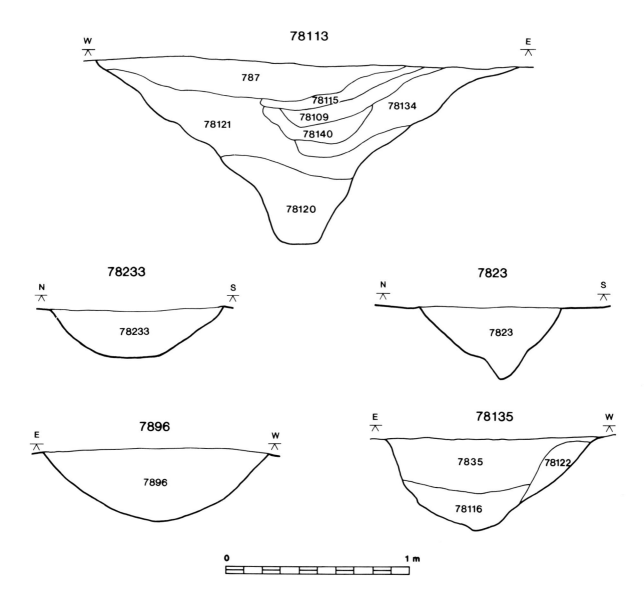

Figure 10 Sections: ditches of Enclosures 2 and 3

Enclosure 2

Enclosure 2 was roughly trapezoidal in plan, *c.* 1020m^2 in size, and overlay the west end of Bronze Age Enclosure 1. Approximately 20m of enclosure ditch *78113* was excavated, showing it to be generally 2.2m wide and 1m deep, with a V-shaped section and some evidence for having been cleaned out or recut (Fig. 10). This may explain why it contained few finds, comprising a mixture of small Iron Age sherds and larger quantities of redeposited Bronze Age pottery and briquetage.

There was no clear evidence for an internal bank associated with the ditch. However, various sections through the ditch showed layer *78109* to have been deposited from within the enclosure and this could, along with a number of related fills (*78115*, *78134*, and *78140*), have derived from a bank.

One or other, if not both undated post-holes *78195* and *78263* may have supported a gateway through the 3m wide entrance in the centre of the southern side of the enclosure. Three shallow gullies, *78233*, all around 0.3m deep (Fig. 9), lay immediately behind the entrance, one to each side with the other appearing to block it. However, the

stratigraphic relationship between these gullies and enclosure ditch *78113* could not be clearly established.

The majority of Enclosure 2 overlapped with ground previously occupied by Bronze Age Enclosure 1, and as few of the features contained finds it has not been possible to attribute many of the pits and post-holes encompassed by Enclosure 2 to phase. Of these, only one post-hole, *78202* (Figs 4 and 9), may be of Iron Age date, while sixteen other features contained only Bronze Age material. Although some of this earlier material may, like that in the ditch, be redeposited, the absence of features to the west of the Bronze Age enclosure may further suggest that the majority of the features within Enclosure 2 should be assigned a Phase 1 Bronze Age date. However, as noted above, few Phase 1 features lie within 3m of the ditch of Enclosure 1 apart from in the area encompassed by Enclosure 2. Some of these post-holes may be of Iron Age date but the matter cannot be resolved.

The presence of large quantities of Iron Age pottery in the upper levels of Bronze Age Enclosure 1 ditch *78145*, particularly in layer *784* (Fig. 5), may represent in part the deliberate infilling of this ditch to level the ground prior

Plate VII 1978 excavation from the air, facing south-east

Plate VIII Enclosure 3 ditch *78135*, facing north. 2m scale

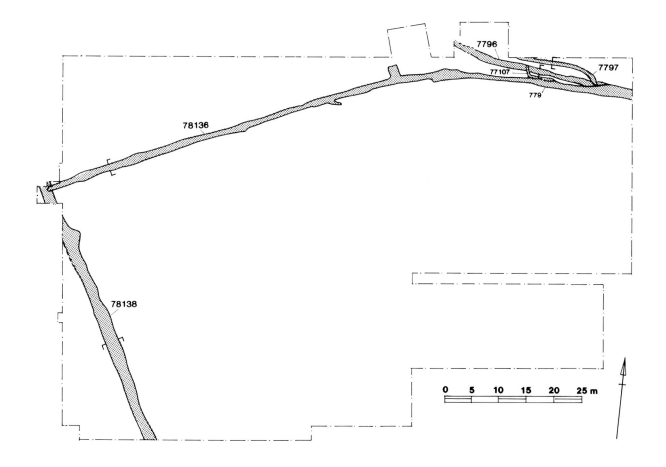

Figure 11 Plan of Phase 4 features

to the building of Enclosure 2 or debris deposited early in the use of this enclosure. However, layer *784* also occurs outside that enclosure so deliberate dumping of debris may not represent the whole answer. In view of the uncertainty of the stratigraphic relationship between Enclosures 2 and 3 it is possible that some of the material in layer *784* derives from occupation in Enclosure 3.

Field system associated with Enclosure 2
(Figs 9 and 10)
Two shallow ditches appear to be aligned on Enclosure 2. The northern terminal of ditch *7896* lies at the south-west corner of the enclosure; the southern terminal of ditch *7823* at its north-west corner. Neither ditch cuts enclosure ditch *78113*, which may suggest that they were aligned on it as an existing earthwork but that they were not intended to discharge drainage water directly into the enclosure ditch.

Enclosure 3
(Fig. 9)
Approximately 8m to the west of Enclosure 2 was the eastern edge of Enclosure 3 (Pl. VIII). Only a small portion of the enclosure, which was slightly larger than Enclosure 2, was excavated and it was shown to be bounded by a comparatively shallow ditch (*78135*) approximately 1.3m wide and 0.5m deep (Fig. 10). What was presumably an entrance some 1.5m wide with two gullies (*78103* and *78129*) aligned on it east–west was found. Post-hole *7885* in the centre of the entrance contained shelly pottery, and

might represent a slightly later Iron Age phase. Within the enclosure was a hearth lined with pebbles, *7894*, approximately 3.5m from the ditch, perhaps in the lee of a bank made from upcast from the ditch. Air photographs indicate a possible roundhouse in Enclosure 3 to the west of the excavated area.

In the north-west corner of the excavation, enclosure ditch *78135* appeared to cut ditch *7823* running up to the north-west corner of Enclosure 2, although it was difficult to discern the stratigraphical relationships.

As ditch *7823* appears to be aligned on Enclosure 2, this would suggest that Enclosure 3 is later than Enclosure 2. By how long is not known, but parts of pots with related inturned rims (Fig. 27: 90, 91 and 92) were found in the upper ditch filling (layer *784*) of Enclosure 1 and in the ditch around Enclosure 3. This may suggest that the interval was not a long one, and it is possible that there was some overlap in the use of Enclosures 2 and 3. Given the notable difference in the size of the ditches of Enclosures 2 and 3, and the number of features and finds which can be attributed to each of them, the use of the enclosures may have been complementary.

One or possibly two brooches were found in the upper filling (*78315*) and another (the Nauheim, Fig. 13: 4) in the lower filling (*78116*) of Enclosure 3 ditch *78135*, and these together with the presence of what appear to be sherds of the same pots in both upper and lower fills (Fig. 27: 94–95) may also suggest that the final filling of the ditch took place over a relatively short time, perhaps in the first half of the 1st century BC.

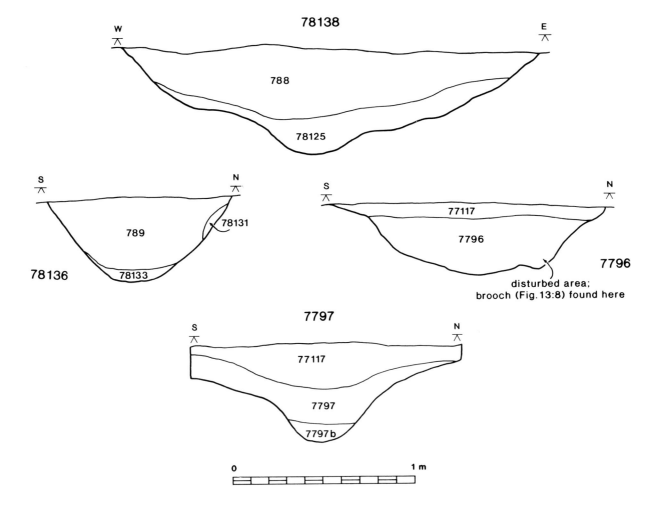

Figure 12 Sections: ditches

Features outside Enclosures 2 and 3

Further evidence for use of the area in the Iron Age comes from the partial recutting of ditch *7710*, the northern side of Bronze Age Enclosure 1. Layers *7710* and *7710b* in the central portion of the ditch (see Fig. 5) contained the smith's 'poker' (Pl. IX) and Iron Age pottery. Farther along the ditch to the west, layer *78225* may also represent recutting of the ditch. In neither case, however, was the feature well defined or particularly deep and in the case of the 'poker' may represent the digging of a pit in a still recognisable old boundary for a formal, votive, deposit. Many pieces of Iron Age ironwork have been found in boundary contexts (Hingley 1990) and the evidence at Billingborough may represent this rather than the wholesale recutting of the northern side of Enclosure 1.

V. Phase 4: Early Romano-British
by A.P. Fitzpatrick and Peter Chowne (1990)
(Fig. 11)

This phase is principally represented by two ditches, *78138* and *779/78136*, probably defining a large field or enclosure. The north–south ditch, *78138*, was the earlier of the two and was cut by *78136*. Ditch *78138* was *c.* 2m wide and 0.6m deep (Fig. 12) and had been recut at least

once. It was on a different alignment to Phase 3 ditch *78135* of Enclosure 3, which it cut on the western edge of the excavation. Ditch *779/78136* was only *c.* 0.65m wide and 0.5m deep and it too had been recut at least once. Towards the eastern edge of the excavation, it cut two gullies running north-west to south-east, *7796* and *7797*, each *c.* 1.5m wide and 0.4–0.5m deep. These may have been earlier boundaries, and ditch *779/78136* was itself cut by later gully *77107*.

Dating
Other than Bronze and Iron Age material which is likely to have been redeposited, ditch *78138* contained few finds. Similarly, although nearly 80m of ditch *779/78136* was excavated, it too contained few finds but amongst these was a small quantity of Romano-British grey wares and a bracelet (Fig. 13: 9) of probable late Roman date from an upper fill. The pottery is not closely datable and the best dating for the sequence of ditches was provided by the discovery of a Hod Hill brooch (Fig. 13: 8) in the lower fill of gully *7796* (see Fig. 12). The brooch seems unlikely to have been made much, if at all, after the 60s AD and it suggests that the excavated sequence of field ditches and reworking of boundaries may have begun during the early 1st century AD.

Chapter 3. The Artefacts

I. Copper alloy objects

by Joanna K.F. Bacon and A.P. Fitzpatrick (1984/1990)
(Fig. 13)

A total of seventeen objects of copper alloy (excluding modern finds) was recovered from the excavation at Billingborough. Of these seventeen objects, four come from Phase 1, three from Phase 3, and two from Phase 4, with the remainder unstratified in medieval plough furrows or topsoil. These objects are discussed by phase rather than by category, although some of the objects were clearly redeposited.

Phase 1

Razor/knife
The fragmentary object illustrated as Figure 13: 1 is almost certainly part of a razor or knife blade. It was found in post-hole *77193* assigned to four-post structure D. The piece is badly corroded, but appears to consist of a fragment of blade with a tang, the other edges being corroded. If it is a razor the angle of the shoulder (which is less marked than it would originally have been, because the original edges are missing) suggests that it is of Piggott's Class II (Piggott 1946). The closest parallel to the Billingborough razor is from Broughton, Lincolnshire (Davey 1973, 99, no. 233; May 1976, 79, fig. 41).

Broad-bladed flat copper alloy tanged knives also occur in the later Middle Bronze Age. One from Salmonby, Lincolnshire was classified as a razor by Davey (1973, 99, no. 234) but later recognised by May (1976, 80, fig. 44, no. 7) to be a knife, similar to that from Black Patch, East Sussex (Drewett 1982, 360, fig. 29, no. 2).

Awls
The single awl from the site is square in section, tapering to a point at one end, and flattened at the other (Fig. 13: 2). It was found in the ditch of Enclosure 1 (layer *7710d*) and is typical of Bronze Age awls, such as that from Owmby, Lincolnshire (Davey 1973, 118, no. 426; May 1976, 95), or the two from Risby Warren, Lincolnshire (Davey 1973, 90, fig. 23, nos 212 and 213; May 1976, 95).

Objects of uncertain function
A single small section of rod, bent into a U-shape, was found in Bronze Age (Phase 1/2) layer *7742* (Fig. 13: 3) as was a single unidentifiable fragment (Fig. 13: 7).

Phase 3

Brooches
Parts of three, possibly four, Iron Age brooches were found, one of which (Fig. 13: 4) provides the key dating evidence for Phase 3. It comes from Enclosure 3 ditch *78135*.

The flattened, wide, bow of the brooch (Fig. 13: 4) is similar to those of Nauheim type which is found widely in continental Europe and is currently thought to have appeared at the end of the 2nd or early in the 1st centuries BC and to have been in use until the middle of the 1st century (Feugère 1985, 226; Miron 1991). Feugère has subdivided the Nauheim into three variants — a, b, and c — on the basis of the shape of the bow. The Billingborough piece compares to variant a, which is the earliest of the three (Feugère 1985, 223–6). However, while the bow of the Billingborough find is similar to the Nauheim, the spring has an external chord; and one of the traits by which the Nauheim is defined is an internal chord. External chords are a distinctive feature of British later Iron Age brooches dating to about the first half of the 1st century BC, while the four coil spring on the Billingborough example suggests that it is a comparatively early example. Related finds which have decorated bows, but two coil springs, are known from Folkestone, Kent (Stead 1976, 410–11, fig. 4, 2) and Meare Village East, Somerset (Coles 1987, 73, 75, no. EE6, fig. 3.13, EE6).

A similar date seems likely for the brooch pin and spring from Billingborough which has an external chord (Fig. 13: 5) and which also came from Enclosure 3 ditch *78135*. Although it is too corroded to be certain, the fragmentary iron object illustrated as Figure 15: 3 also appears to be from a brooch with an external chord, and may be of similar date.

A third copper alloy object from enclosure ditch *78135* is also likely to be from an Iron Age brooch (Fig. 13: 6). Although it has some similarities to ring-headed pins, it lacks their characteristic bend beneath the head (Dunning 1934, fig. 3–4). Instead the piece seems more likely to be the bow and part of the mock-spring of an involuted brooch (*cf* Stead 1979, 66–71, fig. 24–5; Hawkes and Hull 1987, Type 2Ca, 133–5, 157–63, pl. 44–6). Most brooches of this type are in iron, including an example from Ancaster Quarry, Lincolnshire where the return of the foot to the bow is quite pronounced as would have been the case with the Billingborough piece (May 1976, 140, fig.69: 2; Hawkes and Hull 1987, 161, no. 9220, pl. 46, 9220). A 3rd or 2nd century BC date seems likely.

Although comparatively small in number, most of the Billingborough brooches form a homogenous group, none of which need be later than *c*. 50 BC. If the copper alloy pin (Fig. 13: 6) is from an involuted brooch of La Tène II type this extends the chronology back into the 2nd, and possibly 3rd, century BC.

Phase 4

Brooches
Although conceivably an Iron Age import, the Hod Hill brooch (Fig. 13: 8), from gully *7796*, is most likely to be of Claudio-Neronian date (*cf* Mackreth 1987, 150).

Bracelets
The copper alloy bracelet (Fig. 13: 9), from ditch *78136*, is probably also of Romano-British date. Bracelets were never particularly common in the Iron Age (Stead 1979,

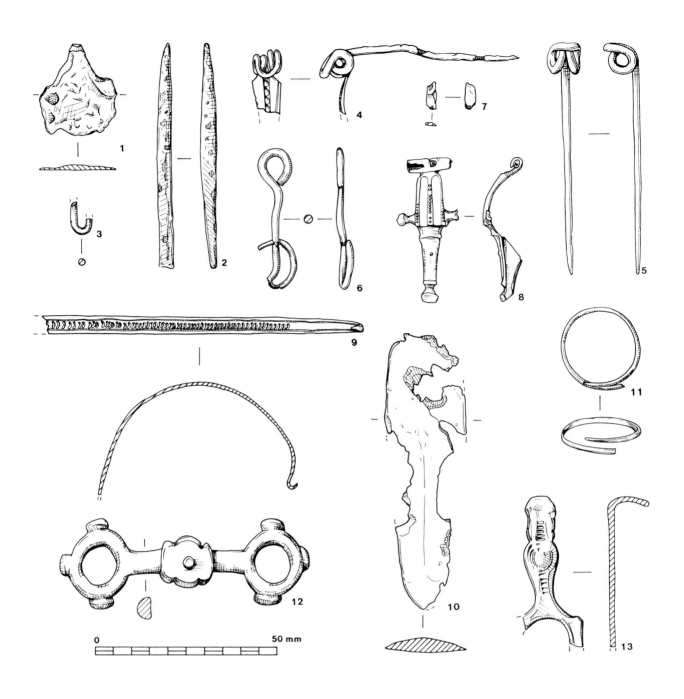

Figure 13 Copper alloy objects

73–7, fig. 27–9), while stamped and grooved decoration is well known on Romano-British bracelets with hook and eye clasps which tend to be late Roman in date (*e.g.* Crummy 1983, 41–4, fig. 44–5), and this would be consistent with the unstratified 4th-century coin from the site.

Unphased

Dagger
The blade illustrated as Figure 13: 10 is without a tang and is fairly narrow, short and double-edged; it is likely to belong to a Middle Bronze Age dirk or dagger. It is similar to the example in the Caythorpe hoard, Lincolnshire (Davey 1973, 113, no. 385) which is of the same proportions but 168mm long. Also similar but larger are more than 50 segments of undistinguished blades

recovered from the Langdon Bay cargo (Muckelroy 1981, 283). The narrower blade from Black Patch (Drewett 1982, 360, fig. 29, no. 8) was identified as a rapier. The nearest parallel to the Billingborough example is a blade from New Barn Down, East Sussex (Curwen 1934).

Rings
A single spiral finger ring of unknown date was recovered (Fig. 13: 11).

Objects of uncertain function
The looped object illustrated as Figure 13: 12 is of iron plated with copper alloy and is likely to be of medieval date. Although the piece has passing similarities with certain later Iron Age strap unions from horse harnesses (*e.g.* Taylor and Brailsford 1985), better parallels are found in the side-links used to attach the reins to the

mouthpieces of bridal bits which have been found on a number of sites with 8th- to 10th-century AD occupation. These include an elaborate decorated example from Old Sarum, Wiltshire, suggested to have Scandinavian affinities (Stevens 1937). Related, but more simple pieces which, like the Old Sarum find, are also plated with non-ferrous metal are known, for example from Goltho, Lincolnshire (Goodall 1987, 184, fig. 160, 160). While bronze on iron objects are known from the Iron Age, the technique was not common and was usually applied to horse-bits (*e.g.* Spratling 1979). Consequently an 8th- to 10th-century date for the Billingborough example appears likely.

A single copper alloy droplet (not illustrated) may derive from metalworking. This was found close to unphased hearths *7816* and *7817*.

Other finds include a decorative fitting of unknown use (Fig. 18: 13), a small fragment of possible brooch pin (not illustrated), and two bronze coins from the second quarter of the 4th century, minted at Trier, found in the topsoil and a medieval plough furrow respectively.

Catalogue of copper alloy objects

(All catalogued objects are illustrated in Figure 13. In the catalogue the context or layer number is followed by the feature type and number (if any), the small find number, and phase).

Fig. 13

1. Fragment of **blade** with flat, wide body, thickened and tapering to handle. Incomplete and very corroded. Max. length 22mm. Max. width 20mm. Thickness 1–2mm. (*post-hole 77193, no. 370, Phase 1*)
2. **Awl**, tapering to round-sectioned point at one end, squared section centrally, flattened into oblong, chisel-shape at other end, slightly askew. Surface corroded. Lab. no. 84/79. Length 58.5mm. Width 1.5–4.0mm. Thickness 1.0–3.5mm. (*7710d, ditch 7710, no. 85, Phase 1*)
3. Small fragment of round-sectioned **rod** bent into U-shape. Length 8mm. Width 6mm. Thickness 1.5mm. (*Layer 7742, no. 224, Phase 1*)
4. **Brooch**. Length 54.5mm. Lab. no. 85/79. (*78116, ditch 78135, sf 349, Phase 3*)
5. **Brooch**. Length 61.5mm. (*7835, ditch 78135, no. 362, Phase 3*)
6. Part of an ?involuted **brooch**. Round sectioned rod bent into ring at top, tapering at other end where returned into larger loop, probably the result of pre-depositional damage. Tip possibly missing. Some corrosion of outer surface especially towards this end, showing construction over inner wire. Length 37.5mm. Width 12mm. Thickness 2mm. (*7835, ditch 78135, no. 105, Phase 3*)
7. **Unidentified object**. Small fragment, pitted surface. Length 7.5mm. Width 3mm. Thickness 1.5mm. (*784, ditch 78145, no. 387, Phase 1*)
8. **Brooch**. Length 38.5mm. Width 17mm. Height 11.5mm. Lab. no. 323/79. (*gully 7796, no. 191, Phase 4*)
9. About one half of a thin, ribbon **bracelet**, tapering to point at surviving terminal which is turned back on itself. Decorated with a groove parallel to the edge on each side, 2mm apart, tapering to V at terminal. Rouletting of small arcs between grooves from 22mm above terminal. Length 88mm. Diameter 55mm. Thickness 0.5mm. Depth 3.5mm. (*789, ditch 78136, no. 274, Phase 4*)
10. **Dagger or dirk**, centrally thickened, hammered very thin at edges and with a flattened, rounded tip. Edges squared towards basal end (*c.* 1mm thick). Tapers lengthways from centre to ends. Tip slightly bent back. Incomplete, corroded. Lab. no. 2. X-ray no. 5/79. Length 72mm. Max. width 22mm. Max. thickness 3mm. (*781, no. 137, topsoil*)
11. One circuit only of **spiral ring**, tapering at one end to pointed terminal. Thin ribbon, oblong in section with squared edges, worn down into narrower strip opposite terminal. Diameter 22mm. Width 1mm. Thickness 1.2–1.8mm. Lab. no. 86/79. (*drain 7746, no. 106, modern field drain*)
12. **Cast object** with flat back and domed surfaces. It appears to be of iron with a copper alloy plating. Squared oval central boss, indented

from below and slightly raised; solid D-sectioned rod, has flat bottom extending from each of two flat sides, each terminating in oval ring bearing three vestigial knobs in cruciform layout. Both rounded sides of boss have vertical groove towards each corner forming trefoil shape. Single small domed knob at centre top of boss has four grooves running from it — one to each corner. Two oval rings are arched inwards from below, slightly raised and narrower at outer ends, and of thin oval section. The knobs have domed outer surfaces, ridged outwards above vague neck onto ring. Much of original outer surface missing, though signs of wear within the two rings. Lab. no. 93/79. Length 69mm. Width 7–24mm. Thickness 1.5–6mm. (*771, no. 57, topsoil*)

13. Flat, narrow **fitting**, with squared edges. Incomplete, slightly asymmetrical. Waisted above open (incomplete) end, widening to roundel, then nipped in, with triangular pointed terminal bent over at right angle. Incomplete end has bevelled edge on underside. Either side of roundel has decorated upper face with rouletting, and a groove across bend towards pointed terminal. Lab. no. 81/79. Length 40mm. Max. width 16mm. Thickness 2mm. Height 11.5mm. (*781, no. 4, topsoil*).

II. Iron objects

by A.P. Fitzpatrick and Joanna K.F. Bacon (1984/1990)
(Figs 14 and 15)

The iron objects included in the catalogue are only a selection of those recovered during the excavation. The majority of pieces were fragmentary and not from stratified contexts; these are omitted here, although they are recorded in the archive. All but Fig. 15: 4 (unphased) are from Phase 3 contexts.

Tools

'Pokers'

The object illustrated as Figure 14:1 may be identified as a blacksmith's 'poker'. It belongs to a well defined group of tools which, though considered to be fire pokers by Rodwell (1976, 45–6) and all-purpose pokers by Jacobi (1974, 101), were probably 'slices' used to move fuel in the fire (Saunders 1977, 16).

Rodwell divided pokers into three types and the Billingborough find is an example of his Type B with a 'Plain, untwisted shaft, square or round in section, often terminating in a knob or suspension loop' (Rodwell 1976, 46). Examples of Type A, which has a twisted shaft, and B were found together at Wetwang Slack (North Yorkshire) (Brewster 1980, 363–5, fig. 217–19, pl. 68) demonstrating that they were contemporary. Whether or not Rodwell's Type C, which is defined as having a 'plain shaft, round in section, without suspension loop, terminal loop or decorative twisting...' existed as a separate category is open to doubt as the type figure from Witham, Essex appears to have the remains of such a terminal (Rodwell 1976, fig. 2,1) and the other examples suggested to be of Type C are fragmentary. Rodwell also suggested that Type C may have been 'insulated with an organic binding at the 'handle end', and that a knob on the rod could have 'contained' an organic handle' (Rodwell 1976, 45, fig 1). The thickening of the rod on the Billingborough poker to form a boss may similarly have served to retain an organic handle.

Rodwell argued that 'there is no evidence to suggest that iron pokers remained popular late into La Tène III' (1976, 49), which may be broadly termed as from the 1st century BC onwards. It is quite possible that the Billingborough slice is contemporary with the Mid–Late Iron Age brooches from the site.

There can be no doubt about the formal deposition of the Billingborough poker, broken in half, with the two pieces being laid side-by-side oriented north–south in the ditch (Pl. IX). The pokers at Wetwang Slack and Madmarston, Oxfordshire (Fowler 1960) were certainly deposited in, or as, hoards and the same may be true for the Witham finds. The boundary context of the Billingborough find echoes the repeated formal deposition of currency bars in boundaries, both of settlements and in the form of other features such as pit alignments (Hingley 1990, table 3).

Awls
An extremely corroded object from Phase 3 ditch *78135* of Enclosure 3 may be an awl (Fig. 15: 2).

Objects of personal adornment or dress

Brooches
The fragmentary object illustrated as Figure 15: 3 appears to be a fragment of a brooch with an external chord. This may, on analogy with the copper alloy brooches of similar form (see above, p. 21) be dated to the late 2nd century BC or first half of the 1st century. It came from a gully within Enclosure 3 dated to Phase 3.

Weapons

Projectile points
The corroded and unstratified object illustrated as Figure 15: 4 may be an Iron Age spear, which are characteristically very small, some no more than 60mm in length (Stead 1991, 74–5), although it could as easily be of medieval date.

Catalogue of iron objects

Figs 14 and 15
1. 'Poker' (Pl. IX). Round-sectioned **rod** flattened at one end to slightly concave trapezoidal-shaped shovel flaring towards edge. Other end flattened slightly and curled around a round-sectioned ring (57mm in diameter, 7–8mm thick) probably for suspension. Rod thickens to form round knob 25mm in diameter at 245mm from shovel end. The rod has been deliberately broken, 158mm above knob. Length 844mm. Diameter 13mm. Shovel head length 90mm, width 45–55mm. (*7710, ditch 7710, Phase 3*)
2. Possible **awl**. Iron rod, square in section, narrowed at both ends and slightly arched. Very corroded. Length 64mm. Width 5–8mm. Thickness 5–8mm. (*78116, ditch 78135, no. 188, Phase 3*)
3. **Brooch** fragment. Very corroded. Length 13mm. Max. width 8mm. (*gully 75103, no. 369, Phase 3*)
4. **Projectile point/ spear**?; round sectioned shank, hollow at base, tapering towards blade. Blade oval in section with thin edges, tapering to point on same line as shank. Bottom edges of blade lopsided. Tip missing. X-ray no. 14/79. Length 48mm. Width 5–14mm. Thickness 3–11mm. (*781, no. 287, topsoil*)

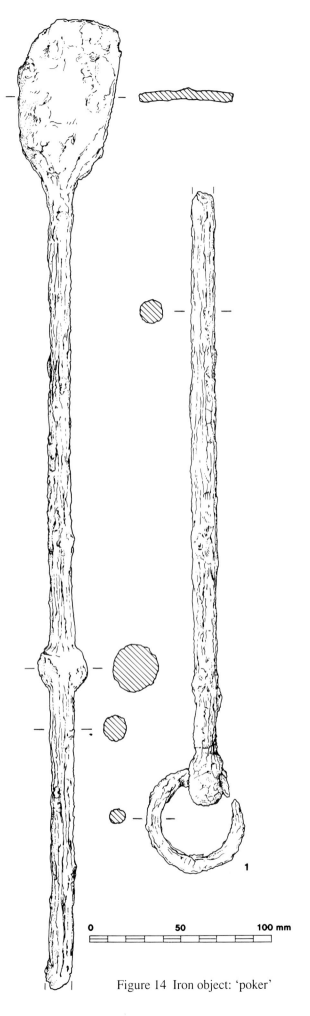

Figure 14 Iron object: 'poker'

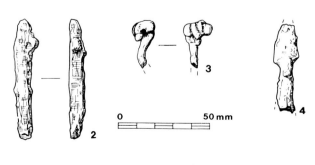

Figure 15 Iron objects

Plate IX Iron 'poker' in upper fill of ditch *7710*. Scale = 170mm

III. Technological Finds
by Justine Bayley (1984)

Assorted finds which were thought to be of technological origin were submitted for examination and identification (AML No.830469, AML Report No. 4259, June 1984). The bulk of the finds were either iron-working slag or fired clay though smaller amounts of other material were also noted. The total weight of the samples was about 4kg. There is little difference in the range of materials present in contexts of different date, which suggests that many of the finds in later contexts are redeposited from earlier deposits. Certainly there is nothing that could not be Iron Age in origin.

The iron slag indicates iron working, though probably on a fairly small scale as the total quantities are not large. The question is whether the iron was being smelted from its ores or just worked by a blacksmith. Some of the slag has the porous, open texture usually associated with smithing but much of it is rather denser and less vesicular which suggests higher temperatures than are normally obtained in a smith's hearth. Some of the slag is small, irregular pieces but some is in the form of plano-convex buns which collected at the bottom of the hearth or furnace. There is no tap slag (a sure indicator of smelting) but this would be very unusual in an Iron Age context as the furnaces in use then were of a non-tapping type. It is therefore possible, but by no means certain, that iron was being smelted at Billingborough. The occurrence of several pieces of ironstone among the finds supports this suggestion but none of them had been roasted, a necessary preliminary to smelting, so their presence could just be fortuitous.

The rest of the slag is fuel ash slag which forms when silicate materials such as sand or clay are heated strongly in contact with the ash of a fire. The alkalis in the ash react with the silicates producing vitreous slags. Fuel ash slags contain far less iron than smelting and smithing slags and so are lighter in weight and often paler in colour. Fuel ash slags are not necessarily an indicator of industrial processes as they can form in any fire at high enough temperatures but they are often found associated with other evidence for metalworking. One specific form of

fuel ash slag is described as hearth lining; the clay lining to a hearth is vitrified on the surface in contact with the fire so a gradient can be observed from a glassy surface through to ordinary fired clay further from the fire. Bellows were often used to obtain higher working temperatures. The usual evidence for this is a tuyère hole, a regular circular hole in the furnace or hearth lining with the immediate surroundings heavily vitrified where the air blast has produced a localised hot spot. The one example from Billingborough had a hole with a diameter of about 40mm, which is rather larger than is usually found.

The majority of the stratified material, including four plano-convex buns of slag and the fragment of tuyère hole, came from Enclosure 3 ditch *78113*, assigned a Phase 3 (Iron Age) date. A smaller quantity of debris came from later, unstratified contexts in this area and it seems likely that iron working, probably smithing, took place within Enclosure 3 or the immediate vicinity.

The rest of the samples can be described as fired clay and come from various contexts almost entirely of Phase 3 or later date. There are a variety of fabrics but most are fairly fine and contain little temper. They show a range of firing conditions from strongly oxidising to reducing. Many of the lumps have some evidence for one or more original surfaces but it is difficult to assign forms and hence to suggest uses when the majority of pieces are so small. A few bits would appear to have been daub as traces of the wattle survive on them. Many of the pieces have a pale-coloured surface, either grey-green, cream or off-white. This decolourisation of fired clay happens when the water mixed with the raw clay is brackish or saline or the clay is calcareous. The soluble salts in the clay tend to concentrate on the surface having migrated there in the water which evaporates as the clay dries out. These salts, particularly chlorides, will react with the iron present in the clay forming ferric chloride which volatilises readily at about 800°C leaving an iron-depleted surface layer to the clay which is pale coloured. The effect has been noted on fired clay associated with salt boiling but is found widely in areas where the ground water is brackish. At Billingborough its occurrence is not unexpected and does not necessarily mean that all the pale-surfaced fired clay was a by-product of salt working.

Two conjoining fragments from one half of a clay mould (Fig. 36: 13) came from Phase 3 ditch *78113*. The mould was probably for a piece of horse harness, such as a side-ring from a three-link snaffle bit.

Two small fragments of copper alloy sheet (unprovenanced) were analysed by X-ray fluorescence and shown to be bronze (copper and tin). This alloy was used from prehistoric times onwards so the composition of the metal cannot be used to date it. The fragments were probably parts of objects rather than waste from a metalworking operation, although one droplet of copper alloy (not analysed) which might conceivably derive from metalworking was recovered close to a pair of ?Phase 2 hearths (*7511* and *7512*) towards the north-east corner of the site.

IV. Flint
by Jill Harden (1981)

Introduction
The excavations at Billingborough produced 653 worked flints, consisting of 30 cores, 11 pieces of irregular workshop waste, 341 non-retouched flakes, and 271 retouched or utilised flakes (Table 3). A large proportion of this assemblage probably derives from pre-Phase 1 (Late Neolithic–Early Bronze Age) activity on the site.

The majority of the raw material could have been obtained from the immediate vicinty of the site, flint nodules and chert occurring in the topsoil and underlying coarse calcareous gravels. This raw material has a thin cortex, covering grey, grey-brown, orange-brown or brown coloured flint.

There are a few pieces of atypical flint from Billingborough which have a thick white cortex and are black in colour. These only occur as retouched pieces (*e.g.* Fig. 16: 2). This type of raw material could be mined flint, the nearest known sources being the Norfolk chalk area although the Lincolnshire Wolds may contain similar deposits. Similar black flint is also present in the gravels at Fengate, Cambridgeshire (Francis Pryor pers. comm.).

How the flint was obtained is not known. It may have been gathered from the ground surface or pits may have been dug into the gravels to find suitably sized nodules (a possible function suggested for Phase 1 pit *7570*).

Patination was present on 23% of the pieces of flint, varying in degree from patchy pale blue to thick white. The majority of these patinated pieces occurred in unstratified contexts.

Analysis
The flints from Billingborough were initially divided into three groups of contexts for finds analysis:

1) Those from Phase 1/2 contexts — 156 flints
2) Those from derived or unphased contexts — 150 flints
3) Those from known medieval or post-medieval contexts, including the plough soil — 347 flints

However, no differences between the assemblages from the three groups of contexts were identified, either in flint knapping techniques or in the types of retouched pieces produced. For the purposes of this report the flint collection has therefore been treated as a single assemblage. Details of the analysis of the three groups of contexts are available in the archive.

The flints have been classified as follows:

Cores
The system adopted in the Hurst Fen, Suffolk, report (Clark *et al.* 1960) has been used, except that any cores which might have had platforms but are definitely keeled have been included in Class D. The only other group of cores consists of those which are thermally fractured or broken.

Irregular waste
Large, heavy pieces which are neither cores nor flakes, but exhibit a few struck flake scars.

Retouched and utilised flakes
These flints have been classified according to the generic term usually attributed to these forms. It should be noted, however, that as no microwear analysis has been carried out on these pieces the inference that they have been used or that they could have been used in a specific way has not been tested. Utilised flakes are classed as those that exhibit tiny flake scars for at least 10mm on one or more edges of the flake.

Scrapers
These are retouched thick flakes and occasionally cores, and this class also includes pieces of irregular waste or thermal pieces which have been retouched. The angle of retouch is always greater than 40°, and retouch occurs along specific edges of the dorsal face producing convex edges and, occasionally, nosed or hollow pieces.

Projectile points
Specific classification of barbed and tanged arrowheads follows that developed by Green (1980) and petit tranchet derivatives follows that of Clark (1934) and Green (1980).

Other retouched pieces
Other retouched pieces have been identified by analogy with similar forms from sites in the south and east of England.

Metrical analysis
In the analysis of the flints from Billingborough the breadth:length ratios of the flakes have been calculated and these are presented in histogram form (Fig. 17). Full details of this analysis are contained in the archive. It should be borne in mind that the arbitrary nature of the divisions used in each histogram do not necessarily reflect the actual variations which are significant to these flakes. The divisions have been chosen for convenience of comparison with other flint assemblages.

Results
(Table 3)

Debitage
(382 pieces — 58.5% of total flints)

Cores
(30 pieces — 4.6% of total flints)
Class A1/A2 — single platform, broken cores: 3 examples
Class B3 — 2 platforms at right angles: 1 example
Class C — 3 or more platforms: 1 example
Class D — keeled cores: 14 examples
Thermally fractured cores: 11 examples

The predominance of the keeled core at Billingborough is not paralleled at other 2nd-millennium BC sites, either in the Fens or further afield. The main type of core on sites such as Fengate (Pryor 1980) and Itford Hill, East Sussex (Holden 1972) was class A1/A2. The few sites where keeled cores formed more than 20% of the core types recovered include Hurst Fen (Clark *et al.* 1960) and Arreton Down, Isle of Wight (Ozanne and Ozanne 1960). At Hurst Fen, an earlier Neolithic site, keeled cores formed 33% of the total cores but class A1/A2 were of even greater importance — 41%. At Arreton Down, a later Neolithic site, keeled cores formed 27% of the total cores but again class A1/A2 were of greater importance — 47%.

	Quantity	Total
Debitage		**382**
Cores	30	
Irregular workshop waste	11	
Non-retouched flakes	341	
Utilised and retouched flakes		**271**
Utilised		126
Scrapers		117
Side/end	35	
Horseshoe	33	
Discoidal	8	
Broken flake	19	
Core	3	
On waste/thermal flint	19	
Projectiles		9
Barbed and tanged	5	
Bifacially retouched, triangular	1	
Bifacially retouched, assymetrical	1	
Possible projectile points	2	
Other retouched		15
Serrated flake	4	
Flat end retouch	4	
Fabricator	2	
Miscellaneous	5	
Other		4
'Chopping tool'	3	
Hammerstone	1	
TOTAL		**653**

Table 3 Flint totals

Non-retouched flakes
(341 pieces — 52.2% of total flints)
Of the 341 non-retouched flakes, 153 (*c.* 45%) were broken, but an indication of the probable shape of the flake was recorded.

Using the categories presented in Figure 17, the predominant shape of flake has a breadth:length ratio of 4:5–5:5. However, when comparing this analysis with other sites it will be noted that 44% of the flakes have a breadth:length ratio of greater than 5:5. Pitts (1978) and Ford *et al.* (1984) highlighted the fact that there is usually a trend from narrow, blade-like flakes in the earlier Neolithic to broad, squat flakes in the Bronze Age. This is illustrated convincingly at Fengate (Pryor 1980, fig. 74) and is paralleled here at Billingborough.

When a comparison of assemblages from a few other Bronze Age East Anglian gravel sites is made, the ratio of debitage to retouched pieces is as follows: at Hurst Fen, Suffolk, debitage (including utilised flakes) formed 95.2% of the assemblage; at Ecton, Northamptonshire (Moore and Williams 1975) 95.5%; and at Fengate (Pryor 1980) 91.9%. If utilised flakes are included in the analysis of debitage from Billingborough, the percentage of workshop waste is only 77.5%. Thus, although some flint knapping had obviously taken place within the area excavated, the working of flint is also presumed to have taken place elsewhere.

Utilised and retouched pieces
(271 pieces: 41.5% of total flints)
Utilised flakes (126 pieces — 19% of total flints)
Of the 127 utilised flakes, 55 (*c.* 44%) were broken, but an indication of the probable shape of the flakes was recorded.

A wide variety of flake shapes appear to have been utilised, from those with breadth:length ratios of 2:5–3:5 to those of 6:5–7:5 (Fig. 17). If only six categories of breadth:length ratios are used the predominant form is that with a ratio of greater than 5:5. The small number of flakes which are *unbroken* means that comparison with other sites would probably be unwise, but there does seem to be a significant difference between the shapes of non-retouched and utilised flakes at Billingborough. This difference is also present amongst the broken flakes. There are approximately the same number of blade-like as non blade-like unbroken or broken flakes in the utilised category, whereas there are are three times as many non-blade-like than blade-like in the non-retouched category. Thus there appears to be a preference for blade-like flakes for utilisation rather than the predominant broad, squat flakes. However, it must not be forgotten that 47% of the utilised flakes were found in the plough soil and that the 'utilisation' may in fact be the result of damage caused by the turning of the soil. The importance of this proviso is lessened somewhat by the fact that the utilised flakes formed 20% of the flints from Phase 1 and 2 contexts and 21% of those from unstratified contexts.

Scrapers
(Fig. 16: 1–10)
(117 pieces — 17.9% of total flints)
The scrapers are closely comparable in style with those from Fengate (Pryor 1980) and Mildenhall Fen, Suffolk (Clark 1936); many retaining areas of cortex and the retouch including examples of bold, stepped edges. As at Mildenhall Fen, the use of thermally fractured pieces is noted, although the lack of disc and end-of-blade scrapers is not paralleled at Billingborough. A decrease in the size of scrapers was noted at Fengate between the later Neolithic and Bronze Age sites. At Billingborough the length, breadth, and thickness of the scrapers are directly comparable with those for the later Neolithic at Fengate. Further afield, the Billingborough scrapers are closely comparable with those from a large number of sites including Itford Hill, Thorny Down, Wiltshire (Stone 1941) and Boscombe Down East, Wiltshire (Stone 1936).

Projectile Points
(9 pieces — 1.4% of total flints)
Projectile points consist of a barbed and tanged arrowhead of Green's (1980) enlarged Green Low type (Fig. 16: 11), three barbed and tanged arrowheads of Green's Sutton (a) type, and one which is probably a Conygar Hill type. There is also a bifacially retouched triangular arrowhead, a bifacially retouched assymetrical arrowhead, and two possible projectile points.

Other retouched flakes
(15 pieces — 2.3% of total flints)
This category is shown by subdivision in Table 3. The predominance of scrapers over other retouched flakes is also a characteristic of sites such as Mildenhall Fen, Itford Hill, and Thorny Down. The only marked variation between the few other retouched flakes from Billingborough and those from Fengate and Mildenhall Fen is the lack of awls and piercers at the former site.

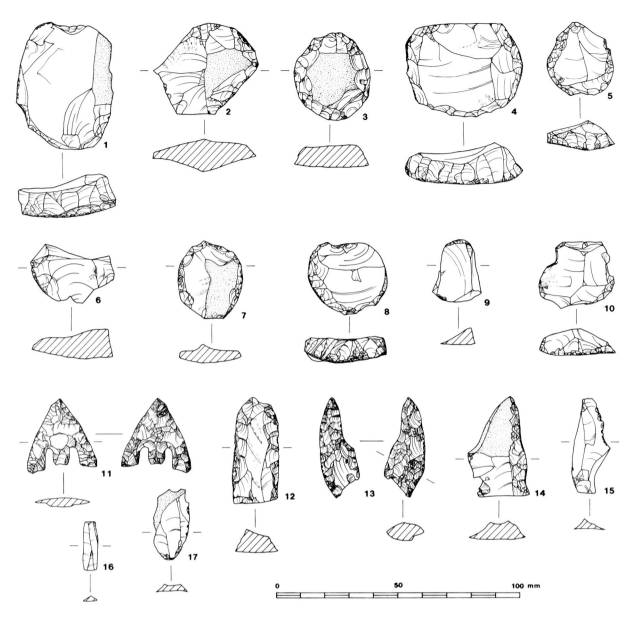

Figure 16 Flint objects

Other objects
There are three 'chopping tools' and one hammerstone in the assemblage.

Discussion
It would be misleading to place too much importance on the comparison of the flint collection from Billingborough with those of similarly dated sites, even if they are located in comparable geological, topographical, and possibly environmental areas. This is largely because of the nature of the flint collection — the majority of the pieces coming from the plough soil rather than the stratified contexts assigned to Phases 1 and 2 (53%:24% from topsoil and Phases 1/2 respectively) — and its small size. However, with this major proviso in mind, some conclusions may be drawn.

The predominant shape of the non-retouched flakes is typical of 'late' flint knapping techniques, as is the less controlled nature of retouch on the scrapers and the lack of finely worked pieces such as leaf-shaped arrowheads or knives. The importance of the keeled cores may also reflect a Bronze Age date, although single platform cores would normally be the predominant type of this period. Alternatively, the number of keeled cores may not reflect the true variety of cores, for the ratio of by-products to implements is not that which would be expected if the majority of flint knapping took place within the area excavated. It should be noted that ploughing may have produced more flakes than was originally the case, so that the number of by-products may even be exaggerated at Billingborough.

The utilised and retouched flake types are similar to those found on other 2nd-millennium BC sites throughout south-east England. However, the short, narrow, thin characteristics of the scrapers from Fengate are not paralleled at Billingborough, although the source of the flint nodules is presumed to be comparable. The only tool type not present at Billingborough, although it was found at Fengate and Mildenhall Fen, is the awl/piercer.

Although the flint collection from Billingborough is small, the anomalies identified may be of importance when further work is considered on Fen margin sites (see Healy 1996). The suggestion that specific activities were dispersed around and within the enclosure may be

28

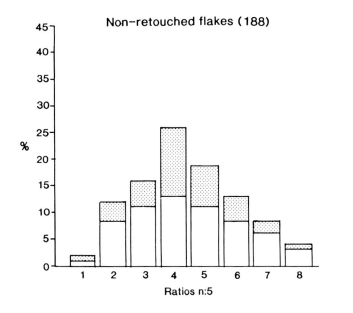

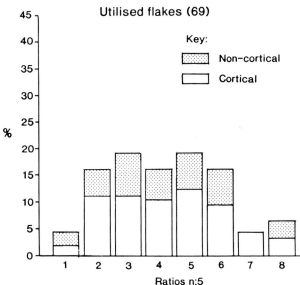

Figure 17 Flint: measurements of non-retouched and utilised flakes

particularly relevant, with flint knapping mainly taking place outside the enclosure, either close to pits dug to extract the flint nodules or near the gathering sites of the raw material (presumably picked from the surface of arable fields). The occurrence of scrapers (which formed 43% of the retouched and utilised pieces) within the enclosure may indicate a specific tool-use related 'industry'.

However, this hypothesis is based on the assumption that the flints from Billingborough are from one assemblage, produced in the Phase 1 occupation of the site. This is possible but it is perhaps more likely that the majority of the flints are of Late Neolithic/Early Bronze Age date and reflect activity on the site prior to the digging of Enclosure 1 in Phase 1. There is some evidence from the pottery and worked stone finds which would support this suggestion of pre-enclosure activity, and this is considered further below (see Chapter 5).

Catalogue of illustrated flint

Fig. 16

1. Horseshoe scraper. (*unprovenanced*)
2. Piece with flat edge retouch. (*post-hole 77180, no. 340, Phase 1*)
3. Discoidal scraper. (*771, no. 29, topsoil*)
4. Horseshoe scraper. (*77117, no. 357, unphased*)
6. Scraper. (*post-hole 77120, no. 401, Phase 1*)
7. Horseshoe scraper. (*7743, ditch 7743, no. 268, Phase 2*)
8. Right side and end scraper. (*1975 excavation, no. 14, surface collection*)
9. End scraper. (*771, no. 203, topsoil*)
10. End scraper. (*7760, no. 109, unphased*)
11. Barbed and tanged arrowhead. (*7721, no. 21, unphased*)
12. Fabricator. (*771, no. 164, topsoil*)
13. Point, bifacial flint tool. (*7743b), no. 379, Phase 1*)
14. Knife. (*7723, no. 94, unphased*)
15. Serrated flake. (*7717, no. 256, unphased*)
16. Broken blade. (*unprovenanced*)
17. Retouched flake. (*unprovenanced*)

V. Jet and Other Worked Stone
by Joanna K.F. Bacon (1984) and Fiona Roe (1996)

Jet

The piece illustrated as Figure 18: 1, from a medieval plough furrow, is part of a jet spacer bead with a V-perforation and pointillé decoration. This type of bead is not uncommon on Early Bronze Age sites, occurring in amber at Upton Lovell, Wiltshire (Annable and Simpson 1964) and in jet at Melfort, Argyll (Inv. Arch. GB. 25). The source of the jet was probably the Whitby area of Yorkshire.

A slightly asymmetric highly polished jet bead (Fig. 18: 2) with rounded sides, flat ends and an oval perforation was found in ditch *78135* of Enclosure 3.

A small block of jet (not illustrated), now broken, from an unphased context, had been cut in preparation for working. It is approximately triangular in section with parallel, flat ends, and measures *c.* 34mm by 26mm by 25mm. The small hole discernible at one end may have been made by a compass point in a similar way to a shale fragment from Maiden Castle, Dorset (Wheeler 1943) which was marked with faint concentric rings around a central indentation.

Stone axe-hammer
by Fiona Roe

An axe-hammer fragment was found on gravel subsoil to the west of Enclosure 1. Only about half of the butt end survives (Fig. 19.3), and part of the shaft-hole, but it appears to have been a Class II variety with a slightly expanded blade end (Roe 1979, 30, fig. 8). There is a slightly hollowed area round the shaft-hole, and also a small cup mark near the butt.

The axe-hammer has been assigned the implement petrology number Li 444, and the stone has been identified as Group XVIII quartz dolerite from Whin Sill in the north of England (Clough and Cummins 1988, 198). There have not been a great many finds of axe-hammers from Lincolnshire (Roe 1979, 28, fig.5; Clough and Cummins 1988), but this material was widely used generally for axe-hammers.

It is difficult to find a close comparison for the cup marks near the butt end of the axe-hammer from Billingborough. A few axe-hammers with secondary borings have been recorded (Roe 1969, 259 and fig. 90), and these borings are either complete or consist of opposing cup marks, always positioned on the broken blade end of an implement. This is a feature more commonly found on the broken blade halves of battle-axes (Roe 1966, 214 and fig. 8; Roe 1969, 85 and fig. 36). The distribution of these battle-axes is centred on Yorkshire, but there are three examples from Lincolnshire, including one of near Group XVIII quartz dolerite from Ancaster (Clough and Cummins 1988, 194, Li 168). However, it is felt that the cup mark on the Billingborough axe-hammer does not compare very well with these examples of secondary borings, which seem to suggest a particular kind of deliberate reuse. It may simply represent the fortuitous reworking of a serviceable piece of stone.

The dating of axe-hammers has become less uncertain with the discovery of a complete example from Cleethorpes, with part of the wooden haft surviving, which produced a radiocarbon date range of 1880-1510 cal BC (weighed mean of OxA-130, 3390±100 BP, and OxA-131, 3330±100 BP) (Leahy 1986, 143). In the present context, it is helpful that this Cleethorpes axe-hammer was also made from Group XVIII quartz dolerite (Leahy 1986, 145).

Associations for axe-hammers have always tended to be somewhat tenuous (Roe 1969, 292), and the axe-hammer from Billingborough is no exception, since it was not directly associated with the Bronze Age occupation or evidence of earlier activity. The only other tentative link between an axe-hammer and a Bronze Age site is from Gwithian, Cornwall, where a fragment from a possible axe-hammer made from Group XII picrite (CO 250) came from plough soil at Site XV (Megaw *et al.* 1961, 213). There are also two axe-hammer fragments from sites of somewhat earlier date. One was a surface find at Windmill Hill, Wiltshire (1010/WI 266), where it may perhaps have belonged with the traces of Beaker and Collared Urn at the site rather than with the Neolithic material (Smith 1965, 80). The other axe-hammer comes from a domestic site at Edingthorpe, Norfolk, where varied Neolithic and Early Bronze Age pottery was recorded (Clough and Green 1972, 154 and fig. 13). This axe-hammer is also a Group XVIII example (N 96), and is one of the few blade halves of axe-hammers with secondary borings, in the form of two opposed cup marks At this site the axe-hammer, if associated in any way, seems more likely to have belonged with the Beaker and Early Bronze Age pottery, rather than with the Neolithic wares. At Billingborough the small amount of Early Bronze Age pottery from the site and the struck flint also seem to provide the most likely context for the axe-hammer fragment, while it must be hoped that future excavations may in time produce more secure evidence for the real associations of axe-hammers.

Other stone finds
A small, oval polishing stone or rubber (not illustrated; maximum dimension *c.* 50mm) is very highly polished and worn, and could have been used to burnish pottery, or for softening resilient material such as leather prior to working. It came from Phase 3 enclosure ditch *78135*.

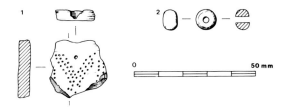

Figure 18 Jet objects

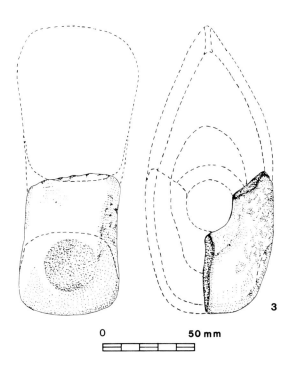

Figure 19 Stone object: axe-hammer

Rubbing stones have been found at many Iron Age sites; a similar flat smoothed oval stone was found at Cold Kitchen Hill, Wiltshire (Nan Kivell 1925, 190, pl. XIV).

Two small fragments of rotary quern were recovered from the topsoil.

Catalogue of jet and stone

Figs 18 and 19
1. Jet **spacer bead**. Small block; two surviving rounded edges with slight bevel. Other sides and back missing. Three round-bottomed holes from the top, one at surviving corner, roughly V-shaped as it returns to edge, others straight. Front decorated by small V-profile indentations (of varying size up to 1mm in diameter) in chevron or cruciform design of three rows of random dots. Some surface scratches. Length 23mm. Width 24mm. Thickness 4–5mm. (*7819, no. 124, medieval plough furrow*)
2. Jet **bead**; slightly assymmetric, rounded sides and flat ends. Almost central oval perforation, slightly larger at one end. Undecorated, highly polished. Height 5–6mm. Diameter 8mm. Thickness 2–3mm. (*78139, ditch 78138, no. 384, Phase 4*)
3. Group XVIII **axe-hammer fragment**. (*78150, flood layer, unphased*)

VI. Prehistoric Pottery

by Rosamund M.J. Cleal (1990)

Introduction

A total of 5644 sherds of pottery weighing 83,873kg was recovered from stratified contexts during the three seasons of excavation at Billingborough. It did not prove possible to either count or weigh the pottery from surface collection and unstratified contexts. The pottery is summarised by Phase in Tables 4, 6, 7, and 8 (these tables also include briquetage and fired clay totals). Pottery from post-Roman and unphased contexts (comprising 1650 sherds weighing 27,215g) is not tabulated here, but full details are included in archive (virtually all of this material is of prehistoric date, comprising grog-tempered (1045 sherds / 20,724g) and shell-tempered (558 sherds / 5003g) wares).

As a result of the long time period over which the Billingborough pottery has been studied and prepared for publication, the report is the product of more than one specialist. It is important that the historical vicissitudes of the collection are made clear, as the decisions reached in the early stages of the project have necessarily affected the later work.

The material was first studied by Aiden Challis who provided the basis for the detailed catalogue of all illustrated sherds. Initially, all sherds from stratified contexts other than plain body sherds were illustrated, in provisional phase order. In addition, some unstratified sherds were also chosen for illustration on the grounds of their unusual nature or that they were good examples of their type. Sherds were individually described, rather than assigned to fabrics, as this was felt to be an appropriate method of dealing with a fairly homogeneous collection. No division was made between pottery and briquetage, and many featured sherds of briquetage containers were illustrated with the pottery. However, unlike the pottery, there are also featured briquetage container sherds from stratified contexts which were not illustrated: illustration of all featured sherds of briquetage containers was not considered feasible because of the very large quantity of the material. Subsequently, the present writer defined criteria on which to separate briquetage from pottery, and all illustrated pieces of briquetage containers referred to in the text have now been grouped separately (see Fig. 29).

During the final phase of post-excavation work the decision was taken to illustrate only the sherds mentioned in the text (123 in total) and they have been remounted for publication here. The illustrated sherds are arranged in phase order and grouped according to various criteria (i.e. form, decoration, stratified assemblage etc.). The context of every illustrated sherd is noted in the Pottery Catalogue. Throughout the text pottery illustrations are referred to by figure and catalogue number, with the earlier 'P' prefix numbers also retained in the catalogue. 'P' numbers, assigned by Aiden Challis, are unique numbers which can refer only to one sherd; they will allow future researchers to cross reference pottery in this report with data in the archive and all 1266 illustrated sherds which were originally drawn and which appear elsewhere (Chowne 1988).

Methods

Because the material had already undergone the first stages of analysis before reaching Wessex Archaeology, an application of standard Wessex Archaeology procedures was not possible, as these include the definition of fabric types mainly on the basis of presence and frequency of inclusions. A complete re-analysis of the material was not practical and, as frequency of inclusions is not recorded in the individual descriptions, it was not possible to establish groupings of sherds into fabrics on the basis of these. However, as the *presence* of inclusions is recorded, it was decided to treat the collection on the basis of type of inclusions alone, and to use these broad divisions instead of fabrics (i.e. fabric *groups* rather than fabrics, with the fabrics constituting each group not individually isolated). With some collections of prehistoric pottery this procedure would undoubtedly mask much variation, but in the case of the Billingborough pottery it seems, as is apparent from the petrological study (see below, p. 45), that only a small amount of extra information would have been gained by a more detailed fabric analysis.

The pottery is treated primarily by site phase. Much of the Bronze Age pottery occurred in contexts in which it was clearly redeposited; this material is treated, as a separate section, with the pottery from Phase 1 contexts. It was not possible to separate the Phase 2, Phase 3, and Phase 4 pottery on the grounds of fabric or form, so this is all treated as belonging to the phase in which it occurs. The pottery which pre-dates the Bronze Age enclosure is dealt with separately, before the Phase 1 enclosure pottery.

Neolithic Pottery

A single sherd (Fig. 20: 1) of a Peterborough Ware bowl was recovered from unphased layer *7725* in the central northern part of the site. The sherd shows the shoulder carination of a bowl decorated with whipped cord impressions in a herringbone or chevron motif. The fabric is flint-tempered, with the temper comprising approximately 15% of the fabric by surface area; the fabric is laminated and the sherd has lost most of the interior surface. Both the decoration and fabric of the sherd fall within the range of the Mortlake and Ebbsfleet sub-styles of Peterborough Ware. At some sites at least whipped cord impressions are more characteristic of the Ebbsfleet sub-style than the Mortlake (Smith 1965, figs 31–33).

The Peterborough tradition is not firmly dated, although Ebbsfleet Ware appears to have developed during the currency of Neolithic bowl styles as it occurs deep in the ditches of the causewayed enclosure at Windmill Hill (Smith 1965; Smith 1974). A date in the late 4th or early 3rd millennium BC would be likely, on present evidence.

Peterborough Ware occurs around the western edge of the Fens (Cleal 1984, figs 9.1, 9.2; Cleal 1985), most notably at the type site, where the Mortlake and Fengate sub-styles are represented (Abbott 1910). A single plain bowl from Grantham (Phillips 1935, 347–8) may be plain Ebbsfleet Ware, as the rim form is one common in that sub-style and rare on bowls of the Early to Middle Neolithic plain and decorated bowl traditions, but in view of the lack of decoration the attribution to the Ebbsfleet sub-style must remain uncertain.

Early Bronze Age Pottery

Five sherds, probably belonging to four vessels, are of Early Bronze Age date.

Two sherds (Fig. 20: 2 and 3) were found in the uppermost layer (*752*) of feature *752*, which is assignable to Phase 2. Both sherds are in grog-tempered fabrics, not dissimilar to that of the Phase 1 Enclosure pottery, but also typical of Early Bronze Age fabrics in central, southern, and eastern England. The everted rim and internal bevel of Fig. 20: 3 strongly suggest that the form is a Food Vessel. Fig. 20: 2, on the grounds of fabric and decoration, may belong to a Collared Urn; it is certainly not cord-impressed Beaker (on the grounds of wall thickness and general appearance).

Two sherds, not conjoining, but almost certainly belonging to a single vessel (Fig. 20: 4) were recovered from the topsoil in the 1975 excavations. One sherd was thin-sectioned (Allen, below) and showed 20% grog and 1% quartz. The everted, internally bevelled rim and ridge suggest that the vessel is a ridged Food Vessel, similar to vessels from the south-eastern fen edge (Healy 1996, P94) and elsewhere in Norfolk (Healy 1988, fig. 83: P226, 73).

A single sherd in a grog-tempered fabric with vertical twisted cord impressions (Fig. 20: 5) from a Phase 3 context may belong to a Collared Urn.

The presence of these few sherds of Early Bronze Age pottery and also the struck flints suggest a low level of activity somewhere in the vicinity in the early 2nd millennium cal BC. Barrows exist at Hoe Hills, Dowsby, approximately 4km to the south, but are unexcavated; Collared Urn sherds have been recovered in the vicinity of these by field walking (P. Chowne pers. comm.).

Phase 1

The pottery recovered from Phase 1 contexts (Table 4) can be assigned to the late Early to Middle Bronze Age on the basis of form and fabric. It is related to the Deverel-Rimbury tradition of central southern England.

Within Phase 1, the fillings of the Enclosure 1 ditch, where undisturbed by later activity, offer a sequence of deposits in which it is possible to trace some changes in form and fabric. That some change through time was discernible within the pottery of the ditch deposits, even within those assigned to Phase 1, was appreciated early on in the post-excavation process, and because of this it has been considered justifiable to submit the material from the one undisturbed length of ditch (*7743*) to a more detailed analysis than was considered feasible for the rest of the collection. This analysis (Table 5) demonstrates that there are forms which only appear in the middle and upper fills, and for this reason the Phase 1 pottery will be considered in four groups:

a) the pottery from the lower ditch deposits in Enclosure 1 (layers *e, g, j, k,* and *h* of *7743*; *d* and *e* of *7510* and *78164*).

b) the pottery from the upper levels in the ditch (layers *b, c, d* and *f* of ditch *7743*).

c) pottery from other Phase 1 contexts.

d) pottery redeposited in later contexts, and from unphased contexts.

Fabric
a) Pottery from the lower ditch deposits
Grog is the most common inclusion in the pottery from the lower ditch deposits; it occurs with varying frequency and size, even within single vessels. Some sand is included in most fabrics, although generally with low frequency, which would suggest that it is a natural inclusion in the clay. Occasionally, grog and shell occur together, and some shell is also present (probably less than 2% surface area) in Fig. 21: 11. A single piece of fossil shell was noted in the thin-section of Fig. 21: 12 which Allen notes is likely to be an accidental inclusion. This low frequency of shell inclusions suggests that, although a source of clay containing some shell was utilised, the potters were not deliberately opting for a fossiliferous

clay; indeed, considering the problems of firing clay containing carbonates (Rice 1987, 98; Rye 1981, 32–3), it may be that they were deliberately avoiding shell-rich clays. Allen suggests the Great Oolite limestones and clays as a possible source for the clay used in Fig. 21: 12.

b) Pottery from the upper ditch deposits
The pottery in the upper layers of the ditch includes both grog-tempered vessels, which are indistinguishable from those in the lower levels, and vessels in fabrics with shell and stone. ('Stone', as used by Challis in the fabric descriptions, generally indicates limestone, or obvious fossil fragments; there are no definite identifications of stone fragments other than this in the entire collection, either in thin-section or macroscopically.) Occasional occurrences of voids are likely to be leached-out shell; on the whole, however, the calcareous inclusions survive *in situ*. The shelly fabrics contain varying frequencies of shell and there is also some variation in the size and sorting of inclusions. Two sherds from these layers were thin-sectioned: Fig. 21: 19 is included by Allen in her group probably derived from the Great Oolite limestones and clays, and Fig. 21: 18 was found to include one fragment of the limestone known as 'ironstone', which occurs in the Ancaster Beds and can be found approximately 12km from the site. The fabrics as a whole from the upper ditch show greater variation in inclusion type than do those in the lower fill although the evidence available does not indicate that sources farther afield were being utilised.

c) Pottery from other Phase 1 contexts
For those features not linked stratigraphically to the ditch deposits it is impossible to suggest equivalence with the two pottery sub-phases, as the ceramics alone are not distinctive enough, but the fact that there may be features equivalent to both is suggested by the preponderance of grog-tempered fabrics in some features, and shelly fabrics in others. Two vessels belonging to Phase 1 contexts other than the ditch fill have been thin-sectioned: Fig. 22: 21, from hollow *7747*, and Fig. 22: 25 from feature *752*. Fig. 22: 21, apart from the fact that a single piece of chert was visible in thin-section, is similar to the grog-tempered fabrics from the ditch of Enclosure 1. Similarly, Fig. 22: 25 is included by Allen in the group of sherds which were probably made from clays of the Great Oolite.

Form
Vessel forms are discussed as they occur in the four separate groups outlined above. As with the fabrics, this is to ensure the separation of material which is possibly of different dates, albeit all belonging to the first phase of use of the site (*i.e.* Phase 1). The terms 'jar', 'bowl', and 'cup' are used to denote, respectively, vessels deeper than they are wide and with some restriction at the neck or mouth; vessels wider than they are deep; and small vessels with capacities less than 1000cc which are generally open, but which may show some degree of restriction. (VT — Vessel Type; DT — Decoration Type. Volumes were calculated by dividing vessel interiors into a series of conic frustra, or a combination of cylinders and frustra, as appropriate and summing their volumes).

a) Pottery from lower ditch deposits
It is not possible to reconstruct with confidence more than three vessel forms from the lower ditch filling. Only one complete profile survives, that preserved by the large slab of Fig. 23: 40. Of the three vessel forms definable, at least one appears in more than one size range.

VT 1: Most complete example: Fig. 23: 40. Vessel with a slightly flared profile, approaching that of a truncated cone rather than a cylinder, and with a simple rim. Decoration: fingernail or fingertip straight on to body wall. Fabric: grog-tempered. Rim diameter (external) of example: 250mm. Capacity: approximately 8000cc.

VT 2: Most complete example: Fig. 21: 8. Cylindrical vessel with simple rim. Decoration/handling aid: cordon around upper body; cordon does not mark change in wall profile. Fabric: grog-tempered. Rim diameter of example (external): *c.* 360mm. Capacity unknown; however, if height calculated as same as external diameter: 31,000cc.

VT 3: Most complete examples: Fig. 21: 11 and 12. Probable examples: Fig. 21: 9 and 10. Vessel with a profile similar to that of VT1 (*i.e.* a truncated cone rather than a cylinder) but with the addition of a slack shoulder set directly beneath the rim. Decoration: row(s) of fingernail impressions directly onto vessel wall (DT 1; Fig. 21: 9 and 10). Fabric: grog-tempered, or grog with rare shell. Diameter (external): *c.* 200mm (Fig. 21: 12), *c.* 400mm (Fig. 21: 11). Capacity: unknown. However, if the height is taken as the same as the diameter at the mouth Fig. 21: 12 has a capacity of just over 4000cc; the form of Fig. 21: 11 suggests that it is unlikely to have been as high as it is wide, so an interior depth of 300mm was used to calculate a possible capacity of 48,000cc.

	Pottery								Briquetage		Fired Clay*	
	Grog		Shell		Other prehistoric		Non-prehistoric					
	No	Wt	No	Wt	No	Wt	No	Wt	No	Wt	No	Wt
PHASE 1												
DITCH [7743]												
Upper fill												
7743b	92(+ 1nw)	1195g	170(+ 2nw)	1532g	2 (sand)	23g	-	-	163	783g	49	523g
7743c	79(+ 1nw)	1331g	56(+ 2nw)	579g	-	-	-	-	32	158g	7	94g
7743d	86	1619g	37(+ 1nw)	345g	-	-	-	-	63	236g	26	173g
Lower fill												
7743e	1	40g	-	-	-	-	-	-	3 (grog)	62g	-	-
7743f	17	651g	2	47g	-	-	-	-	1 (grog)	13g	-	-
7743g	25	1361g	-	-	-	-	-	-	1	2g	6	104g
7743h	26	2705g	-	-	-	-	-	-	-	-	6	162g
7743j	2	114g	-	-	-	-	-	-	-	-	-	-
7743k	(1 nw)	-	-	-	-	-	-	-	-	-	-	-
DITCH [7710]												
7710c	8	286g	1	4g	-	-	-	-	2	13g	4+ (+ frags)	404g
7710d	6	175g	-	-	-	-	-	-	-	-	4	201g
7710e	5	36g	2	59g	-	-	-	-	1	3g	2	43g
DITCH [78145]												
78164	7	327g	-	-	-	-	-	-	1	5g	4	371g
Totals	**354 (+ 3nw)**	**9840g**	**268 (+ 5nw)**	**2566g**	**2**	**23g**	-	-	**268**	**1275g**	**108**	**2075g**

PROBABLE PHASE 1 - Features with grog-tempered pottery only (and no stratigraphic evidence to suggest that they are later than Phase 1)

	Grog No	Grog Wt									Fired Clay* No	Fired Clay* Wt
[7537] not on plan	3	109g	-	-	-	-	-	-	-	-	-	-
[7545] not on plan	2	30g	-	-	-	-	-	-	-	-	-	-
[7566] not on plan	1	13g	-	-	-	-	-	-	-	-	-	-
[7568]/[7570] not on plan	1	3g	-	-	-	-	-	-	-	-	-	-
[776]	1	7g	-	-	-	-	-	-	-	-	-	-
[7726c]	1	11g	-	-	-	-	-	-	-	-	-	-
[7726h]	1	12g	-	-	-	-	-	-	-	-	-	-
[7726h]	1	12g	-	-	-	-	-	-	-	-	-	-
[7726i]	2	9g	-	-	-	-	-	-	-	-	-	-
[7726k]	1	7g	-	-	-	-	-	-	-	-	-	-
[7738]	3	109g	-	-	-	-	-	-	-	-	-	-
[776l]	1	8g	-	-	-	-	-	-	-	-	-	-
[7781]	1	19g	-	-	-	-	-	-	-	-	7	72g
[7784]	1	9g	-	-	-	-	-	-	-	-	-	-

	Pottery								Briquetage		Fired Clay*	
	Grog		Shell		Other prehistoric		Non-prehistoric					
	No	Wt	No	Wt	No	Wt	No	Wt	No	Wt	No	Wt
[77120]	1	9g	-	-	-	-	-	-	-	-	-	-
[77122]	1	69g	-	-	-	-	-	-	-	-	-	-
[77142]	1	21g	-	-	-	-	-	-	-	-	-	-
[77154]	1	95g	-	-	-	-	-	-	-	-	-	-
[77157]	3	34g	-	-	-	-	-	-	-	-	-	-
[77166]	1	6g	-	-	-	-	-	-	-	-	-	-
[77171]	2	30g	-	-	-	-	-	-	-	-	-	-
[77193]	2	54g	-	-	-	-	-	-	-	-	-	-
[7816]	1	40g	-	-	-	-	-	-	-	-	1	6g
[7845]	2	105g	-	-	-	-	-	-	-	-	-	-
[7846]	1	61g	-	-	-	-	-	-	-	-	-	-
[7855]	1	10g	-	-	-	-	-	-	-	-	-	-
[7857]	2	108g	-	-	-	-	-	-	-	-	-	-
[7858]	4	44g	-	-	-	-	-	-	-	-	-	-
[7871] (not illus.)	27(+ 3nw)	757g	-	-	-	-	-	-	-	-	-	-
7879	1	37g	-	-	-	-	-	-	-	-	-	-
[78143]	2	19g	-	-	-	-	-	-	-	-	-	-
[78144]	2	23g	-	-	-	-	-	-	-	-	-	-
[78153]	3	70g	-	-	-	-	-	-	-	-	-	-
[78162]	3	23g	-	-	-	-	-	-	-	-	-	-
78171 [78183]	2	51g	-	-	-	-	-	-	-	-	-	-
78182 [78173]	1	13g	-	-	-	-	-	-	-	-	-	-
[78191]	2	52g	-	-	-	-	-	-	-	-	-	-
[78213]	3	42g	-	-	-	-	-	-	-	-	1	170g
[78223]	1	23g	-	-	-	-	-	-	-	-	-	-
[78255]	1	57g	-	-	-	-	-	-	-	-	-	-
Totals	**90**	**2179g**	-	-	-	-	-	-	-	-	**9**	**248g**

PROBABLE PHASE 1 (briquetage probably from mixed ?layer)

	Pottery								Briquetage		Fired Clay*	
	Grog		Shell		Other prehistoric		Non-prehistoric					
	No	Wt	No	Wt	No	Wt	No	Wt	No	Wt	No	Wt
7747 (concentration of sherds, not within a feature)	144	5072g	1	3g	-	-	-	-	3	5g	12*	392g
Totals	**144**	**5072g**	**1**	**3g**	-	-	-	-	**3**	**5g**	**12***	**392g**

PROBABLE PHASE 1 – FOUR-POST STRUCTURE

	Pottery								Briquetage		Fired Clay*	
	Grog		Shell		Other prehistoric		Non-prehistoric					
	No	Wt	No	Wt	No	Wt	No	Wt	No	Wt	No	Wt
[7541]	-	-	1	10g	-	-	-	-	-	-	-	-
[7734]	-	-	1	4g	-	-	-	-	-	-	-	-
[7790]	-	-	1	10g	-	-	-	-	-	-	-	-
Totals	-	-	**3**	**24g**	-	-	-	-	-	-	-	-

PHASE 1 – PROBABLY CONTEMPORARY WITH UPPER FILL OF DITCH [7743] (on ceramic phasing)

| | Pottery | | | | | | | | Briquetage | | Fired Clay* | |
| | Grog | | Shell | | Other prehistoric | | Non-prehistoric | | | | | |
	No	Wt	No	Wt	No	Wt	No	Wt	No	Wt	No	Wt
752a [752]	1	40g	-	-	(1nw; sand) -		-	-	-	-	-	-
752b [752]	7	137g	1	29g	-	-	-	-	13	66g	16	398g
752c [752]	1	36g	1	19g	-	-	-	-	4	11g	5	52g
752d [752]	1	63g	1	20g	-	-	-	-	-	-	9	168g
752e [752]	-	-	11	614g	-	-	-	-	1	2g	-	-
Totals	**10**	**276g**	**14**	**682g**	**1nw**		-	-	**18**	**79g**	**52**	**618g**
PHASE 1— CONTEXTS ASSIGNED TO PHASE 1 ON STRATIGRAPHIC EVIDENCE												
[7749]	3	152g	-	-	-	-	-	-	-	-	-	-
[7774]	2	15g	-	-	-	-	-	-	2	5g	-	-
7774b	1	12g	1	11g	-	-	-	-	-	-	-	-
[77180]	-	-	1	6g	-	-	-	-	-	-	-	-
Totals	**6**	**179g**	**2**	**17g**	-	-	-	-	**2**	**5g**	-	-
PHASE 1 or 2												
7719	55	433g	6	59g	-	-	-	-	14	33g	2	6g
7720	1	7g	-	-	-	-	-	-	-	-	-	-
7742	248+ (+3nw)	3537g (+1nw)	54	274g	-	-	-	-	417	887g	91	906g
77168	59	1074g	6	41g	-	-	-	-	65	227g	5	8g
[7884]	1	9g	4	35g	-	-	-	-	4	11g	-	-
78208	-	-	1	11g	-	-	-	-	-	-	-	-
Totals	**364 (+ 3nw)**	**5060g (+ 1nw)**	**71**	**420g**	-	-	-	-	**500**	**1158g**	**98**	**920g**
GRAND TOTAL	**968**	**22,246g**	**359**	**3712g**	**2**	**23g**	-	-	**791**	**2522g**	**279**	**4253g**

NB **Counts** were not carried out for all material.
'nw' indicates sherd(s) not weighed.
[ ] indicates feature.
* does not include material treated as technological finds.

Table 4 Pottery and other ceramic material from Phase 1 contexts

Layer (phase)		Rim forms														Briquetage Rim forms		Angled body			
		1	1b	2	3	4	4b	5	5b	7	8	10	11	12	13	Cut	Other	1	2	3	4
Layer (phase)																					
7743	(2)			1		2	2	2						1	1	8	7				1
UPPER																					
7743b	(1)	5				5	1	2		1								3		1	
7743c	(1)	4	1	1		3	2	2	2		1							1			
7743d	(1)	1				3	3	1				1	1			2	3		1		
LOWER																					
7743e	(1)						1														
7743f	(1)	2	1		1			1								1					
7743g	(1)				1			1													
7743j	(1)				1																
7743k	(1)							1													
7743h	(1)				1		1														

KEY:

Rim form
1= simple*, pointed (*e.g.* P6, P40)
1b= simple, pointed, incurved (*e.g.* P23)
2= simple, pointed, everted (*e.g.* P3)
3= simple, internally bevelled (*e.g.* P1)
4= simple, rounded (*e.g.* P7, P59)
4b= simple, rounded, incurved (*e.g.* P7, P59)
5= simple, flat-topped (*e.g.* P7, P59)
7= extended symmetrically (T-shaped) (*e.g.* P116)
8= rounded above slightly concave neck (*e.g.* P44)
10= internally extended (*e.g.* P64)
11= simple, externally bevelled (*e.g.* P65)
12= internally bevelled, with pronounced internal extension with concave bevel surface (*e.g.* P419)
13= externally extended (*e.g.* P436)

Angled body form
1= sharp shoulder angle (*e.g.* P46)
2= slack shoulder (*e.g.* P80)
3= concave neck (*e.g.* P80)
4= rounded shoulder angle (*e.g.* P129)

* *i.e.* no extra clay added to vessel wall

Table 5 Pottery: rim and body forms from Enclosure 1 ditch

Although these figures are hypothetical, they are based on reasonable suppositions and illustrate, more clearly than diameter alone, that there are vessels of widely different size in this vessel type.

It is difficult to estimate the relative occurrence of Vessel Type 1 as compared with VT 2 in the assemblage because the angle of lie of the rim is uncertain in most cases, but it is clear that together they outnumber the vessels of VT3.

b) Pottery from upper ditch deposits

Vessel Types 1 and 2 occur in the upper ditch silts, although it is not possible to be certain whether they were still in use as the upper ditch filling formed, or were already entering the ditch only as sherds residual from earlier occupation. Fig. 21: 13 may represent a smaller version of VT1; it has a rim diameter of 120mm and a capacity (from the illustrated reconstruction) of 600cc. There are no certain examples of VT3. Three new forms appear, and the existence of others is hinted at by the presence of angled sherds among the body sherds (e.g. Fig. 21: 14, 15 and 16) and by the single example of a concave neck sherd (Fig. 21: 17) (Table 5, Angled body Type 3). The new forms are represented only by fragmentary vessels, for two of which it is not possible to establish certain diameter or capacity.

VT 4: Most complete example: Fig. 21: 18. Open vessel, possibly a bowl (i.e. if the projected height is correct). The rim angle appears to be correct as illustrated, and although the diameter is uncertain the thin walls suggest a fairly small vessel. Decoration: circular impressions (possibly the hollow end of a reed or bone, arranged diagonally and in horizontal rows; DT 7 and 18). Fabric: grog-tempered. A sherd of Fig. 21: 18 was thin-sectioned and found to contain 30% grog and 7.5% quartz; a single piece of limestone recorded as 'ironstone' was noted.

VT 5: Most complete example: Fig. 21: 19. Small truncated conical bowl or cup with everted rim. Decoration: none. Fabric: a sherd of Fig. 21: 19 was thin-sectioned and found to contain 10% fossil shell, 5% quartz, and 10% grog. The likely source for the clay is the Great Oolite. Rim diameter (external) of example: c. 120 mm. Minimum capacity (i.e. of body part represented by sherd) 300cc.

VT 6: Most complete example: Fig. 21: 20. Closed vessel with a simple upright rim, probably above a rounded body. The only example is represented by a small rim sherd, but a new form is clearly indicated. Decoration: non-plastic fingernail and groove (DT 15 and 16). Fabric: grog-tempered. Rim diameter: greater than 22cm.

c) Pottery from other Phase 1 contexts

With the exception of the large vessel from feature 752 the material from other Phase 1 contexts is as fragmentary as that from the upper ditch filling. Vessel types 1 and 2 are present, as in context 752 (Fig. 22: 22 and 23), but no vessels of Vessel type 3 are identifiable. Two types not present in the ditch deposits are recognisable (VT 8 and 9, although the latter may be intrusive) and one further type, which may be present but unrecognisable in the ditch, may also be defined (VT 7).

VT 7: Most complete example: Fig. 22: 24. Small truncated conical vessel. Decoration: fingernail directly onto vessel wall (DT 1). Fabric: grog-tempered. Rim diameter (external) of example: 120mm. Capacity of example: at least 500cc (i.e. capacity of body part represented by sherd); the capacity of the complete vessel is unlikely to be much greater than this, on the basis of the projected profile.

VT 8: Most complete example: Fig. 22: 25. Jar with everted rim. Decoration: none, but the body is covered with shallow finger smoothing marks. On the upper body these run vertically, but on the lower they run obliquely. Fabric: shelly. Thin-sectioning of Fig. 22:25 showed that it contained c. 30% shell and 1% quartz; the clay is likely to be from the Great Oolite. Rim diameter (external) of example: 320mm. Capacity of reconstructable body part: 18,600cc; projected capacity (taking depth to be equal to rim diameter: 21,000cc.

VT 9: Most complete example: Fig. 27: 96. Bowl with round shoulder angle. Decoration: none. Smooth finish, but not burnished. Fabric: only quartz sand visible. Diameter around shoulder: c. 150mm. On the grounds of fabric, this vessel may belong to the Iron Age phases of the site and be intrusive in the context in which it occurs (7742); it is included below in the Phase 3 illustrated pottery.

The vessel represented by Fig. 22: 26 may belong to a small version of VT8, or represent a new type, but insufficient of the form survives to enable this to be established. Similarly, it is possible that both Fig. 22: 27 and 28 belong to vessel types not otherwise represented. For example No. 28 recalls a cordoned beaker, but too little of the profiles of Fig 22: 27 and 28 survive to be certain of the form of the lower body in either case.

d) Redeposited Phase 1 pottery

Because of the distinctive nature of the Phase 1 grog-tempered fabrics it is possible to identify Phase 1 sherds where they occur in later contexts and in unphased contexts, and it is clear that vessels of types VT 1 and 2, and probably 3, occur (e.g. Fig. 23: 29, 30, 31 and 32). Three vessel types not previously represented may be identified among the unphased material, although it is likely that at least VT 10 occurs in other contexts (e.g. perhaps incurved rims such as Fig. 23: 33) but that the lack of profile has disguised this.

VT 10: Most complete example: P1147 (Fig. 23: 34). Weakly shouldered or ovoid-bodied vessel with incurved rim (the hooked rim shown in Fig. 23: 34 is a product of the irregularity of the rim; the 'hook' only occurs on approximately 10mm of the length of the rim surviving; the remainder is a simple incurved form). Decoration: none. Fabric: grog-tempered. Diameter: uncertain, but greater than 200mm. Capacity: uncertain.

VT 11: Most complete example: Fig. 23: 36. Shouldered vessel, probably a jar. Decoration: fingernail impressions directly onto body wall. Fabric: grog-tempered. Rim diameter (external): approximately 21mm. Capacity of body part represented by surviving profile: 2500cc; if the vessel is assumed to be as deep as it is wide at the mouth, the capacity would be approximately 4500cc.

VT 12: Most complete example: Fig. 23: 37. Bowl or jar with shoulder angle. Decoration: none. Fabric: grog-tempered. Rim diameter (external) of example: c. 220mm. Capacity: uncertain.

A single rim sherd (Fig. 23: 38) from the topsoil may belong to a strongly biconical vessel, and might be termed a Biconical Urn, in that it has an apparently sharp shoulder angle marked by slight fingernail impressions. However, the form of the vessel is not certain, as the break is along the angle, and to identify it as a Biconical Urn *sensu stricto* in an assemblage in which even sub-biconical forms are not strongly represented, would seem to be stretching the evidence.

Decoration

Fingernail impression is the most common form of decoration throughout Phase 1. Both plastic and non-plastic fingernail impressions are used (e.g. Fig. 23: 39 and 40), as are both single and paired impressions (e.g. Fig. 21: 13 and Fig. 22: 28); impressions are placed both directly onto the body wall and onto cordons (e.g. Fig. 23: 41 and Fig. 25: 9). The use of columns of horizontal fingernail impressions occurs only once (the Fig. 23: 42). Most commonly the impressions are arranged in horizontal rows, usually single (e.g. Fig. 22: 24 and Fig. 23: 40) but there are examples of more than one row occurring (e.g. Fig. 23: 43, where one row is applied to the body wall and one to a cordon). Fingernail rustication also occurs, although there are fewer examples of this than of simple rows (e.g. Fig. 23: 32 and 44). Impressions occur occasionally on a shoulder angle (e.g. Fig. 23: 36).

Other decorative techniques are restricted to impression, grooves and incision. The circular impressions on Fig. 21: 18 and Fig. 23: 45 (which may belong to the same vessel) are similar to impressions occasionally found on Beakers, and possibly made with a hollow reed. Vessels stamped with a hollow bone or reed are also known from Bronze Age contexts in the Thames Valley. A single example of round-toothed comb occurs (Fig. 23: 46): this technique is generally rare, but occurs in the large assemblage from Grimes Graves, Norfolk (Longworth et al. 1988, fig. 32: 247). Incision or grooving is rare at Billingborough, and the use of oblique grooves below the rim of Fig. 23: 47 is unique within the site, as is the combination of grooves parallel to and perpendicular to a fingernail-decorated cordon (Fig. 23: 48)

Function

The occurrence of sooting on some vessels, and of carbonised residues within others (noted in the Catalogue) indicates that at least some were utilised as cooking pots, although as the range of forms is so restricted it seems that there was no formal distinction between these and vessels used for other purposes. The virtual absence of bowls from this assemblage, as from Middle Bronze Age assemblages in general, suggests that non-ceramic containers were used as 'tableware'. The single form which can be termed a bowl (represented only by Fig. 23: 37) is not from the Enclosure 1 ditch, although the fabric is indistinguishable from the pottery which occurs there. The rim angle as illustrated is correct, and the vessel appears to represent the adoption of the bowl form into the Middle Bronze Age ceramic tradition at the site, although whether this is a real precursor of later bowls, or the product of a single idiosyncratic episode is uncertain.

Few very large vessels seem to be present. This is in contrast to the classic Deverel-Rimbury sites of southern central England, where very large urns seem to have been used for storage, and were probably moved only rarely, or not at all. Fig. 21: 8 and 11 may be such vessels, although the capacities suggested above for these pots are based on estimated depths (see VT2 and VT3, above). This paucity of very large vessels may be a feature of Middle Bronze Age pottery in the East Midlands, as Allen *et al.* note that over 60% of measurable pots from the cemeteries of Coneygre Farm, Nottinghamshire, Pasture Lodge Farm, Frieston and Belton Lane (all Lincolnshire) are below 4000cc in volume, and that this is unlike the majority of Deverel-Rimbury urns used by Barrett to illustrate vessel capacity in the Middle Bronze Age to early Iron Age, among which capacities of between 4000cc and 16,000cc are common (Allen *et al.* 1987, 216; Barrett 1980, 298, 300, fig. 2).

Cut vessels
At least one vessel in the upper ditch filling of Enclosure 1 (represented by Fig. 24: 49 and 50), one (Fig. 24: 51) in the fill of structural gully *77102* (Phase 2), and two or three (Fig. 22: 21 and Fig. 24: 52, 53 and 54) in hollow *7747*, have been cut before firing. The deep grooves cut part way through the vessels appear to have been intended to facilitate tearing of the vessels before firing or snapping after firing. The colour of the breaks strongly suggest that the breaks are pre-firing, although there is some possibility that leaching might produce a pale surface similar to the partially oxidised surface of the vessel. This type of treatment is often associated with salt extraction, and these vessels are discussed further below in the section on briquetage.

Post-firing holes
Six vessels exhibit holes which have been drilled after firing (Fig. 24: 55–60). Such holes are generally assumed to belong to pairs of repair holes, which enabled cracks or breaks to be bound. This practice must have been fairly common as drilled holes are a not unusual feature of Middle Bronze Age assemblages and often occur in cemeteries (*e.g.* at Kimpton, Hampshire, Dacre and Ellison 1981, and Pasture Lodge Farm, Allen *et al.* 1987, 216, fig. 14: 17).

Discussion
Because of the greater diversity of forms and fabrics in the upper ditch levels of the Phase 1 Enclosure 1 ditch *7743*, as compared with the lower deposits, it seems justifiable to treat the material from the lower layers as a distinct assemblage, although both upper and lower fillings are classified as Phase 1 for the purposes of the site interpretation. The nature of the activities which led to the formation of the upper levels of ditch *7743* and the incorporation of the pottery within it are not clear, but even if the ditch was no longer functioning as an enclosure boundary some contemporary occupation seems to have occurred. The differences between the pottery in the upper and lower fillings are such that it seems extremely unlikely that all the types present in the upper levels were in use during the formation of the lower layers but failed to enter the deposit. The existence of pottery datable to the Late Bronze Age on typological grounds (Fig. 22: 25) in a Phase 1 feature also suggests that Phase 1 covers a considerable period. For the purposes of this report the pottery from the lower ditch levels and similar vessels from elsewhere on the site is discussed separately.

The pottery from the initial use of the enclosure is datable to the mid to late 2nd millennium BC, and is related to the Middle Bronze Age Deverel-Rimbury tradition of central southern England. A radiocarbon determination from charcoal from an early silting layer within Enclosure 1 ditch *7710* (layer *7510d*) produced a date of 1530–1260 cal BC (BM-1410; 3148 ± 57 BP). Billingborough is unusual in that there are few settlement sites of this date known in eastern England, unlike the areas of classic Deverel-Rimbury settlement sites in the south. As such it was felt that the detailed analysis of forms given above was justified in order to focus attention on the vessel types occurring on a site of a non-funerary nature.

The Billingborough Bronze Age assemblage, as represented by the material firmly stratified in the lower levels of ditch *7743*, is limited, but the distinctive nature of the fabric enables material from other features to be added to this with some confidence. It cannot be certain that this added material was also in use during the early filling of ditch *7743*, but it seems reasonable to assume that it was, and with only one or two exceptions these additional vessels do not present forms or decoration which are radically different from the material stratified in the ditch. As the Vessel Types have already been presented separately from the upper and lower ditch and other contexts, and can therefore be distinguished if necessary, the grog-tempered vessels from all contexts may be amalgamated into the 'earlier Phase 1' assemblage.

Earlier Phase 1 pottery
This contains a limited range of forms which may loosely be described as 'bucket-shaped', and which range from flared 'flowerpot' shapes (VT1, VT2 and VT7), to vessels with incurved rims above slack shoulders (VT3), to vessels with weakly shouldered or ovoid bodies (VT10). These forms almost certainly occur in a range of sizes although it is impossible to establish their relative frequency. Bowls and/or shouldered jar forms may also be present (VT11 and VT12); although represented only by two vessels from unphased contexts the fabric and general appearance of these vessels is comparable to the material in the lower levels of ditch *7743*. In terms of decoration the earlier Phase 1 pottery is fairly restricted. The techniques used are confined almost entirely to applied cordons (which are in any case presumably largely functional) and fingernail decoration. Decoration appears to be restricted mainly to the upper body; decoration of the rim top is rare, as is decoration of the lower body.

The vessel forms displayed by the earlier Phase 1 assemblage are clearly related to the Deverel-Rimbury tradition of the Middle Bronze Age, but whether the application of this term to assemblages outside central southern England is justified is a matter for debate. The 'Deverel-Rimbury' tradition *sensu stricto* comprises three elements: Barrel Urns, Globular Urns, and Bucket Urns, of which the latter is the least well-defined. In reality this disguises a considerable wealth of variation, which has been the subject of detailed research in southern England (Ellison 1975). In addition, the development of Middle Bronze Age pottery traditions in central and south-eastern Britain is, at least in part, a product of the development of Biconical Urns in the later Early Bronze Age (Tomalin 1983; 1988).

The earlier Phase 1 assemblage at Billingborough is comparable with other sites in East Anglia, the East Midlands, and Yorkshire, but, with few exceptions, the pottery is associated with burials. Two cemeteries, at Coneygre Farm, Nottinghamshire (formerly known as Hoveringham), and Pasture Lodge Farm, Lincolnshire (formerly known as Long Bennington), 40 and 30 kilometres respectively north-west of Billingborough, show close parallels to the Billingborough assemblage (Allen *et al.* 1987). Both show a restricted range of vessel forms, mainly of truncated conical type, and a limited range of decoration. Rim top decoration is rare, and decoration is largely executed with the fingernail or fingertip, and is restricted mainly to the upper body (Allen *et al.* 1987, figs 6–10, and 13–15). Rows of impression are the usual decorative motif, but fingernail impression does occur on the lower body at Pasture Lodge Farm. The only decorative motif not represented or at least closely paralleled at Billingborough is the incised ladder motif on vessel 12 at Coneygre Farm. This motif does not occur at Pasture Lodge, nor at Belton Lane, Grantham, nor at Frieston Lane north of Grantham (approximately 20km east and 20km north-east of Billingborough). This motif may perhaps be one more popular to the north, as it occurs both on a bucket-shaped urn from Beverley, Yorkshire, and at Rudston Wold (Manby 1980, figs 5:9 and 8:1).

That a number of cemeteries existed in the Grantham area is well-established, but apart from the Frieston and Belton Lane pottery, now published (Allen *et al.* 1987, fig. 16), very little survives of the finds made during building and during gravel and limestone extraction in the past (Phillips 1933). However, the grog-tempered vessels from the cemeteries at Old Somerby, Ropsley and Humby (*c.* 15km west of Billingborough), although represented only by base and lower body fragments, are also almost certainly of the same tradition as the Billingborough pottery (Chowne and Lane 1987).

The Billingborough pottery, coming as it does from a settlement where normal activities (*e.g.* trampling *etc.*) are likely to have led to the breaking up of discarded vessels, may well include vessels of types other than the ones identified above, but of which too little survives to enable a definition of form to be made. The presence of incurving rims at Billingborough (*e.g.* Fig. 23: 25) may indicate not only the presence of vessels of type VT 10, but also of forms such as that of vessels 20 and 29 at Coneygre Farm (Allen *et al.* 1987, figs 8 and 10).

To the south and south-east there are certainly similarities with the Middle to Late Bronze Age pottery of Norfolk, which like much of that from Lincolnshire, is mainly from funerary contexts. With the exception of the pottery from the fen-edge (Healy 1996) and that from Grimes Graves (Longworth 1981; Longworth *et al.* 1988) there are no certain settlement sites known (Lawson 1980, 275). The vessels from Norfolk illustrate the two strands of development visible in East Anglia during the Middle Bronze Age. On the one hand the bucket-shaped urns such as those from Shouldham (Lawson 1980, fig. 4:A and B), Snettisham (Lawson 1980, fig. 5:D) and Witton (*e.g.* Lawson 1983, fig. 25) would not be out of place in a classic Deverel-Rimbury assemblage, while on the other the presence of Biconical Urns and related forms (Lawson 1980, fig. 3: A–E and F) indicate the presence of a tradition not well-represented in the area around Billingborough. Two collections of major importance to the region, because they are the only groups of material in a settlement context of this date, are those from Grimes Graves, Norfolk, (Longworth 1981; Longworth *et al.* 1988) and from the margins of the Fenland in the Hockwold/Methwold area (Healy 1996).

Although Ellison (in Longworth *et al.* 1988), in her discussion of the material from the Grimes Graves assemblages, notes the influence of both the Ardleigh and Biconical traditions, she also comments on the difference between the development of the Ardleigh tradition in southern East Anglia and the strong Biconical tradition of Norfolk which gave rise to diverse ceramic styles such as occur at Grimes Graves. Although there are similarities between the Grimes Graves pottery and that from Billingborough there are also important differences. Punctuation through the body wall is a feature both of northern and southern East Anglia (Longworth *et al.* 1988, Appendix I), but does not occur at the cemeteries cited

above, and only rarely occurs at Billingborough and its immediate vicinity (Fig. 24: 61 is the only sherd from stratified contexts with a pre-firing hole, but others were apparently observed from surface collection in the area). Horseshoe applied cordons are a characteristic feature of Ardleigh Urns, and occur both at Grimes Graves and elsewhere in Norfolk, on both vessels identifiable as Ardleigh Urns and on Biconicals (Longworth *et al.* 1988, appendix I), but they do not occur at Billingborough. Other notable differences between Grimes Graves and Billingborough include the preference at the former for slashed decoration on rim top and cordon, and the frequency of rim top decoration of all types. Slashed decoration is not present in the stratified material at Billingborough (there was one example from surface collection in the area), and rim top decoration is rare. This applies also to the cemetery assemblages in the region (Allen *et al.* 1987; May 1976).

Although there are general similarities with the East Anglian pottery of the middle to late 2nd millennium cal. BC, it is difficult to trace clearly either of the two lines of development outlined by Ellison (in Longworth *et al.* 1988); the connection between Biconical Urns and pottery of Billingborough type seems at best tenuous. In view of the lack of absolute dates for Phase 1 the assemblage from Billingborough cannot shed much light on the development of ceramic traditions in the mid to late 2nd millennium cal BC in the East Midlands. Unlike much of Wessex there is in Lincolnshire no development from grog-tempered traditions in the Early Bronze Age to a preference for flint temper in the Middle and Late Bronze Age. This may be partly due to a paucity of raw material, but flint is present in the area, albeit mainly in the form of gravel. The lack of evidence for a strong influence from Biconical Urns distances this material from that of East Anglia, but it must be presumed that in a loosely associated way the developments in this area are related to the more widespread development of largely bucket-shaped traditions over much of England at this time.

Later Phase 1 pottery
The difference between the earlier and later Phase 1 deposits in ditch *7743* is best exemplified by the occurrence of angled body sherds (Table 5). Of the seven angled body sherds which occur in the Phase 1 contexts of the undisturbed length of ditch *7743*, none occur in a context deeper than layer *7743c* or *7743d* (see Fig. 5). Similarly, shell-bearing fabrics, rare in the lower fill, only become common in layers *7743b*, *c*, and *d*. In part the greater variety of forms may be a reflection of the greater amount of pottery in the upper ditch fill, and it may also be due to the mixing of material from overlying layer *7743* of Phase 2, which was felt to account for the presence of briquetage in the Phase 1 contexts of the upper ditch. However, the existence elsewhere on the site of material datable to the Late Bronze Age strongly indicates that the change in the pottery within the ditch could be due to change through time. At least one vessel (Fig. 22: 25), from basal layer *752e* of feature *752*, is identifiable as probably of Barrett's Post-Deverel-Rimbury plain ware tradition, in which it is classifiable as a Class I jar (Barrett 1980, 302–303). In contrast, the hooked-rim profile of (Fig. 23: 34), which also seems reminiscent of Barrett Post-Deverel-Rimbury pottery, is in fact misleading, as the 'hook' only occurs in one small length of rim; this vessel

is in a grog-tempered fabric, in contrast to Figure 22: 25 which is shelly.

Vessels which may be assigned to the Post-Deverel-Rimbury tradition include the cup or small bowl Fig. 21: 19 (VT5) and possibly the small bowl Fig. 21: 18 (VT4), both from the upper fill of ditch *7743*. Neither have close parallels, although the bowl Fig. 21: 19 may be related to bowls with marked out-turned rims such as vessel 39 at Aldermaston Wharf, Berkshire (Bradley *et al.* 1980, fig. 13), or, nearer to Billingborough, at Washingborough, Lincolnshire (Coles *et al.* 1979, fig. 3:9). The Washingborough collection, recovered after construction of a pump-house on the River Witham, also includes a vessel not dissimilar to Fig. 22: 25 (Coles *et al.* 1979, fig. 3:12) and an antler cheek piece of a type found elsewhere with Ewart Park type metalwork.

The circumstances of recovery at Washingborough were such that the internal association of the group is not strong, and the radiocarbon date of 410–120 cal BC (Q-1163, 2253±70 BP) seems of doubtful validity in dating the pottery. If the pottery at Washingborough is contemporary with Ewart Park metalwork, and the parallel with later Phase 1 at Billingborough is correct, this implies that the end of Phase 1 and the inception of Phase 2 may not be long separated in time. There is, for example, a considerable degree of similarity between vessel 12 at Washingborough (Coles *et al.* 1979, fig. 3), Fig. 22: 25 from a Phase 1 context (*752e*) at Billingborough, and Fig. 25: 63 and 64 from pits *78256* and *78257* belonging to Phase 2.

Phase 2

The ceramic material from Phase 2 includes ceramic containers which were certainly involved in salt extraction as well as pottery. The former are considered separately below. The fabrics of the Phase 2 pottery (Table 6), unlike those of the Phase 1 vessels, are shelly and are indistinguishable in fabric to the majority of the Phase 3 and Phase 4 pottery. As the Phase 2 pottery is not distinctive in either form or fabric it is, therefore, impossible to identify redeposited Phase 2 pottery in later phases, although it is likely that such material is present. The amount of pottery securely stratified in Phase 2 contexts is small (see Table 6) and much of this is clearly redeposited Phase 1 material; it is therefore not suitable for the detailed analysis applied to the Phase 1 material.

Fabric
The pottery of Phase 2, excluding the grog-tempered material redeposited from previous occupation, is almost entirely shell-bearing. A single angled shoulder sherd (Fig. 25: 70) is in a fabric with small irregular limestone fragments with no visible shell.

Only one sherd from this phase was thin-sectioned (Fig. 25: 63). The sherd contained 20% shell, including fossils of the Jurassic limestone, and 1% quartz. The source for the clay is likely to be the Great Oolite limestone and clays, as is also the case with the shelly fabrics of both Phase 1 and the later phases.

Form
Although the vessels are represented only by sherds giving very incomplete profiles the following types may be identified:

Long-necked vessels: with a slack angle between body and a slightly everted neck. Rims are simple. (Fig. 25: 62).

Jars with weakly shouldered or ovoid bodies and upright to everted externally expanded rims: (Fig. 25: 63 and 64).

Vessels with rounded bodies and T-shaped rims: (Fig. 25: 65). This is a form which is also represented in the upper layers of Enclosure 1 ditch

7743 in a Phase 1 context and in a combination of fabric and firing colour which is indistinguishable from that of salt containers.

Vessels with an upright upper body with marked interior bevel or internal flange, concave in profile and formed by the addition of clay to the interior of the rim (Fig. 25: 66 and 67). The degree of protrusion of the bevel or internal flange in the case of at least Fig. 25: 67 suggests that it may have been intended to form the seating for a lid, although no lids are identifiable among the Phase 2 pottery. The internally thickened rim of Fig. 25: 68 may be a form related to Fig. 25: 66 and 67, although in this case the thickening is not in the form of a distinct bevel or flange.

Probable bowl form with everted, flattened rim: (Fig. 25: 69).

Discussion
The radiocarbon date of 840–390 cal BC (HAR-3101, 2500±100 BP) provides a *terminus ante quem* for the deposition of the pottery in pit *78256*, and is likely, on the grounds of the appearance of the deposit, to not long succeed it. This date places pit *78256* in the Late Bronze Age to Early Iron Age, and contemporary with either the Ewart Park metalworking tradition, or metalwork of Hallstatt C or D. In the terms set out by Knight (1984) it is impossible to classify the assemblage from the pits because of the small number of vessels represented: the absence of angled sherds from the pit may not be significant. However, the presence of two weakly shouldered, ovoid or globular forms (Fig. 25: 63 and 64) may indicate that it belongs to his Group 2 assemblages rather than to Group 1 (Knight 1984, 39–40). From Phase 2 contexts overall there is only a single angular sherd (Fig. 25: 70), which strengthens the impression that the pottery of this phase does not belong to Knight's Group 1 assemblage. However, the pottery from Phase 2 contexts is difficult to interpret not only because of the fragmentary and partial nature of the evidence, but also because the nature of the activities, attested by the salt-working debris from features of this phase, suggests that the range of vessels represented may be more restricted and specialised than that occurring on the settlement sites used for comparison.

Comparable vessels to those present in Phase 2 at Billingborough occur at a number of sites, but no single site affords a convincing parallel for the collection. The pottery recovered at Washingborough shows some similarity to that from Billingborough (Coles *et al.* 1979, Fig. 3:11) and is thought to be Late Bronze Age. The vessel illustrated as fig. 3:11 at Washingborough is similar to Fig. 25: 63 and 64 from Billingborough which, as already noted, also resemble Fig. 22: 25 from Phase 1, although the firing colour and surface finish differ. The sherd apparently from a bowl with a flat-topped rim (Fig. 25: 69) is perhaps related to the form of vessel 9 at Washingborough (Coles *et al.* 1979, fig. 3) and vessel 35 from the pre-Period 1 phase at Werrington, Cambridgeshire (Rollo 1988, 110). The assemblage from Werrington also includes at least one weakly shouldered, globular or ovoid jar with an everted rim, broadly similar to Fig. 25: 63 and 64 at Billingborough, although lacking the squared-off rim (Rollo 1988, fig. 25: 7). The Werrington pre-Period 1 pottery is tentatively dated to the 5th century BC, but there is no independent evidence for this (Rollo 1988, 112).

Closer matches for the Billingborough pottery of this phase seem to be provided by the Late Bronze Age/Early Iron Age pottery from field OS 124 at Maxey, 20km to the south of Billingborough. Two rim sherds from area J at Maxey (May 1981, fig. 9: 2 and 3) offer parallels for Fig.

Table 6 is oriented sideways on the page. "Pottery" spans the Shell, Other prehistoric and Non-prehistoric column groups.

	Grog		Pottery						Briquetage		Fired Clay*	
			Shell		Other prehistoric		Non-prehistoric					
	No	Wt	No	Wt	No	Wt	No	Wt	No	Wt	No	Wt
752	11	155g	3	35g	-	-	-	-	-	1516g	-	433g
[751]1	2	23g	-	-	-	-	-	-	1	8g	-	-
[751]2	-	-	1	6g	-	-	-	-	14	150g	-	-
7554	1	12g	-	-	-	-	-	-	-	-	-	-
[778]	2	11g	5	41g	1 (sandy)	14g	1 (post-med)	3g	6	20g	1	5g
[7736]	101	1502g	23	116g	-	-	1 (R-B)	3g	447	1284g	125 (+ frags)	807g
7743	44	636g	44	417g	-	-	-	-	1128	3514g	140	1104g
[7756]	-	-	-	-	-	-	-	-	1	11g	-	-
7779	-	-	-	-	-	-	-	-	1	21g	-	-
[7795]	28	464g	6	26g	-	-	-	-	511	1243g	88	455g
77101	4	63g	-	-	1	3g	-	-	11	30g	-	-
77101a	1	9g	-	-	-	-	-	-	-	-	1	18g
77101b	86	1472g	-	-	-	-	-	-	-	-	-	-
77101c	19	163g	2	21g	-	-	-	-	19	62g	6	52g
77101d	14	96g	4	9g	-	-	-	-	30	132g	-	-
[77102]	1 (+ 1nw)	92g	1	8g	-	-	-	-	30	182g	3	12g
[78256]	16	525g	-	-	-	-	-	-	-	-	1	62g
[78257]	-	-	75	973g	-	-	-	-	1541	4688g	88	1729g
GRAND TOTAL	330(+ 1nw)	5223g	164	1652g	2	17g	2	6g	3740+	12,861g	453+	4677g

NB **Counts** were not carried out for all material. 'nw' indicates sherd(s) not weighed. * does not include material treated as technological finds

Table 6 Pottery and other ceramic material from Phase 2 contexts

25: 69 at Billingborough, and are interpreted by May as covers or shallow bowls or dishes. May cites continental Urnfield and Hallstatt parallels for the form, and the related, but poorly dated rim sherd at Washingborough (Coles *et al.* 1979 fig. 3:9). The form is also known from the Late Bronze Age site at Runnymede Bridge, Surrey, where it occurs in association with metalwork of the Ewart Park metalworking tradition (May 1981, 57; Longley 1980, fig. 21: 38 and 39). The strongly internally bevelled or flanged rims Fig. 25: 66 and 67 are not paralleled at Runnymede, but may be a form peculiar to the East Midlands: close parallels for them occur at Gretton, Northamptonshire, in an assemblage which, on the basis of the other pottery in the assemblage, is thought to be contemporary with pottery in use from the period of Ewart Park metalwork to that of La Tène I (Jackson and Knight 1985, 82). The sherds similar to Billingborough Fig. 25: 66 and 67 are from a layer in Ditch A at Gretton which also produced a virtually complete iron ring-headed pin (Jackson and Knight 1985, 81–82, fig 8: 51, 53 and 54; fig. 10:7) for which a date in La Tène I, or possibly Hallstatt C/D is suggested (Jackson and Knight 1985, 81); the condition of the pottery in Ditch A is such as to suggest that the pottery is not residual. This dating is not inconsistent with the radiocarbon date from pit *78256* (840 – 390 cal BC, HAR-3101, 2500±100BP), that is, early 8th to late 6th centuries BC, a date which would place the pottery within the earlier (*i.e.* Hallstatt C/D) rather than the later end of the range suggested by the Gretton ditch A assemblage.

Phase 3

The pottery of Phases 2, 3 and 4 and the briquetage are all in shelly fabrics. Thin-sectioning of sherds from all phases has led to the identification of the possible source for the shelly clays as the Great Oolite. This is true of almost all the shelly pottery thin-sectioned, and as such it is not possible to separate pottery of these three phases on the grounds of fabric. Redeposited sherds are therefore difficult to isolate. In the following three sections (*i.e.* Phase 3 pottery, Phase 4 pottery, and the briquetage) it must be understood that an element of redeposited material is present in each phase, but that it is not possible to identify it. Pottery from Phase 3 contexts is tabulated below (Table 7).

Fabric
Four sherds from Phase 3 were thin-sectioned (Fig. 26: 71–74), and all contained fossil shell (see below). Fig. 26: 74 differed from the rest of the shelly fabrics from the site, as the limestone fossil fragments in this vessel are not weathered. Allen does not suggest a source for the clay, although she suggests that it need not be at any great distance. A single illustrated sherd (Fig. 27: 97) occurs in a sandy fabric, and three other body sherds also contain sand alone.

Form
A greater range of vessel forms occur in Phase 3 than in the previous two phases, but the fragmentary nature of much of the pottery renders the creation of detailed vessel type descriptions impossible. In most cases the profile only survives for a short distance below the rim, or bases and upper bodies cannot be reconstructed into complete profiles. The general paucity of angular sherds suggests that carinated vessels were not frequent but slack and rounded shoulders do occur. The following forms are represented in the collection:

Large, possibly necked, vessels with expanded to T-shaped rims. Fig. 26: 74 is the best example of this type; Fig. 26: 75 and 76 probably also belong to it. It is impossible to determine the shape of the lower body, although the very slightly concave profile to Fig. 26: 74 suggests the presence of

at least a slack shoulder, if not an angular carination. Fig. 26: 74 and 75 have shallow grooves running around the rim top.

Globular to ovoid, weakly shouldered, jars with simple upright or everted rims (Fig. 26: 77–81; Fig. 27: 82). It is likely that rims such as Fig. 27: 83 and 84 also belong to globular or ovoid, weakly shouldered jars, but no profile survives below the rim. The rim sherd Fig. 27: 85 from a massive vessel, possibly also represented by the lower body (Fig. 27: 86) may also be of this type, although the rim form, which is inturned above a sharply concave neck, is distinctive.

A number of vessels appear to have had longer necks than those cited above, although because of the lack of body profile in all cases the proportion of body to neck cannot be estimated. Neck types certainly present include markedly concave forms (Fig. 27: 87), upright forms (Fig. 27: 88) and concave forms with incurved rim (Fig. 27: 89).

Bowls and/or jars with markedly inturned rims (Fig. 27: 90–92). The angle of the rim sherd (Fig. 27: 92) is not certain and may be more upright than illustrated; it could, therefore, belong to the same type of vessel as Figure 27:90, which appears to be a necked jar.

Bowls with slack or round shoulders (Fig. 27: 93–5). Fig. 27: 96 is also likely to be an Iron Age example of this form, though apparently intrusive in an earlier context.

Decoration
Fingernail/tip decoration continues in use in Phase 3, although the emphasis in this phase is on the rim top rather than the body, and scoring appears as an important part of the repertoire. Fingernail/tip decoration: always single, and usually lacking the impression of the nail. It occurs exclusively on the rim top, or, rarely, on the exterior vessel surface just below the rim (Fig. 27: 90 and 92; Fig. 28: 97–101).
Grooves around the rim top on two vessels with expanded rims (Fig. 26: 74 and 75). Incision: occurs once on the rim top (Fig. 28; 103), and once on the body of a small bowl (Fig. 27: 95).
Scoring: both shallow scoring, possibly executed with a bundle of twigs, and deep scoring, are present (*e.g.* Fig. 26: 80 and 81, and Fig. 27: 82 show the former; and Fig. 28; 104 the latter). Shallow scoring appears to be the preferred method.

Discussion
The majority of pottery from Phase 3 contexts was found in the recut length of the Phase 1 Bronze Age Enclosure 1 ditch *7710*, in upper fill *78145* of the same ditch where it appeared to have been filled in at the time that Enclosure 2 was constructed, and in Iron Age Enclosure 3 ditch *78135*. Associated metalwork was found in ditch *7710* (Fig. 18: 2) and in both the upper (*7835*) and lower (*78116*) levels of ditch *78135* (Fig. 15: 4, 5, 6, and Fig. 15: 3). In view of the unrefined chronology of the Middle to Late Iron Age in the East Midlands these associations are of particular importance.

The length of occupation represented by the Phase 3 contexts is unknown. The pottery from the upper levels (*78145*) of ditch *7710* where it lies within Enclosure 2 probably belongs to the period when the latter was laid out, while that from the upper fill of Enclosure 3 ditch *78135* would seem likely to date from the end of the life of that enclosure. Very little pottery was recovered from Iron Age ditch *78113* of Enclosure 2 and, although there is no certain stratigraphic link between this enclosure and that bounded by ditch *78135* (Enclosure 3), they have been interpreted as complementary in function and likely to belong to a single phase of use of the site (*i.e.* Phase 3).

Several elements of the Phase 3 pottery are identifiable in other collections from the East Midlands and from the fen edge, although nowhere is the dating well-defined.

Scored pottery is ubiquitous in the Middle to Late Iron Age and beyond in the East Midlands, but the date of both its inception and disappearance are uncertain. A key site for this style of decoration is Ancaster Quarry (18km to the north-west of Billingborough), at which scored wares appear in large quantities. May (1976, 138–140)

	Grog		Shell	Pottery	Other prehistoric		Non-prehistoric		Briquetage		Fired Clay*	
	No	Wt	No	Wt	No	Wt	No	Wt	No	Wt	No	Wt
7710 [7710]	6	169g	242	3248g	-	-	4 (R-B)	27g	575(+ 3nw)	1785g	228	2111g
7710b [7710]	4	60g	5	64g	-	-	-	-	107	610g	113	143g
7787	18	182g	4	27g	-	-	-	-	786	865g	32	89g
7787b [7787]	-	-	-	-	-	-	-	-	1	3g	-	-
7787e [7787]	2	11g	-	-	-	-	-	-	-	-	-	-
[77128]	-	-	3	19g	-	-	-	-	44	394g	17	144g
784 [78145]	68	1009g	140	1609g	-	-	-	-	292(some nw)	2326g	124	126g
786	2	113g	-	-	-	-	-	-	1	26g	-	-
787 [78113]	51	919g	122	1234g	-	-	2 (R-B)	16g	956 (+ 1nw)	4553g	57	782g
7810	1	34g	4	194g	-	-	-	-	1	7g	-	-
7835 [78135]	53	511g	525	4325g	3	21g	-	-	319	1005g	69	513g
[7844]	1	19g	7	18g	-	-	-	-	1	3g	-	-
[78103]	-	-	14	131g	-	-	-	-	18	55g	1	20g
78112 [78135]	3	17g	4	116g	-	-	-	-	4	19g	-	-
78115 [78113]	1	12g	2	9g	-	-	-	-	81	235g	10	26g
78116 [78113]	3	52g	95	1423g	2	7g	-	-	44	135g	70	109g
78120 [78113]	9	188g	7	70g	-	-	-	-	12	59g	4	26g
78121 [78113]	4	60g	1	4g	-	-	-	-	20	126g	4	27g
78122 [78135]	-	-	6	36g	-	-	-	-	1	6g	-	-
[78127] [78135]	-	-	1	5g	-	-	-	-	1	5g	-	-
[78129]	-	-	12	168g	-	-	-	-	9	44g	2	17g
78134 [78113]	20	320g	11	78g	-	-	-	-	97	398g	4	26g
78137 [78113]	1	28g	1	6g	-	-	-	-	18	90g	1	5g
78140 [78113]	9	198g	5	62g	-	-	-	-	132	542g	7	74g
78141 [78145]	16	106g	4	53g	-	-	-	-	15	80g	6	74g
78142 [78145]	14	339g	2	10g	-	-	-	-	2	4g	-	-
78147 [78145]	2	58g	-	-	-	-	-	-	-	-	-	-
78148 [78145]	1	57g	-	-	-	-	-	-	-	-	-	-
78225 [78145]	7	108g	9	103g	-	-	1 (CBM)	6g	37 (+1 nw)	150g	12	90g
78229 [78145]	-	-	-	-	-	-	-	-	1	8g	1	126g
78233 [78113]	3	36g	-	-	-	-	-	-	1	8g	-	-
78251 [78145]	-	-	-	-	1 vitrified?	3g	-	-	2	33g	1	63g
GRAND TOTAL	299(+ 1nw)	4606g	1226	13,012g	6	31g	7	49g	3568+	13,574g	763	8008g

NB **Counts** were not carried out for all material. 'nw' indicates sherd(s) not weighed. * does not include material treated as technological finds

Table 7 Pottery and other ceramic material from Phase 3 contexts

favours a date for the main use of this site in the 3rd century BC, partly on the basis of the likely dating of two La Tène brooches. The date of the end of occupation at Ancaster Quarry is uncertain but there is no evidence that it extended beyond 100 BC (May 1976, 140).

An early beginning for scored pottery has been suggested by Pryor on the basis of the material found in a well, *F3*, at the Padholme Road sub-site, Fengate, Peterborough. There, a radiocarbon date of 2300±46BP (GaK-4198) was obtained from wood in the lowest layer of F3 (Pryor 1974, 38, figs 20–22) which calibrates to 410 – 240 cal BC. The association of this date is with the pottery in layer *5* of the feature. The section (Pryor 1974, fig. 18) suggests that the formation of layers *4* and *5* was not long separated in time, as the wooden lining extends through both, but the slightly different character of the upper layers (layers *1–3*; Pryor 1974, 26, fig. 18) might be taken as an indication that their formation was separated by a considerable time-lapse from the two lower layers. Layers *4* and *5* contain two distinctive rims with internal corrugations (Pryor 1974, fig. 21:20, and fig. 22:10), a form which appears in the early Iron Age around the western fen edge and further afield. A similar rim occurs at Gretton in a probable La Tène I context (Jackson and Knight 1985, 82, fig. 6:24), and another at Brigstock in occupation probably pre-dating the enclosure (Jackson 1983, fig. 8:45). The reconstructable pot from Fiskerton found 'crushed under the cross timbers of the causeway', constructed of timbers felled at intervals between 456 BC and 375 BC (Hillam 1989, 140), also has a rim of this type. This rim form, therefore, is clearly consistent with the radiocarbon date for layer *5* of Padholme Road *F3*, and there is certainly *some* scored pottery present in that feature, including one of the vessels with a corrugated rim. This date, however, *cannot* be used with the same confidence in relation to the typical scored ware jars of the upper fill of *F3* (Pryor 1974, fig. 20), which could therefore belong to the Middle rather than Early Iron Age, of which they would seem more characteristic.

Although radiocarbon dating can clearly be of assistance in broad terms, the lack of precision in the radiocarbon chronology of the 1st millennium is still such that dating on the basis of metalwork associations must be given precedence. Knight, writing in the mid-1980s, could state that no scored ware had then been found with metalwork associations earlier than La Tène II (*i.e.* unlikely to be earlier than late 4th/early 3rd century BC) (Knight 1984, 81, fig. 25). At most then, the Padholme Road date indicates an early inception for the technique, approximately a century earlier than the earliest metalwork associations, but does not date the classic scored ware jars, such as occur at Ancaster Quarry, and at Billingborough.

In the case of the Billingborough scored jars (Fig 26: 80 and 81; Fig. 27: 82) an early date is also excluded by the occurrence in the same layer (*7710*) of the 'poker' (Fig. 14: 1) which is most likely to be of Middle to Late Iron Age date.

The relationship between the upper filling of the recut Bronze Age enclosure ditch *78145* outside the area occupied by Enclosure 2 and the upper levels of the same ditch where they lie inside the area of the enclosure is not certain, but both are likely to belong to Phase 3. The length of ditch inside Enclosure 2 may have been deliberately backfilled to provide a level surface within the enclosure

and so is likely to be contemporary with or earlier than the construction of that enclosure. The material within this length of ditch (*i.e.* from the four excavated sections) is therefore of considerable importance. The illustrated pottery from the uppermost layer of the ditch in these sections comprises Fig. 27: 90; Fig. 28: 97, 98 and 105–120.

This pottery, apart from including obviously redeposited pieces (*e.g.* Fig. 20: 5; Fig 23: 31 and 32; and probably all the briquetage) includes one of the vessels with a long neck and markedly inturned rim (Fig. 27: 90), a necked vessel with fingertip decoration on the rim top, and one piece (Fig. 28: 115) with shallow, but clear, scoring.

The inturned rims (Fig. 27: 90–92) may, like those in Phase 2, be loosely related to those at Gretton, which, it has been suggested, may date to the period from Ewart Park metalwork to La Tène I (Jackson and Knight 1985, 82). This dating would appear to be too early for Phase 3 at Billingborough, in contrast to the good match between the radiocarbon date for Phase 2 feature *78256* (840–390 cal BC, HAR-3101, 2500±100 BP) with similar rims and the proposed date for the Gretton pottery. However, although the similarity between both Fig. 25: 66 and 67, and Fig. 27: 90–92, and the Gretton examples is not strong, in some of the Gretton examples and in the two rims of Phase 2 the internal extension is more of a bevel or flange than an inturning of the rim, whereas in the three rim sherds from Phase 3 the latter is the case. Strongly inturned forms do occur rarely in later assemblages, such as at Twywell, Northamptonshire (Harding 1975, fig. 22:30), and it is possible that it is a local idiosyncracy which persists through time and at present is not well dated. The rim from the upper fill (*7835*) of Enclosure 3 ditch *7835* (Fig. 27: 92) at least seems unlikely to be early; unless it is redeposited it is likely to be of 1st century BC date.

In contrast, the use of fingertip and fingernail decoration on the top of out-turned or expanded rims (*e.g.* Fig. 28: 97, 100 and 101), a feature which is also represented in the top of ditch *78145* (*i.e.* by Fig. 28: 97), is entirely typical of the Twywell assemblage, and may be dated within the time span late 5th to the end of the 2nd century BC (Harding 1975, 73).

Twywell and Billingborough resemble each other not only in what is present in the assemblages, but also in what is absent from them. Harding notes, at Twywell, the unusual lack of fine globular bowls with short or incipient bead rim, and the paucity of curvilinear ornament, which is usually an accompaniment of the type (Harding 1975, 72). This is also true of Billingborough, where no curvilinear decoration occurs. The only vessel from Billingborough with what may be contemporary decoration is the cup or small bowl found represented by two (non-joining) sherds (Fig. 27: 95) from both the lower and upper fill of ditch *78135*. The continuous single chevron motif in incision or grooving is found on vessels over a long period (Knight 1984, 23–26), but the form of P616 is more suggestive of the former than the latter. The fabric of this vessel is black, well-fired, and noticeably finer than that of the majority of the material from the site, although it is in a shelly fabric. Weekley, Northamptonshire, *c.* 57km to the south-west, has produced an unusually large collection of decorated pottery, some of which is decorated in a linear style (rather than the more usual curvilinear style) in which chevrons are a common motif (*e.g.* Jackson and Dix 1986–87, fig. 34: 60, 63, 64, 69; Jackson and Ambrose 1978, 174).

The assemblage from Enclosure 3 ditch *78135* appears to belong to the final stage of settlement on the site, as the ditches of Phase 4, which cut it, seem unlikely to represent occupation in the immediate vicinity. Most of the material in Phase 4 contexts is likely to be redeposited from the earlier use of the site, the settlement associated with this period presmably lying at some distance along the fen edge. The date of the end of the Phase 3 occupation is therefore clearly of importance, in that it dates a fairly radical change in the history of land-use in that area.

The assemblages from the lower and upper fill of ditch *78135* do not differ markedly in character, and two vessels are represented by sherds which occur in both layers (Fig. 27: 94 and 95). In neither case are the sherds in the upper fill markedly more worn than those in the lower, and there seems no reason to propose a long history for the filling of this ditch. The proportion of scored ware is low: only 19 sherds are scored from a total of 601 sherds (*i.e.* 3%) in the shelly fabric from the ditch (*i.e.* excluding the grog-tempered sherds which are likely to be residual). The assemblage also includes at least one large jar (Fig. 27: 86, possibly belonging to the same vessel as the rim Fig. 27: 85), necked jars (*e.g.* Fig. 27: 83 and 84), vessels with sharply inturned rims (Fig. 27: 92; Fig. 28: 121) and small bowls (Fig. 27: 94 and the probably decorated Fig. 27: 95). Rims are generally simple and plain, although seven are finger-decorated (Fig. 27: 92; Fig. 28: 99–102, 122 and 123). These features have been discussed in general terms above, but their association in this ditch, with metalwork, is an important addition to the number of well-associated assemblages in the area. On the basis of the pottery alone a date for the assemblage within the 2nd or 1st centuries is possible. Apart from the similarity between Fig. 27: 95 and the Weekley pottery of Ceramic Phase 1 (Jackson and Dix 1986–87, fig. 34) some of the jars with short upright rims in the same Ceramic Phase at that site bear comparison with vessels from ditch *78135* (*cf* Fig. 26: 77 and 79, and Jackson and Dix 1986–87, fig. 30). At Weekley the use of related decorated pottery is dated by a series of radiocarbon determinations (HAR-1725, 2050±70 BP; HAR1779, 1910±80 BP; HAR-1844, 2120±90 BP; HAR-2007, 2160±70 BP; HAR-2008, 2000±70 BP) (Jackson and Dix 1986–87, 49, 77). Jackson and Dix suggest, on the basis of the sequences of ditch cutting and short-lived use of some features, that this pottery, while pre-dating the Ceramic Phase 2 assemblages of the second and third quarters of the 1st century AD, may not have been in use for a long period, probably less than the century or so indicated by the range of the radiocarbon dates (Jackson and Dix 1986–7, 70, 79).

If Fig. 27: 95, which is represented only by a small proportion of its profile, is correctly identified this could be taken, in conjunction with the Weekley evidence, as an indication of a date anywhere within the later 2nd or 1st century BC for the assemblage. However, the identifications of the brooches in the ditch at Billingborough are crucial to the dating of the pottery associated with the use of this enclosure. The Nauheim type is unlikely to have been made earlier than the late 2nd century nor later than the mid 1st century BC. It is most likely to have been in use in the first half of the 1st century BC (see above, p.21). Although the possibility cannot be ruled out that it and the other brooches were old when they entered the ditch, the lack of later brooch forms, combined with the pottery assemblage which contains no forms which *must* be later than mid 1st century BC, suggests that the likeliest date for the whole assemblage, and therefore for the abandonment of the enclosure, is the first half of the 1st century BC. In support of this is also the fact that there seem to be no points of comparison between the Billingborough Phase 3 and Dragonby assemblages (Elsdon and May 1987), nor between Billingborough and Old Sleaford (Elsdon 1982). Both of these assemblages have extensive cordoned and stamped decoration which is likely to date to the later 1st century BC, although the absence of these traits could reflect the social status of the inhabitants of a site rather than its date.

The dating of comparative material is so uncertain or unrefined in many cases that it seems reasonable to give precedence to the internal evidence from Billingborough, particularly as this includes the two associations with metalwork discussed above. Taken together these strongly suggest a date of no later than the mid 1st century BC for the Phase 3 pottery, and there is certainly nothing in the pottery assemblage itself which demands a date later than this. The inception of Phase 3 is even more uncertain than its end, but if the the heavy rims in the upper fill in the back-filled length of ditch 78145 are accepted as middle rather than earlier Iron Age a date in the 4th to 2nd centuries would seem reasonable.

Phase 4

The pottery recovered from stratified contexts of this phase appears to be largely redeposited, as it is mostly of fabric, form, and decorative types occurring in previous Phases (Table 8). However, there is a small collection comprising 19 sherds of Romano-British pottery, with the majority (10 sherds) from ditch *78136*. These are grey wares which are not closely datable, but a Hod Hill brooch (Fig. 13: 8) from a broadly contemporaneous context suggests that these belong to the second half of the 1st century AD. The paucity of material contemporary with the use of the site in this phase reflects agricultural activity represented by two field ditches and several small, related gullies, with no known settlement in the immediate vicinity. Other, unstratified material is reported below.

Fabric Analysis
by Carol S.M. Allen (1984 with revisions)
Seventeen sherds of pottery were examined in thin section. A short summary of the identity and possible sources of the inclusions is given below with full details available in archive. The percentages of materials included in the fabric of the sherds, which are quoted above by Cleal in the discussion of the pottery, are estimates expressed by area using Flugel (1982). The full results of the fabric analysis, comparisons with material from other sites and the implications of the results are discussed fully elsewhere (Allen 1988 and 1991).

Shell inclusions
The shell in the eleven samples of shelly wares is of fossil type. Echinoid, bryozoa and brachiopod have been identified, and this association is considered diagnostic of the middle Jurassic. The Great Oolite limestone and clays, which are not oolitic in spite of their name, contain this material and are suggested as the likely source of this fossil

	Pottery								Briquetage		Fired Clay*	
	Grog		Shell		Other prehistoric		Non-prehistoric					
	No	Wt	No	Wt	No	Wt	No	Wt	No	Wt	No	Wt
[759]	1	158g	2	5g	-	-	-	-	6	60g	4	370g
[779]	30	427g	-	331g	-	-	13 (R-B)	81g	-	11069g	-	1537g
7752	-	-	-	-	-	-	-	-	1	10g	-	-
[7796]	4	58g	17	147g	-	-	-	-	254	1005g	62 (vitrified clay?)	495g
7797 [7797]	2	18g	16	108g	-	-	1 (R-B)	12g	282	724g	51	226g
7797b [7797]	-	-	-	-	1 (vitrified pot?)	5g	-	-	70	185g	11	114g
[77107]	-	-	8	64g	-	-	1 (R-B)	34g	207	761g	15	82g
[788]	31	373g	267	2055g	1 (organic) / 2 (oolitic)	1g / 52g	3	100g	853	2759g	26	209g
789 [78136]	19	557g	91	616g	1 (sandy)	4g	4 (R-B)	42g	1023	1710g	97	430g
78125 [78138]	4	74g	38	309g	1	5g	1 (R-B)	12g	174	602g	13	75g
78132 [78136]	-	-	-	-	-	-	-	-	1	2g	-	-
78133 [78136]	-	-	2	10g	-	-	-	-	26	91g	1	4g
[78136]	2	26g	2	9g	-	-	-	-	23	105g	1	6g
[78138]	-	-	2	31g	-	-	-	-	-	-	-	-
78139 [78139]	3	48g	29	299g	-	-	-	-	60	188g	5	13g
GRAND TOTAL	**96**	**1739g**	**474 +**	**3994g**	**6**	**67g**	**23**	**281g**	**2980 +**	**19271g**	**286 +**	**3561g**

NB **Counts** were not carried out for all material. 'nw' indicates sherd(s) not weighed. * does not include material treated as technological finds

Table 8 Pottery and other ceramic material from Phase 4 contexts

46

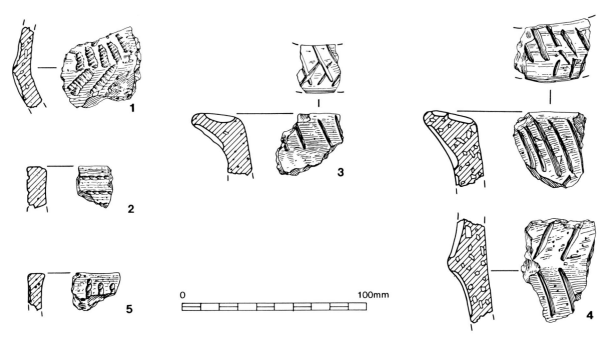

Figure 20 Pottery. Late Neolithic and Early Bronze Age

shell combination and of the oyster shell seen (Swinnerton and Kent 1976, 48; Kent and Gaunt 1980, 49). It is possible that the differing shell content could be a reflection of natural variation within the clays. However, thin-section analysis indicates that the sherd shown in Fig. 26: 73 contains such dense shell that deliberate addition of fossil shell from a weathered outcrop is suggested. The nearest limestone of this type to Billingborough lies within 2km of the site (Tom Lane, pers. comm.).

The size of the shell in the pottery sections does not vary much from sample to sample (details in archive). However, the inclusions in the sherd shown in Fig. 26: 73 present a different appearance as the shell pieces are mainly very small fragments of around 0.25mm. Most of the other shell inclusions vary between 0.5mm and 1mm.

The sherd shown in Fig. 21: 12 contains a fossil shell, an oyster, and this one piece of limestone can be seen by eye in the sherd. This seems to be an accidental inclusion and samples of clay from the site would be required in order to determine whether the source could be local.

Other Limestone Inclusions
The inclusions seen in the clay fabric of the other pottery sections are described as naturally occuring inclusions rather than having been deliberately added tempering materials. Such inclusions may be inherent in the clay or even be trapped by accident.

The thin section of the sherd shown in Fig. 26: 18 exhibited a piece of limestone of ironstone type, composed of ooliths and sparry cement. Such limestone can be seen in the Ancaster Beds, and similar material lies about 12km from the site (Swinnerton and Kent 1976, 38–9). The fabric of another sherd (not illustrated) also contains pelloidal limestone, probably from a similar source.

The fossil limestone seen in the section of sherd Fig 26: 74 has not been weathered in the same manner as in the other fabrics on this site, as calcite can be clearly seen around the fossil shell. The unweathered inclusions are different and unique to this sample, but unfortunately it is not possible to determine the source more accurately. A

sample of material from the limestone uplands 1km to the west of Billingborough might assist in identifying the source, for it is unclear why local limestone was not always used on the site unless for some reason the potting traditions considered that it was unsuitable. However, the pottery need not have been manufactured on site.

Pottery catalogue
by Aiden Challis with M. Laidlaw (1984/1996)

Fig. 20: Neolithic and Early Bronze Age (Pre-Phase 1)
1. Body sherd from carinated bowl with cord impressed chevron decoration; flint < 5mm. Ext: brown, coarse, gritty. Int: black to brown. Sec: black. *Context 7725. P149.*
2. Rim sherd possibly Collared Urn with horizontal twisted cord impressions; grog < 2mm, sand. Ext: buff to black, hard. Int: black. Sec: black. *Context 752, pit 752. P411.*
3. Everted rim with internal bevel, probably Food Vessel; grog < 2mm. Ext: orange buff, coarse. Int: black. Sec: orange buff to black. *Context 752, pit 752. P414.*
4. One everted rim with internal bevel and external ridge, and one body sherd belonging to the same vessel, both have deep scored decoration; grog < 6mm, sand. Ext: brown, burnished, coarse. Int: black. Sec: buff to brownish black. *Context 771. P1222.*
5. Rim sherd, possibly Collared Urn; sand, grog < 5mm. Ext: orange buff, soft, unevenly hand moulded. Int: orange buff. Sec: light buff to orange buff. *Context 784, ditch 78145. P542.*

Fig. 21: Middle Bronze Age (Phase 1)
6. Base sherd; shell mm, grog < 4mm. Ext: grey buff to orange buff, coarse, friable, hand moulded. Int: grey buff to orange buff. Sec: grey buff to orange buff. *Context 7743h, ditch 7743. P27.*
7. Rim sherd with fingertip decoration on rim top (VT1); sand and grog < 10mm. Ext: black to light buff, hard, coarse; Int: black to light buff. Sec: grey. *Context 7743f, ditch 7743. P7.*
8. Flattened, externally expanded rim and applied cordon on upper body of cylindrical vessel (VT2); grog < 12mm, sand. Ext: orange buff to grey, coarse, sandy, uneven. Int: orange buff to grey buff. Sec: black to orange. Smoothing marks. *Context 7743g, ditch 7743. P30.*
9. Simple rim, slack shoulder directly beneath with fingertip decoration on wall (VT3); sand and grog < 5mm. Ext: grey black. Int: light brown. Sec: dark grey. *Context 7743e, ditch 7743. P1.*
10. Simple rim, slack shoulder directly beneath with fingertip decoration on wall (VT3); sand and grog < 4mm. Ext: orange buff to grey buff, coarse, sandy, hand moulded. Int: orange buff. Sec: grey to buff. *Context 7743e, ditch 7743. P2.*

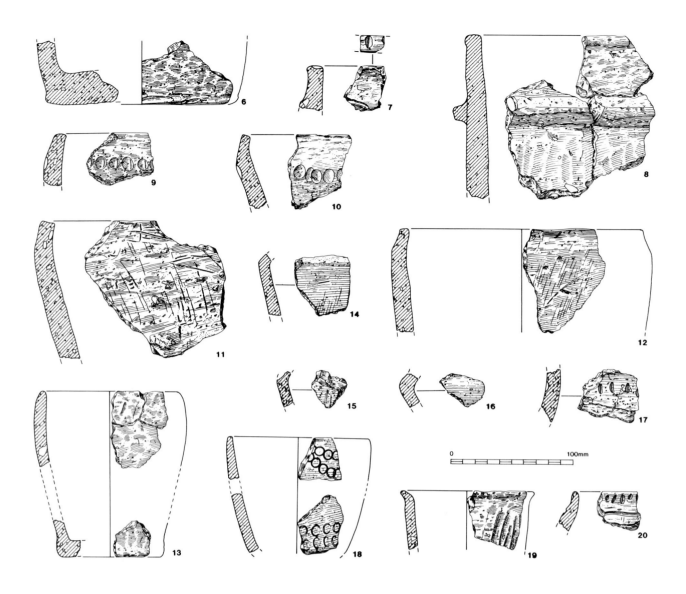

Figure 21 Pottery. Middle Bronze Age (Phase 1)

11. Simple rim, slack shoulder directly beneath (VT3); sand, grog < 8mm, rare shell mm, water-rolled stone < 3mm. Ext: grey buff to buff, hard, coarse, moulding and smoothing marks. Int: grey buff to black, iron pan. Sec: black. *Context 7743h, ditch 7743. P29.*

12. Simple rim, slack shoulder directly beneath (VT3); sand, grog < 8mm. Ext: grey buff to buff, hard, coarse, hand moulded. Int: grey buff to buff. Sec: black. *Context 7743k, ditch 7743. P20.*

13. Rim and base sherd of a smaller version of VT1; shell < 2mm, sand, grog < 7mm. Ext: grey buff to orange buff, hard, coarse, abrasive. Int: buff to black. Sec: black to buff. *Context 7743f, ditch 7743. P26.*

14. Angled body sherd, part of shoulder; shell < 3mm, sand. Ext: black to buff, hard, fine, sandy. Int: mid-brown. Sec: black. *Context 7743b, ditch 7743. P111.*

15. Angled body sherd, part of shoulder, vertical groove; dense shell < 3mm. Ext: orange buff, gritty, friable. Int: black. Sec: grey black to red. *Context 7743b, ditch 7743. P117.*

16. Body sherd, part of rounded shoulder; shell < 3mm. Ext: orange buff, hard, sandy. Int: black, pitted. Sec: black. *Context 7743b, ditch 7743. P129.*

17. Body sherd of vessel with a concave neck, fingernail decoration; shell < 6mm. Ext: reddish brown, hard, brittle. Int: greyish brown, horizontal brushing marks. Sec: black to reddish brown. *Context 7743b, ditch 7743. P110.*

18. Rim and body sherd of a possible bowl decorated with small circular stamps (VT4); small stones and sand, grog, limestone. Ext: orange buff to grey buff, hard, sandy. Int: light buff to black. Sec: black. *Context 7743b, ditch 7743. P112.*

19. Small truncated conical bowl with everted rim (VT5); shell < 3mm, sand, grog, rolled stone mm up wall. Ext: grey buff, hard, vertical smoothing marks. Int: black. Sec: black. *Context 7743c, ditch 7743. P31.*

20. Simple upright rim sherd, closed vessel probably rounded body, fingertip decoration and groove (VT6); sand and grog. Ext: light buff to black, coarse, sandy. Int: black. Sec: grey black. *Context 7743b, ditch 7743. P93.*

Fig. 22: Middle Bronze Age (Phase 1)

21. Rim internally thickened and base sherd of bucket shaped vessel, finger impressions, broad deep groove across exterior of base extending up ext. of body, pre-firing; grog 7mm, flint < 9mm, sand. Ext: orange buff, sandy, hand moulded. Int: black to brown and orange, coarse. Sec: orange buff to buff. *Context 7747, hollow. P153.*

22. Simple rim with slight flared profile, fingertip impressed (VT1); grog < 5mm, sand. Ext: grey buff, hard, sandy, hand moulded. Int: black to orange buff. Sec: black to orange buff. *Context 752b, pit 752. P196.*

23. Simple rim with cordon around upper body (VT2); limestone < 2mm, sand. Ext: orange buff, hard, sandy, hand moulded. Int: orange to buff. Sec: red to buff. *Context 752b, pit 752. P204.*

24. Rim sherd of small truncated conical vessel, fingertip impressed (VT7); grog < 2mm, sand. Ext: grey buff, hard. Int: grey black. Sec: black. *Context 77101c, structure. P269.*

25. Jar with everted rim, horizontal smoothing marks on rim and neck, vertical smoothings on lower body (VT8); shell < 4mm. Ext: orange

48

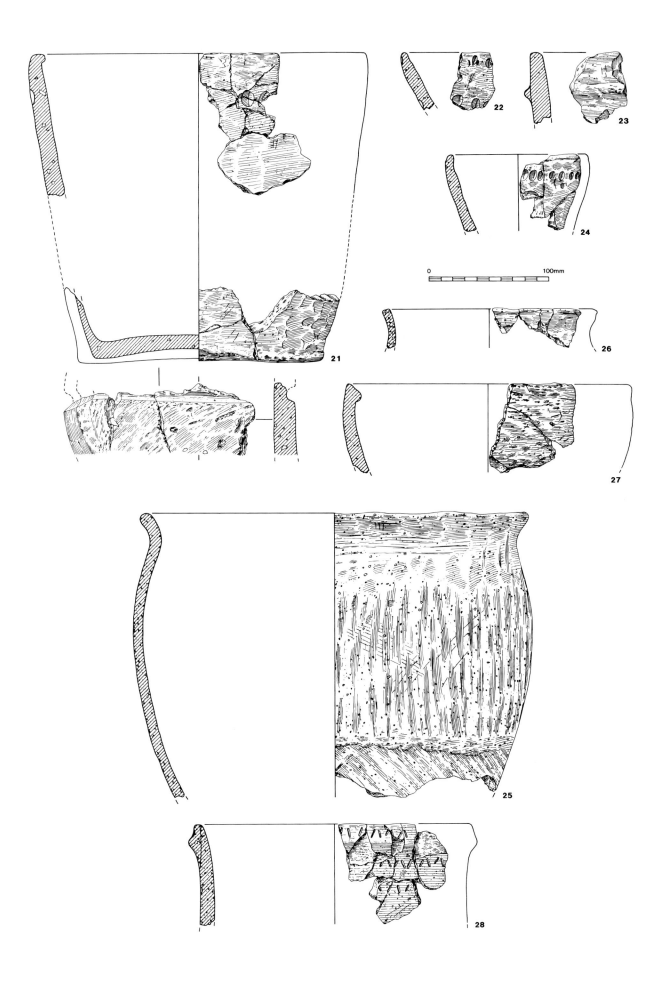

Figure 22 Pottery. Middle Bronze Age (Phase 1)

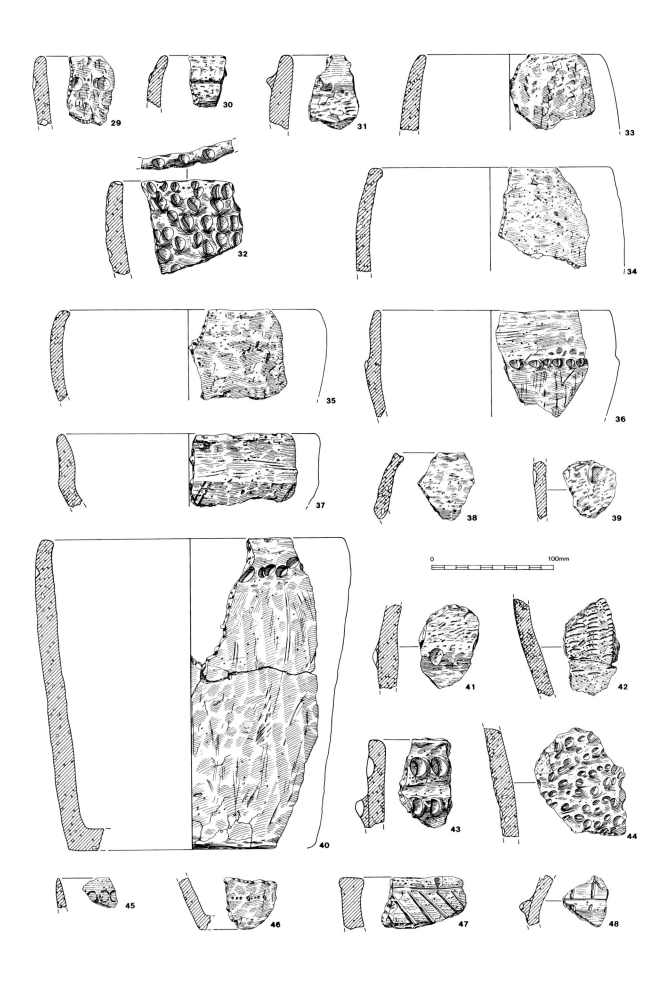

Figure 23 Pottery. Middle Bronze Age (Phase 1)

50

to grey buff, hard, gritty, hand moulded. Int: orange to grey buff. Sec: orange. *Context 752e, pit 752. P190.*

Although the form of this vessel is similar to ones of Middle/Late Iron Age date (Fig. 26: 80 and 81), the fabric is shelly and the surface is smeared, not scored.

26. Jar with expanded rim, small version of VT8; shell < 6mm. Ext: orange buff, hard, brittle, hand moulded. Int: grey buff. Sec: black. *Context 77118, pit 7718. P207.*

27. Rim with internal bevel; grog < 3mm. Ext: buff to black, hard, coarse. Int: buff to black. Sec: black. *Context 7517. P208.*

28. Rim sherd with applied external expansion, fingernail impressions; grog < 4mm, sand. Ext: orange brown, sandy. Int: orange brown. Sec: black. Although the form has some resemblance to a cordoned Beaker, the fabric would be atypical and instead is consistent with the Late Bronze Age date suggested by the stratigraphy. *Context 7742. P211.*

Fig. 23: Middle Bronze Age (Phase 1)

29. Simple rim slightly outflaring, fingertip impressions (VT1); grog < 6mm, stone < 2mm, sand. Ext: orange buff, hard, coarse. Int: orange buff. Sec: black. *Context 7736, hearth. P383.*

30. Simple incurved rim, applied cordon (VT2); stone and grog < 3mm, sand. Ext: light grey buff, coarse. Int: black. Sec: black to orange buff. *Context 7736, hearth. P384.*

31. Simple rim with applied cordon (VT2); sand. Ext: red to reddish buff, sandy. Int: red to light buff. Sec: red to light buff. *Context 784, ditch 78145. P524.*

32. Simple rim fingertip impressions on top of rim and ext. wall; grog < 4mm, stone < 2mm, sand. Ext: black to buff, hard, sandy. Int: orange buff. Sec: grey black. *Context 784, ditch 78145. P527.*

33. Simple incurved rim; sand, grog < 2mm. Ext: buff, slightly friable, sandy. Int: grey buff. Sec: black to grey buff. *Context 7743c, ditch 7743. P33.*

34. Weakly shouldered, ovoid vessel with incurved rim (VT10); grog < 11mm, sand. Ext: reddish buff. Int: grey brown. Sec: black to buff. *Context 7845, post-hole. P1147.*

35. Weakly shouldered, ovoid vessel with incurved rim (VT10); shell < 3mm, grog < 6mm. Ext: grey brown, coarse. Int: buff to grey brown. Sec: black. *Context 7743d, ditch 7743. P86.*

36. Shouldered vessel, probably a jar, fingertip impressions on wall (VT11); grog < 3mm, sand. Ext: buff to brown to black. Int: grey black. Sec: black. *Context 7754, post-hole. P1113.*

37. Bowl or jar with shoulder angle (VT12); grog < 7mm. Ext: orange buff. Int: grey brown to black. Sec: black. *Context 77119, gully. P1090.*

38. Rim sherd from biconical vessel; grog < 5mm, sand. Ext: grey buff to buff. Int: light orange buff. Sec: grey black to light buff. *Context 781. P1204.*

39. Body sherd, fingertip decoration; shell < 4mm; grog < 3mm. Ext: grey brown, coarse. Int: dark brown. Sec: grey buff to brown. *Context 7743f, ditch 7743. P13.*

40. Bucket shaped urn, single row of fingertip impressions on upper body near rim; grog < 11mm, sand. Ext: light buff to orange brown, coarse vertical hand smoothing. Int: light orange buff to black. Sec: orange buff. *Context 7743h, ditch 7743. P4.*

41. Body sherd with fingertip decoration on applied cordon; sand, grog < 5mm. Ext: orange buff, soft, unevenly hand moulded. Int: orange buff. Sec: light buff to orange buff. *Context 7743g, ditch 7743. P5.*

42. Body sherd decorated with columns of horizontal fingernail impressions; sand, grog < 3mm. Ext: black, hard, coarse, pitted. Int: light orange buff to grey buff. Sec: black. *Context 7743. P84.*

43. Rim sherd with two rows of fingertip impressions, one occurs on the wall and one on the cordon; grog < 4mm, stone < 3mm. Ext: dark grey brown. Int: orange to light buff. Sec: black. *Context 77104. P1065.*

44. Body sherd decorated with fingernail rustication; grog < 6mm, sand. Ext: orange buff. Int: orange buff to black. Sec: orange buff to grey buff. *Context 77104. P1087.*

45. Simple rim with circular impressions; sand, grog < 2mm. Ext: grey black, hard. Int: light orange buff. Sec: black. *Context 7743c, ditch 7743. P40.*

46. Base sherd with round-toothed comb impressions; grog < 2mm, sand. Ext: orange, hard. Int: buff. Sec: black. *Context 752, pit 752. P416.*

47. Flattened rim sherd with oblique grooves below rim; grog < 2mm, sand. Ext: black. Int: light buff. Sec: black. *Context 7727, modern drain. P991.*

48. Body sherd with applied cordon, fingernail impressions on cordon, grooves parallel and perpendicular above cordon; stone, sand, grog.

Ext: orange brown to brown black, hard, sandy. Int: light buff. Sec: grey black. *Context 7835, ditch 78135. P667.*

Fig. 24: Middle Bronze Age (Phase 1)

49. Rim sherd incised on top; grog < 15mm, sand. Ext: reddish brown, rough, coarse, sandy. Int: dark brown. Sec: buff. *Context 7743f, ditch 7743. P10.*

50. Cut rim sherd, possibly briquetage vessel; grog < 3mm. Ext: reddish brown. Int: reddish brown. Sec: reddish brown to grey. *Context 7743d, ditch 7743. P67.*

51. Base sherd with pre-firing groove; grog < 5mm, sand. Ext: orange to grey buff, hard, coarse. Int: grey brown. Sec: black. *Context 77101d, gully 77102. P306.*

52. Base sherd with pre-firing groove; grog < 4mm, sand. Ext: buff to orange buff, hard, sandy. Int: orange. Sec: buff to orange. *Context 7747, hollow 7747. P166.*

53. Body to base sherd with pre-firing almost vertical groove; grog < 4mm, sand. Ext: orange buff, coarse, sandy. Int: black to orange. Sec: black to buff. *Context 7747, hollow 7747. P174.*

54. Base sherd with deep pre-firing groove; grog < 5mm, sand. Ext: orange buff, coarse, sandy. Int: grey buff. Sec: buff. *Context 7747, hollow 7747. P178.*

55. Body sherd with post-firing hole; grog < 6mm. Ext: buff to grey buff, coarse, vertical fingermarks. Int: buff to grey buff. Sec: black. *Context 752d, pit 752. P197.*

56. Rim sherd with post-firing hole; grog < 5mm, sand. Ext: grey buff, coarse, hand moulded. Int: grey buff. Sec: buff to black. *Context 7517. P210.*

57. Rim sherd with fingertip impression and post-firing hole; grog < 3mm, sand. Ext: buff to reddish brown. Int: light buff. Sec: buff. *Context 77170. P321.*

58. Rim sherd with post-firing hole; grog < 5mm, sand. Ext: reddish buff. Int: grey brown. Sec: black. *Context 7727, modern drain. P996.*

59. Body sherd with post-firing hole; grog < 8mm, sand. Ext: grey buff, vertical smoothing marks. Int: grey brown. Sec: black to buff. *Context 77122, post-hole. P1107.*

60. Rim sherd with post-firing hole; grog < 4mm, sand. Ext: orange brown. Int: light orange brown to grey brown. Sec: orange brown to black. *Context 771. P1224.*

61. Body sherd with pre-firing hole; grog < 5mm, sand. Ext: orange buff, hard, coarse. Int: black. Sec: black to orange buff. *Context 7742. P250.*

Fig. 25: Late Bronze Age/Early Iron Age (Phase 2)

62. Long necked vessel with simple rim; shell < 2mm, stone < 1mm, sand. Ext: orange buff to grey buff, coarse. Int: grey black. Sec: grey black. *Context 78257, ditch 78145. P345.*

63. Weakly shouldered, ovoid jar with externally expanded rim; shell < 2mm, sand. Ext: grey buff. Int: black to orange buff. Sec: black. *Context 78256, pit 781. P346.*

64. Weakly shouldered, ovoid jar with externally expanded rim; shell < 3mm, stone < 4mm, sand. Ext: brown to grey black. Int: brown to yellow buff. Sec: black. *Context 78257, ditch 78145. P347.*

65. T-shaped rim from vessel with rounded body, finger impression on outer edge of rim; shell < mm. Ext: black. Int: black. Sec: black. *Context 7736, hearth. P385.*

66. Rim with internal bevel or flange and fingertip impressions; shell < 4mm, limestone < 4mm, sand. Ext: black, hard. Int: black. Sec: black. *Context 78257, ditch 78145. P348.*

67. Rim with internal bevel or flange; shell < 5mm. Ext: grey buff, hard. Int: orange brown. Sec: grey brown. *Context 7743, ditch 77743. P419.*

68. Rim internally thickened; shell < 5mm. Ext: brownish black, hard. Int: orange brown. Sec: grey brown. *Context 752, pit 752. P417.*

69. Bowl with everted, flattened rim; shell < 5mm. Ext: grey brown, hard. Int: grey brown. Sec: grey brown to reddish brown. *Context 7743, ditch 7743. P436.*

70. Angular body sherd; limestone < 3mm. Ext: buff to grey buff, hard, fine, burnished. Int: black. Sec: black. *Context 752, pit 752. P415.*

Fig. 26: Middle to Late Iron Age (Phase 3)

71. Flattened, slight bead rim, scored decoration; shell < 2mm. Ext: reddish buff, hard. Int: orange buff. Sec: black. *Context 787. P462.*

72. Simple rounded rim; shell < 1.5mm, sand. Ext: brown buff to grey black, fine. Int: grey black. Sec: grey black. *Context 78116. P598.*

73. Base and lower body; shell < 4mm, grog < 5mm. Ext: black to orange buff. Int: black to orange buff. Sec: black to orange buff. *Context 7710. P870.*

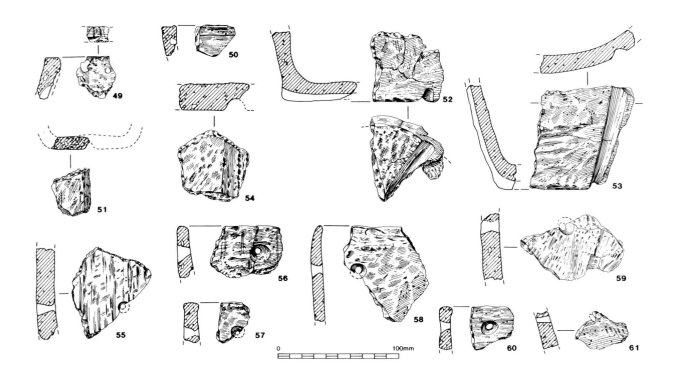

Figure 24 Pottery. Middle Bronze Age (Phase 1)
(Nos 49–54 are possible briquetage in grog-tempered fabric)

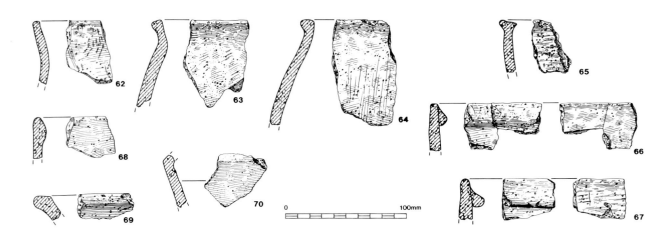

Figure 25 Pottery. Late Bronze Age/Early Iron Age (Phase 2)

74. Large vessel with T-shaped rim, grooved on top; shell < 4mm. Ext: reddish brown, hard. Int: reddish brown. Sec: grey brown. *Context 7810, ditch 78145. P521.*

75. Large vessel with T-shaped rim, grooved on top; shell < 6mm, stone 3mm. Ext: light orange buff, gritty. Int: grey black. Sec: grey black. *Context 787. P466.*

76. Large vessel with T-shaped rim; shell < 3mm, stone < 2mm. Ext: reddish brown, hard. Int: reddish brown. Sec: grey brown. *Context 7810, ditch 78145. P519.*

77. Globular jar with simple upright rim; shell < 4mm, stone < 6mm. Ext: grey brown to brown buff, hard. Int: brownish black. Sec: brownish black. *Context 78116. P571.*

78. Globular jar with everted rim; stone < 6mm, shell, sand. Ext: orange buff to grey black. Int: brownish black. Sec: grey black. *Context 7835, ditch 78135. P591.*

79. Ovoid jar with everted rim; shell < 4mm. Ext: black to brown grey, hand moulded. Int: brown buff. Sec: grey black to brown grey. *Context 78116. P610.*

80. Ovoid jar with everted rim; shell < 8mm, stone < 3mm. Ext: grey brown, shallow scoring. Int: reddish brown. Sec: reddish brown. *Context not recorded. P857.*

81. Ovoid jar with everted rim; shell < 8mm, stone < 3mm. Ext: grey brown, shallow scoring. Int: reddish brown. Sec: reddish brown. *Context not recorded. P861.*

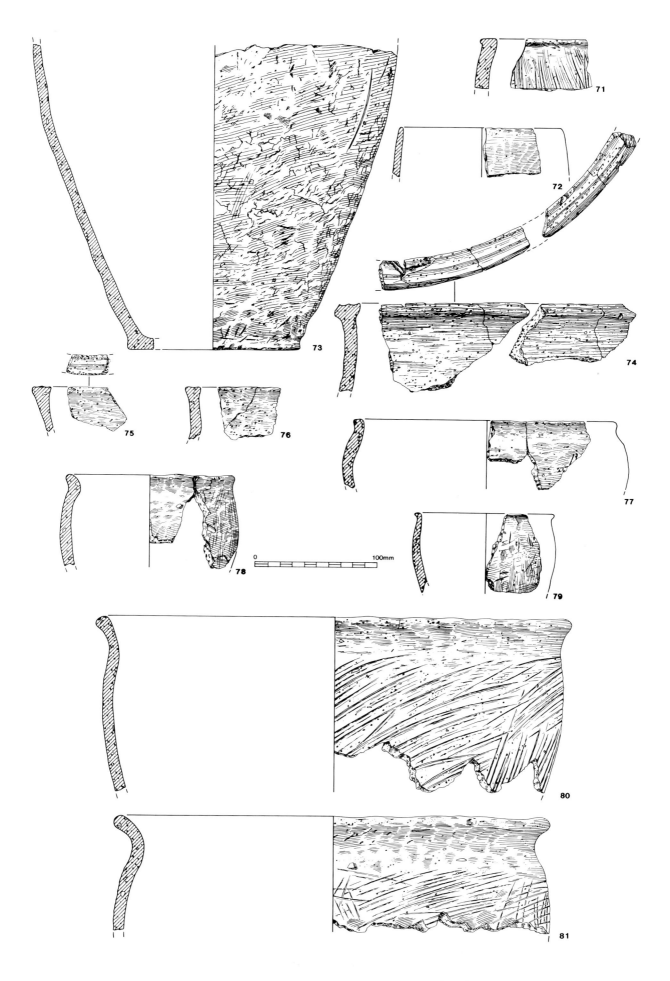

Figure 26 Pottery. Middle–Late Iron Age (Phase 3)

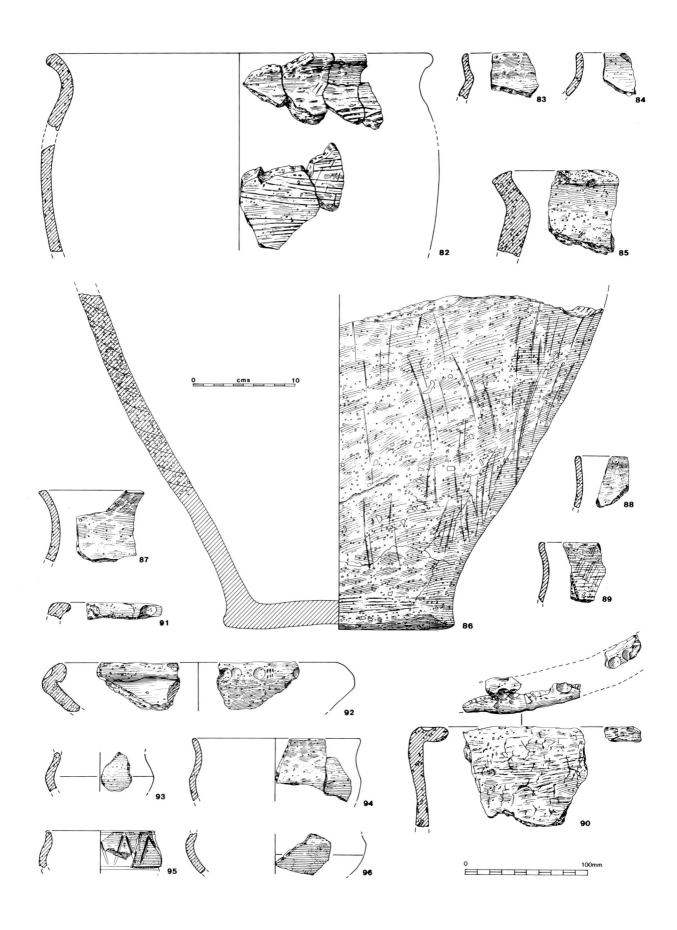

Figure 27 Pottery. Middle–Late Iron Age (Phase 3)

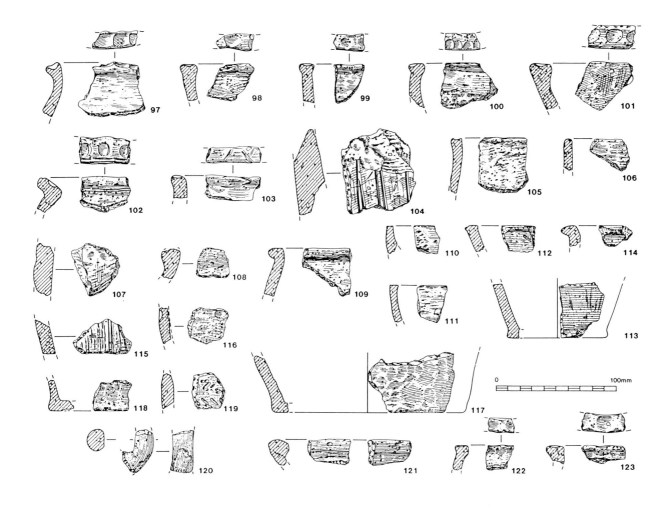

Figure 28 Pottery. Middle–Late Iron Age (Phase 3)

Fig. 27: Middle to Late Iron Age (Phase 3)

82. Globular jar with everted rim; shell < 6mm, stone < 2mm. Ext: black to orange, shallow scoring. Int: grey brown. Sec: grey to orange brown. *Context 7710, ditch 7710. P866.*

83. Upright rim sherd possibly from a globular/ovoid jar; shell < 2mm, stone < 1mm. Ext: light orange buff to grey, sandy. Int: black. Sec: black. *Context 7835, ditch 78135. P593.*

84. Simple upright rim sherd possibly from a globular/ovoid jar; sand, grog < 3mm. Ext: black, hard, coarse, pitted. Int: light orange buff to grey buff. Sec: black. *Context 7743c, ditch 7743. P637.*

85. Incurved rim from a large vessel with a sharply concave neck; shell < 8mm, stone < 5mm. Ext: orange buff, gritty. Int: grey black. Sec: grey black. *Context 78116. P588.*

86. Base and lower body of large vessel, coil construction visible in section; shell < 10mm, stone < 9mm. Ext: black to orange buff. Int: grey buff to black. Sec: grey. *Context 78116. P710.*

87. Vessel with a long, concave neck; shell < 2mm, stone < 3mm, sand. Ext: light grey buff, hard. Int: brown buff. Sec: black. *Context 7835, ditch 78135. P579.*

88. Vessel with long, upright neck; shell < 3mm, sand. Ext: black to light buff. Int: black to grey buff. Sec: black to light buff. *Context 7835, ditch 78135. P600.*

89. Vessel with long, concave neck and incurved rim; shell < 2.5mm. Ext: orange buff. Int: grey brown. Sec: grey. *Context 78135, ditch 78135. P599.*

90. Bowl/jar with inturned rim, fingertip impressions on rim; shell < 10mm. Ext: black to reddish brown, coarse. Int: black to reddish brown. Sec: black to reddish brown. *Context 784, ditch 78145. P520.*

91. Bowl/jar with inturned rim; shell < 2mm, stone < 2mm. Ext: grey to reddish brown. Int: grey brown. Sec: grey brown. *Context 7810, ditch 7710. P532.*

92. Bowl/jar with inturned rim, fingertip impressions on rim; shell < 11mm. Ext: reddish buff to black. Int: reddish buff to black. Sec: grey buff. *Context 7835, ditch 78135. P568.*

93. Small bowl with rounded shoulder; shell < 3mm. Ext: grey black to brown grey, fine. Int: black brown. Sec: grey black. *Context 787. P487.*

94. Slack-shouldered bowl with rounded rim; shell < 2mm, sand. Ext: reddish buff to grey brown. Int: orange buff to grey brown. Sec: black. *Context 7835, ditch 78135. P603.*

95. Small bowl with rounded shoulder, incised decoration; shell < 2mm. Ext: black, fine. Int: black. Sec: black. *Context 7835, ditch 78135. P616.*

96. Bowl with rounded shoulder; sand. Ext: grey brown, fine. Int: black. Sec: black. *Context 7742. P248.*

Fig. 28: Middle to Late Iron Age (Phase 3)

97. Out-turned rim sherd with fingertip impressions on rim top; sand. Ext: black to buff to red, hard. Int: black to buff to red. Sec: buff to orange buff. *Context 784, ditch 78145. P523.*

98. Rim sherd with fingertip impressions on rim top; shell < 4mm. Ext: black. Int: black. Sec: brown to black. *Context 784, ditch 78145. P559.*

99. Rim sherd with fingertip impressions on rim top; shell < 4mm, sand. Ext: reddish brown. Int: red. Sec: grey brown. *Context 78135, ditch 78135. P585.*

100. Inturned and expanded rim sherd with fingertip impressions on rim top; shell < 6mm. Ext: grey black to grey brown. Int: red. Sec: grey black. *Context 7835, ditch 78135. P586.*

101. Expanded rim sherd with fingertip impressions on rim top; shell < 14mm. Ext: reddish brown. Int: grey brown. Sec: reddish brown. *Context 7835, ditch 78135. P612.*

102. Rim sherd with fingertip impressions on rim top; shell < 2.5mm. Ext: grey black to reddish brown. Int: light brown buff to grey black. Sec: black to reddish brown. *Context 78135, ditch 78135. P629.*

103. Rim sherd incised on rim top; shell < 5m, stone < 3mm, sand. Ext: red to orange grey, hard. Int: red to reddish brown. Sec: grey. *Context 7835, ditch 78135. P580.*

104. Body sherd with deep vertical scoring; shell < 4mm. Ext: light orange buff. Int: light orange buff. Sec: grey. *Context 7835, ditch 78135. P657.*

105. Simple upright rim; stone < 3mm. Ext: reddish brown, friable. Int: reddish brown. Sec: reddish brown. *Context 784, ditch 78145. P525.*

106. Simple upright rim; shell < 3mm. Ext: reddish brown. Int: grey buff to reddish brown. Sec: brown. *Context 784, ditch 78145. P530.*

107. Body sherd with fingertip impressions; grog, sand. Ext: light orange buff. Int: black. Sec: black to buff. *Context 784, ditch 78145. P552.*

108. Incomplete rim sherd, top of rim missing; shell < 3mm. Ext: grey brown, hard. Int: brown buff. Sec: black. *Context 784, ditch 78145. P556.*

109. Bead rim; shell < 3mm. Ext: grey brown, hard. Int: grey brown. Sec: grey black. *Context 784, ditch 78145. P526.*

110. Slightly inturned rim; stone < 2mm. Ext: red to orange buff. Int: red to orange buff. Sec: red to grey black. *Context 784, ditch 78145. P533.*

111. Slightly inturned rim; sand. Ext: red. Int: red. Sec: red. *Context 784, ditch 78145. P539.*

112. Simple flared rim; stone < 1mm. Ext: red. Int: red. Sec: red. *Context 784, ditch 78145. P540.*

113. Base and lower body; stone < 2mm, sand. Ext: grey brown, hard. Int: grey brown. Sec: black. *Context 784, ditch 78145. P558.*

114. Externally expanded rim sherd; shell < 3mm. Ext: black. Int: brown buff. Sec: black. *Context 784, ditch 78145. P547.*

115. Body sherd with scored decoration; shell < 4mm. Ext: orange buff. Int: black. Sec: grey black. *Context 784, ditch 78145. P549.*

116. Body sherd with fingertip impressions; inclusions dissolved. Ext: orange buff. Int: grey black. Sec: grey black to buff. *Context 784, ditch 78145. P553.*

117. Base and lower body; stone < 2mm. Ext: brownish buff. Int: grey black. Sec: grey black. *Context 784, ditch 78145. P557.*

118. Base sherd; shell < 2mm, stone < 2mm, sand. Ext: orange, friable. Int: light grey. Sec: orange brown. *Context 784, ditch 78145. P560.*

119. Body sherd decorated with pointed tooled impressions; stone < 3mm, sand. Ext: brown, hard. Int: brown. Sec: black to reddish brown. *Context 784, ditch 78145. P548.*

120. Handle fragment; shell < 2mm. Ext: orange buff to black, hard. Int: buff to black. Sec: buff to black. *Context 784, ditch 78145. P551.*

121. Inturned rim; shell < 3mm. Ext: brown grey. Int: grey black. Sec: brown black. *Context 7835, ditch 78135. P606.*

122. Expanded rim with finger impressions on rim top; shell < 2mm. Ext: grey brown. Int: grey brown. Sec: grey black. *Context 78116. P611.*

123. Expanded rim with finger impressions on rim top; shell < 6mm. Ext: grey black. Int: grey black. Sec: grey black. *Context 78116. P635.*

VII. Post-Iron Age pottery from later features and deposits
by Hilary Healey (1984)

A small quantity of post-Iron Age pottery was found in the upper levels of the excavation, in the disturbed soil of the former medieval ridge-and-furrow. In total this comprised 83 Romano-British sherds, with 181 sherds of medieval and 57 sherds of post-medieval pottery. Both the Romano-British and medieval sherds are very much abraded, presumably owing to their movement in the sandy soil during medieval and later ploughing.

Romano-British

The presence of Romano-British pottery in this assemblage is not unexpected. There are sites of this period, generally quite small, all along the length of the Roman watercourse, the Car Dyke, which runs north–south along the fen edge about 400m east of the excavation. Apart from the few ditches on site ascribed to the early Romano-British period, the two nearest Roman sites lie some 500m to the north-east and north-west of the excavation respectively, and there is a crop/soil mark of a typical Romano-British enclosure less than 200m to the west.

The sherds are characteristic of wares to be found on local sites. Of the 83 sherds, only three are of Nene

Valley-type colour-coated ware, dated from the 2nd century AD onwards, the remainder comprising assorted grey wares with no distinctive characteristics. There is also one rim fragment of a frilled grey ware jar thought to date from the 4th century AD.

Medieval

Field survey in the area has led to the expectation of a general scatter of medieval pottery on the former ridge-and-furrow east of the medieval fen edge villages, such as would be consistent with the practice of manuring. Aerial photographs show that the arable of the medieval village of Billingborough extended at one time over a width of approximately 1.5km between the village and the edge of the uncultivated fen which served both as meadow and summer pasture. What appears to have been a substantial medieval building within a moat, possibly a grange of nearby Sempringham Priory, lies only 400m to the south-east of the Billingborough excavation, and field walking has produced a concentration of medieval pottery immediately north of the surviving earthwork as well as evidence of a perimeter stone wall.

The majority of the medieval sherds, 146 out of 181, are of Bourne B ware type (Healey 1969). The Bourne kilns lie only 14km south of the site and this type of ware can be expected to be predominant. No closer dating of this ware is possible other than a date somewhere between about AD1250 and AD1350. Two sherds of Bourne A ware were also noted. There is a physical difference, but as yet no distinct chronological difference between the two fabrics. A small amount of the late/post-medieval fabric classified as Bourne D ware, dating from the 16th century onwards, is present in some contexts (Healey 1969).

Post-Medieval

The amount of post-medieval material is rather more than might be expected in this particular location, about 1km from the centre of the present village of Billingborough. Local tradition states that there was formerly a cottage at the extreme north-east corner of the excavated area, although this had disappeared by the time of the 1903 revision of the six inch to one mile Ordnance Survey map. The finds are certainly consistent with there having been a building here in the 19th century.

VIII. Briquetage
by Rosamund M.J. Cleal and Joanna K.F. Bacon (1984/1990)

Introduction
Salt production was an important industry in prehistoric Lincolnshire, most extensively on the coast as would be expected (May 1976, 143). There were three principle uses for salt: flavouring, preserving, and as a medium of exchange with areas that did not produce their own (Bradley 1975). The earliest methods of production left little or no evidence. In the European Early Bronze Age, evaporating vessels filled with briny sludge were heated on a stove. This simple, but essentially inconsistent method, gradually evolved to expand production and improve quality, and during the later Bronze Age in the Saale Valley, Central Germany, the foot of the container was elongated and became progressively separated, adapted into pedestals of several types (Gouletquer 1974).

From the Bronze Age in Europe, these more sophisticated techniques reached Britain and Lincolnshire by the Late Bronze/Early Iron Age. Bradley (1975) suggests that in the Middle Iron Age the manufacture of vessels and supports was a seasonal occupation, based on analysis of the vegetable tempering which proved to be winter sown crops, although not necessarily for immediate usage.

The occurrence of salt extraction as an activity at Billingborough is attested by the presence of fired clay pedestals and bars known to be associated with salt extraction, and by the large numbers of sherds which are identifiable as belonging to containers used in the boiling of brine, and possibly also in the moulding and transport of the salt produced (Fig. 29).

Some features on the site (see Fig. 8) could also be identified as likely to have taken some part in the process. The main period of this activity was clearly, on the basis of the first appearance of large amounts of briquetage, Phase 2 (Table 9; see also Table 6); the briquetage present in the two later phases is almost certainly entirely redeposited (Table 9; see also Tables 7 and 8). Some briquetage was present in the upper fill of the Phase 1 enclosure ditch but, during excavation, it was difficult to distinguish the boundary between the upper ditch fill and layer (*7743*) of Phase 2, which overlay it, and this may account for the presence of much of the briquetage in contexts assigned to Phase 1 (Table 9; see also Table 4). The fact that the division between these two contexts was not clear is also attested by the fact that the radiocarbon date from layer *7743c*, in the Phase 1 upper ditch fill, falls in the period 800–370 cal BC (HAR-2523, 2410±80 BP), a date comparable with that from Phase 2 pit 78256 of 840–390 cal BC (HAR-3101, 2500±100 BP). The majority of the briquetage identifiable in the upper Phase 1 fill of ditch *7743* is identical to that found in secure Phase 2 contexts. However, there is also a ceramic element in ditch *7743* and elsewhere which is comparable in fabric with the Phase 1 grog-tempered fabric rather than with the Phase 2 briquetage, but which appears to share some of the latter's distinctive formal features. As the possibility that this material is also briquetage is dependent on its similarity to the certain material from Phase 2, the Phase 2 briquetage is discussed first.

Briquetage containers
by Rosamund M.J. Cleal (1990)

Methods
As the briquetage from Phase 2 and the pottery from both that phase and later phases are in similar fabrics, which appear to have utilised similar clay resources, criteria had to be established on which to separate featureless briquetage body sherds from featureless pottery. The following characteristics were felt to separate adequately briquetage from pottery:

1) Presence of cut edges.
2) Surfaces oxidised to orange, pale orange, or orange-red all over, and usually throughout the section.
3) Fabrics containing a high density of shell.

Sherds with cut edges were automatically counted as briquetage, on the basis of the unusual nature of this feature and its well-known occurrence in briquetage from salt production sites elsewhere. Sherds lacking cut edges

Phase	Briquetage		Fired clay	
	No.	*Wt (g)*	*No.*	*Wt (g)*
1	791	2522	279	4253
2	3740	12861	453	4677
3	3568	13574	763	8008
4	2980+	19271	286	3561
Unphased	4195	15438	706	7794
Total	**15,274**	**63,666+**	**2,487**	**28,293**

Table 9 Briquetage and fired clay by phase

had to possess both completely oxidised, orange surfaces and a very shelly fabric before they were counted as briquetage (*e.g.* Fig. 29: 1). This was felt to be necessary because, although the pottery is generally *unoxidised*, occasional oxidised sherds of undoubted pottery occur, and it was felt that the additional occurrence of frequent shell inclusions was needed to confirm the identification. The use of a high frequency of shell inclusions as an indicator of briquetage was based on the fact that all the cut sherds were in shelly fabrics, usually with a high frequency of shell. Undoubtedly some briquetage has been mis-identified as pottery, and *vice versa*, but by following this method at least internal consistency has been maintained.

Phase 2 briquetage containers

Fabric
Typically the fabric was soft, often friable and almost powdery when rubbed, and oxidised throughout to shades of orange. No surface treatment appears to have normally been given to the sherds, apart from the most superficial smoothing.

Only one sherd of briquetage (Fig. 29: 2) was thin-sectioned. It contained 30% fossil shell and less than 1% quartz. The source of the clay is likely to have been the same as, or similar to, that used for the pottery.

Form
Although the briquetage was extremely fragmentary and the form of the vessels represented is uncertain the following features could be identified:

1) Rims which had been cut before firing, giving a flat, smooth, surface. Typically the rims show little curvature; although this may be in part be due to the generally small sherd size, the few larger sherds include both some with curvature, and some in which there is none (*e.g.* Fig. 29: 5).
2) Uncut, simple rims (*e.g.* Fig. 29: 6).
3) Bases which had been cut before firing (*i.e.* with the cut parallel to or at 90° to the plane of the base) (*e.g.* Fig. 29: 7–9).

In the case of types 1 and 2, different treatments of the rim are clearly present, but as the cut base is cut *across* rather than *along* the base it is possible that uncut base fragments, which are also present, actually belong to cut bases. No rim sherds with cuts perpendicular to either an uncut or a cut rim were observed.

No quantification of featured briquetage sherds was carried out. Recording of featured briquetage sherds was attempted, but it soon became apparent that because of the many thousands of sherds present the task was not practicable. In the early stages of the work featured sherds were at least separated from body sherds for storage, but even this had to be abandoned as the scale of the problem became clear.

The little evidence available could be interpreted as representing the following forms:

A) The presence of bases showing curvature suggests that round or oval vessels were present; the occurrence of cut bases indicates that these might be cut before firing, probably in half, although there is no other evidence for this. The fact that no straight-sided bases were noted suggests that the pans were not square or rectangular, an interpretation which is supported by the absence of corners.

B) The homogeneity of the fabric suggests that the bases and rims belong to the same vessels. Therefore, the cut rims, and the uncut rims, including the rims showing no curvature, are all likely to belong to the same vessels as the bases, which do show curvature.

A possible interpretation of this combination of features is that vessels which were round in plan (*i.e.* cylindrical or conical in section), and therefore possessed bases with curvature in plan, were cut in half before firing to form two trough-like sections with cut rims. This interpretation of similar evidence has been suggested for material from southern England (Farrar 1975, Poole 1987), and certainly the cut bases and rims are indistinguishable from briquetage associated with Middle to Late Iron Age pottery on the Isle of Purbeck, Dorset (Cleal 1991). In Dorset it appears that complete troughs may have been formed by closing cylindrical vessels at the top before cutting, to form two complete troughs (termed by Farrar 'Fitzworth troughs'), but at Danebury, Hampshire, salt appears to have been transported in vessels which were cut, but which had not formed complete troughs, possessing normal, uncut, rims at one end (Poole 1984). The practice of cutting vessels before firing for use in salt extraction or transport appears to have a long history on the south coast, extending perhaps from early in the Iron Age until well into the Romano-British period (Calkin 1948, 56, pl. V; Farrar 1975, 147; Cleal 1991, 147), but does not appear to have previously been attested from Lincolnshire (Baker 1975). The single 'sawn' sherd from Padholme Road Sub-site IX, Fengate, appears to be a vessel of this type, although in this case the possible cut is at an angle of 90° to a simple rim. The sherd, which is in a shelly fabric, was recovered from the uppermost layer of a 2nd-millennium ditch (Pryor 1980, 18, 181, fig. 13:1) and was not associated with diagnostic pottery.

Briquetage in grog-tempered fabrics

The association between salt production and the pre-firing cutting of vessels is well-established in the south of England, and as yet there appear to be no other activities clearly associated with vessels treated in this way. The occurrence at Billingborough of this type of treatment on vessels which on the grounds of fabric, form and decoration are classifiable as Bronze Age is clearly of importance.

Grog-tempered sherds with cut surfaces were recorded as featured sherds and illustrated where they occurred in stratified contexts, in the same way as the pottery, but because of the quantity of the material and the decision not to count sherds from topsoil and surface contexts, such sherds from those contexts may have been missed. The total recorded from features is nineteen, of which four were recovered from ditch *7743* (Phase 1), fourteen from hollow *7747* (Phase 1) and one from structural gully *77102* (Phase 2). The sherds from the Enclosure 1 ditch fill (Fig. 24; 49 and 50; Fig. 29: 3 and 4) comprise four cut 'rims', three of which are probably from the same vessel: two of the sherds join (Fig. 29: 3 and 4) and show slight curvature in plan. The cut sherds from feature *7747* include only basal sherds. Fig 22: 21 appears to have been snapped successfully along a cut groove, but Fig. 24: 53 appears less successful as the snapped surface runs parallel, but alongside, the cut groove. In addition there is one vessel (Fig. 24: 52) in which the cut groove stops at the angle between base and body, thus casting doubt on the interpretation of the cut grooves as intended to facilitate division of the vessels. The appearance of these sherds, and those from ditch *7743* differs slightly from that of the Phase 2 briquetage in that the cuts are groove-like, as they are broad at the exterior surface and narrow towards the interior. However, this difference may be largely due to the greater thickness of the grog-tempered sherds and the presence of large inclusions, necessitating a wider opening for the cut. Despite the doubts occasioned by the slight differences in form, and by the incomplete nature of the cut on sherd (Fig. 24: 52), the similarities between these sherds and the cut Phase 2 briquetage seem compelling. In both the Phase 1 and Phase 2 vessels the cut surface often does not extend all the way through the vessel wall, and must be interpreted as intended to create a linear weakness in the vessel wall which could then be exploited by snapping or tearing, rather than intended in itself to sever the two parts of the vessel. In both periods vessels have cuts which are perpendicular to the base, and in both periods the technique occurs before firing. This occurrence of similar techniques in two phases of the same site may be taken as an indication that they relate to the same activity, although this cannot be demonstrated.

Two interpretations of this material seem possible. Either the interpretation of the grog-tempered vessels as connected with salt production is correct, and Billingborough either produced salt or received it in Phase 1; or the resemblance between the techniques is entirely fortuitous and the grooving of the earlier vessels was intended for another purpose. As the latter appears to stretch the bounds of coincidence rather far, the former is the preferred interpretation, although further work may be able support or refute this in time. It may be that the vessels were used for boiling a saline solution or mud rather than producing salt by solar evaporation. The landscape evidence suggests that salt production at Billingborough would have been unlikely in the mid 2nd millennium BC and, therefore, that the vessels may have been containers in which salt was brought to the site.

Catalogue of briquetage containers

Fig. 29

1. Large base sherd with one cut edge and vertical smoothing marks; shell < 10mm. Ext: reddish brown, coarse, friable. Int: reddish brown. (*'Structure'* 77102. P366).

2. Flat topped rim, cut pre-firing; shell < 8mm. Ext: orange buff, friable. Int: orange buff. Sec: orange buff. (*Hollow 772. P931*).

3. Incurved, flat topped rim, cut pre-firing; sand, grog < 5mm. Ext: grey brown, coarse, sandy. Int: light grey buff. Sec: grey brown. (*7743d, ditch 7743. P60*).

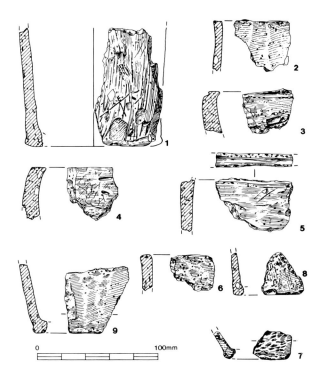

Figure 29 Briquetage containers

4. Incurved, flat topped rim, cut pre-firing; sand, grog < 8mm, carbonaceous material. Ext: orange brown, coarse. Int: orange brown. Sec: grey brown to buff. (*7743d, ditch 7743. P62*).

5. Flat topped rim, broken along pre-firing groove, straight wall; grog < 6mm, sand. Ext: orange buff. Int: buff. Sec: grey buff to orange. (*post-hole 7738. P1060*).

6. Uncut, simple rim; shell < 7mm, stone < 2mm. Ext: light orange buff, friable. Int: greyish orange buff. Sec: orange buff. (*Hearth 7512. P369*).

7. Base with finished surface on one edge, cut pre-firing; shell < 3mm, stone < 4mm. Ext: greyish orange buff, coarse. Int: reddish buff. Sec: reddish buff. (*?Hearth 7736. P400*).

8. Base sherd, cut pre-firing; shell < 4mm. Ext: orange, friable. Int: orange. Sec: red. (*Hollow 772. P945*).

9. Base sherd, edge cut vertically, pre-firing; shell < 6mm. Ext: orange to orange buff. Int: red. Sec: red. (*Modern disturbance. P1008*).

Non-container briquetage

by Joanna K.F. Bacon (1984)

The non-container briquetage from Billingborough has been divided into five basic categories with several subdivisions within some of these groups (Figs 30–34).

Category 1: small pedestals

Small pedestal (Fig. 30: 12, and 13; Fig. 31: 28; Fig. 32: 46 and 47; Fig. 33: 74 and 75). Generally no longer than *c.*100mm; a narrow, usually oval-sectioned, rod with rounded head and flared foot.

Category 2: pedestals

Pedestals (in three subdivisions which are not necessarily clearly differentiated).

(a) Fishtail or spatulate terminal (Fig. 30: 1, 7–10; Fig. 31: 18, 23, 26 and 27; Fig. 32: 34, 36–44, 54–59; Fig. 34: 82) are by far the largest group. Figure 30: 1 could be intrusive in Phase 1 since the majority of these occur in later phases. These pedestals are found in the Halle/Saale area of Central Germany in the Early Bronze Age (Matthias 1976), and in Britain in the Late Bronze Age at Mucking, Essex (Jones 1977), Northey, Peterborough (Gurney 1980) and Fengate (Pryor 1976). They are also present at Helpringham, Lincolnshire (Healey 1999, nos B57, B58, B61) in the Iron Age.

(b) Oval-sectioned, sharply tapering rods (Fig. 30: 2 and 3). Since the two examples have both ends missing it is impossible to determine terminal type but they are possibly paralleled by oval-sectioned pedestals with T-bar top and bottom from the Halle/Saale area of Germany in the Early Bronze Age (Matthias 1976), and one from the Caucasian Black Sea Coast (Riehm 1954).

(c) Gently tapering bar with flared foot (Fig. 30: 14; Fig. 32: 33; Fig. 33: 69–73). Fig. 32: 72 and 73 have squared section, others have round section. Both types are found in the Iron Age at Red Hills, Essex (de Brisay 1975), and there is a square-sectioned tapering bar from Verulamium, Hertfordshire (Wheeler and Wheeler 1936). Cylindrical pedestals appear to be the next step from the vessel foot (Riehm 1960) in the Bronze Age. Fragments of three cylindrical rods were found at Orsett, Essex (Hedges and Buckley 1978) and four from Helpringham (Healey 1999, B23–B26) all Iron Age. Almost all of those from Billingborough are unphased.

Category 3: blocks

(a) Rectangular blocks with parallel sides and faces (Fig. 31: 24; Fig. 32: 35 and 52; Fig. 33: 60–67, 78). These are all incomplete and could well be of the same sub group as (b) but more probably parallel the short, squared pedestals with 60mm base from Helpringham (Healey 1999, B11–B21) of Iron Age date.

(b) Tapering or wedge-shaped blocks, either trapezium-shaped or with straight sides and flared foot (Fig. 30: 4–6, 15; Fig. 31: 17, 19, 20, 30–32; Fig. 32: 48–51, 53; Fig. 33: 79 and 80; Fig. 34: 81, 83–86). Some of these are incomplete. Similar blocks have been found at Halle/Saale, Germany (Matthias 1976) and one with T-bar top from L'Ileau near Nalliers (Riehm 1960, 186 fig.2). Mucking, Essex (Jones 1977) has the nearest parallels in Britain. There is a fragment of an apparently large one (200mm wide) from Helpringham (Healey 1999, B10).

(c) Flat plaque with perforation (Fig. 31: 21 and 22). A similar perforated slab of Middle/Late Bronze Age date was found at Mucking (Jones 1977).

Category 4: spacers/luting

(Fig. 30: 11; Fig. 33: 68, 76 and 77)

With numerous thin-walled evaporating vessels balanced on props within the hearth it became necessary in the later Bronze Age/Early Iron Age to give extra support and also keep the dishes from overlapping. 'Spacers', 'bridging pieces', or 'luting' — clay doodles moulded by hand and stuck like plasticine between vessels, became fired during the evaporating process, and survive bearing imprints of rims (May 1976, 150, fig. 74, nos 1–3; Swinnerton 1932, 249, fig. 9).

Billingborough Figure 30: 11 could be a spout fragment or possibly part of the wall of a small vessel. It is from Phase 2.

Figure 33: 68 is from a Phase 4 context, and Figures 33: 76 and 77 are unphased, though Figure 33: 76 bears a close resemblance to a bridging piece from Helpringham (Healey 1999, B28) of Iron Age date.

Category 5: oven floor (Fig. 31: 16)

A single fragment of perforated oven flooring of Barford type Bi (P. Barford, pers. comm.) of probable Late Bronze Age date. Similar to perforated oven floors from Little Woodbury, Wiltshire (Brailsford 1949, 160, fig. 2), Maiden Castle, Dorset (Wheeler 1943, 321) and Verulamium, Hertfordshire (Wheeler and Wheeler 1936), although these examples were not clearly associated with salt working and may well have served other purposes.

Catalogue of non-container briquetage

(The objects are illustrated in Figures 30–34 and are ordered broadly by phase)

Fig. 30

1. Thick, oval-sectioned bar tapering very sharply, both ends missing. Sandy fabric; some grog inclusions; soapy texture with pitted surface. Oxidised; very red in colour. Height 70mm. Width 43–74mm. Thickness 37mm. (*7743d, ditch 7743, Phase 1*).
2. Pedestal. Thick, oval-sectioned bar tapering very sharply, both ends missing. Height 110mm. Width 34–64 mm. Thickness 30mm. (*7743d, ditch 7743, Phase 1*).
3. Block. Wedge-shaped brick. Incomplete. Heavily tempered — flint and shell. Sandy fabric, crumbly texture from heavy firing. Reddish–brown colour. Height 104mm. Width 66mm. Thickness 25–40mm. (*78164, ditch 78145, no. 547, Phase 1*).
4. Pedestal. Fragment of pedestal with fishtail head. Flattened tapering to top. Height 42mm. Width 45mm. Thickness 19–23mm. (*752d, ditch 752, Phase 1*).
5. Block. Incomplete wedge-shaped block. Height 85mm. Width c. 65mm. Thickness 44–50mm. (*7743b, ditch, 7743, Phase 1*).
6. Block. Incomplete wedge-shaped block. Soapy fabric with some vegetable temper, grog and the odd large (c.5mm) flint. Sandy, vesicular surface. Oxidised. Pink fabric with white/grey outer deposit. Height 108mm. Width c. 90mm. Thickness 32–57mm. (*Pit 78257, Phase 2*).
7. Pedestal. Fragment of top of fishtail or spatulate pedestal. Height 43mm. Width 70mm. Thickness 24mm. (*7743, ditch, 7743, Phase 2*).
8. Pedestal. Fragment of top of fishtail pedestal. Height 40mm Width 57mm Thickness 22–27mm. (*752, pit 752, Phase 2*).
9. Pedestal. Top part of fishtail pedestal. Height 139mm. Width 76mm. Thickness 45mm. (*Pit 78257, Phase 2*).
10. Pedestal. Fragment of top of spatulate or fishtail pedestal. Height 68mm. Width 60mm. Thickness 33–42mm. (*Pit 78257, Phase 2*).
11. Luting? Piece of curved tapering (tubular) fired clay. Height 42mm. Width 46mm. Thickness 7–8mm. (*Pit 78257, Phase 2*).
12. Small pedestal. One end of small rod of clay, flat oval in section. Height 58mm. Width 18–24mm. Thickness 14mm. (*7743, ditch 7743, Phase 2*).
13. Small pedestal. Part of small rod of clay, slightly curved flat section, both ends missing. Height 34mm. Width 25–30mm. Thickness 15mm. (*7743, ditch 7743, Phase 2*).
14. Pedestal. Fragment of foot of thick round-sectioned pedestal (original diam. 90mm). Height 66mm. Width 57mm. Thickness 45mm. (*Hearth 7736, Phase 2*).
15. Block. Incomplete wedge-shaped block. Height 114mm. Width 105mm. Thickness 45–71mm. (*Pit 78257, Phase 2*).

Fig. 31

16. Oven flooring. Small fragment of perforated block — only well defined edges are to the perforations. Thickness 61mm. Width 50mm. Length 55mm. (*787, ditch 78113, Phase 3*).
17. Block. Fragment of foot or block. Height 34mm. Width 65mm. Thickness 49mm. (*784, ditch 78145, Phase 3*).
18. Pedestal. Incomplete spatulate or fishtail pedestal. Sandy fabric with much vegetable temper, soapy texture. Heavily fired; Oxidised. Very pink/red core. White coating to outer surface which is also vesicular. Height 78mm. Width 70mm. Thickness 12–26mm. (*78115, ditch 78113, Phase 3*).
19. Block. Fragment of foot of block. Height 32mm. Width 59mm. Thickness 40mm. (*784, ditch 78145, Phase 3*).
20. Block? Fragment of foot of block or pedestal. Height 31mm. Width 52mm. Thickness 48mm. (*784, ditch 78145, Phase 3*).

21. Block. Top of wedge-shaped or flat trapezium-shaped block with single central perforation made pre-firing (edges of hole raised). Height 80mm. Width 60–83mm. Thickness 18–24mm. (*78109, ditch 78113, Phase 3*).
22. Block. Part of wedge-shaped block with single central perforation. All edges missing. Height 58mm. Width 76mm. Thickness 25–34mm. (*787, ditch 78113, Phase 3*).
23. Pedestal. Fragment of fishtail pedestal. Height 44mm. Width 42mm. Thickness 20mm. (*787, ditch 78113, Phase 3*).
24. Block. Fragment of top of squared block. Height 23mm. Width 58mm. Thickness 46 mm. (*78137, ditch 78113, Phase 3*).
25. Block. Fragment of foot of block. Height 32mm. Width 53mm. Thickness 30mm. (*78137, ditch 78113, Phase 3*).
26. Pedestal? Small fragment of one edge of tapering pedestal, flaring towards top as narrows. Height 31mm. Width 24mm. Thickness 20–30mm. (*787, ditch 78113, Phase 3*).
27. Pedestal? Part of tapering flat edged bar, both ends missing. Possibly pedestal or small block. Height 68mm. Width 64mm. Thickness 25–38mm. (*787, ditch 78113, Phase 3*).
28. Small pedestal. Base of small round-sectioned pedestal; original diameter 28mm. Height 19m. Width 26mm. Thickness 18–25mm. (*787, ditch 78113, Phase 3*).
29. Daub. Fragment of daub showing wattle impressions. Height 40mm. Width 50mm. Thickness 7–18mm. (*Post-hole 77121, unphased*).
30. Block. Large part of foot of wedge-shaped block. Height 101 mm. Width 103 mm. Thickness 44–68mm. (*784, ditch 78145, Phase 3*).
31. Block. Large, thick, foot of tapering block, possibly wedge-shaped. Height 84mm. Width 90–103mm. Thickness 55–82mm. (*784, ditch 78145, Phase 3*).
32. Block. Incomplete wedge-shaped block. Fabric has large quartzite inclusions and glass tempering. Oxidised, red core with white/grey deposit on outer vesicular surface. Height 98mm. Width 95mm. Thickness 38–59mm. (*784, ditch 78113, Phase 3*).

Fig. 32

33. Pedestal. Part of base of round-sectioned pedestal; original diameter 53mm. Height 23mm. Width 48mm. Thickness 26mm. (*784, ditch 78113, Phase 3*).
34. Pedestal. Fragment of top of fishtail pedestal with both tails missing. Slightly curved in section. Height 65mm. Width 64mm. Thickness 34mm. (*784, ditch 78113, Phase 3*).
35. Block. Fragment of foot of block. Height 32mm. Width 50mm. Thickness 26mm. (*784, ditch 78113, Phase 3*).
36. Pedestal. Part of top of fishtail or spatulate pedestal. Height 34mm. Width 56mm. Thickness 28mm. (*784, ditch 78113, Phase 3*).
37. Pedestal. Fragment of top of fishtail pedestal. Height 39mm. Width 30mm. Thickness 25mm. (*Gully 78103, Phase 3*).
38. Pedestal. Part of top of spatulate pedestal. Height 60mm. Width 60mm. Thickness 25–28mm. (*7710b, ditch 7710, Phase 3*).
39. Pedestal. Part of top of spatulate or fishtail pedestal. Height 35mm. Width 44mm. Thickness 17–22mm. (*789, ditch 78136, Phase 4*).
40. Pedestal. Fragment of top of fishtail or spatulate pedestal. Height 44mm. Width 50mm. Thickness 23–32mm. (*7710, ditch 7710, Phase 3*).
41. Pedestal. Fragment of top of fishtail pedestal. Height 49mm. Width 59mm. Thickness 27.5mm. (*Ditch 759, Phase 4*).
42. Pedestal. Fragment of corner top of narrow spatulate pedestal, with slightly wider flattened top edge. Height 25mm. Width 41mm. Thickness 9–14mm. (*7710, ditch 7710, Phase 3*).
43. Pedestal. Part of top of narrow fishtail or spatulate pedestal. Height 52mm. Width 50mm. Thickness 14–17mm. (*Ditch 7530, unphased*).
44. Pedestal. Top of narrow fishtail pedestal, almost wedge-shaped tapering towards top. Height 56mm. Width 63–72mm. Thickness 13–28mm. (*Ditch 779, Phase 4*).
45. Small pedestal. Top of small rod with rounded top, flattish squared section. Height 38mm. Width 24mm. Thickness 14mm. (*7530, unphased*).
46. Small pedestal. Top of narrow small rod, flat in section with rounded edges. Roughly pointed end. Height 36mm. Width 29mm. Thickness 11mm. (*7710, ditch 7710, Phase 3*).
47. Small pedestal. Fragment of small rod, oval in section, both ends missing. Height 37mm. Width 26.5mm. Thickness 18.5mm. (*Ditch 779, Phase 4*).
48. Block. Incomplete wedge-shaped block, very regularly shaped. Soapy texture, fabric grog- and vegetable-tempered. Oxidised, pink with whitish outer vesicular surface. Height 113mm. Width 76–105mm. Thickness 21–70mm. (*Pit 77128, Phase 3*).

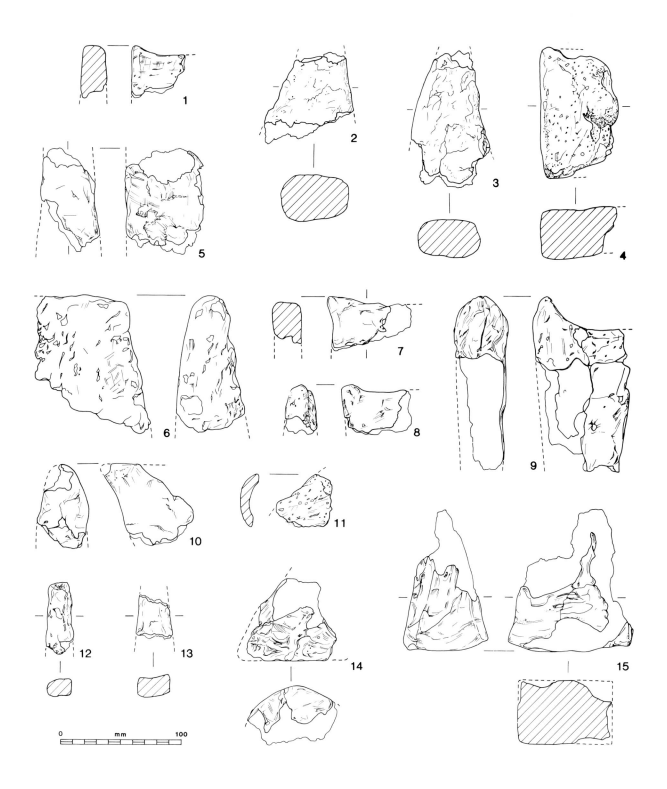

Figure 30 Fired clay: briquetage

49. Block. Fragment of foot of block. Height 41mm. Width 37mm. Thickness 42mm. (*78225, ditch 78145, Phase 3*).

50. Block. Fragment of foot of tapering block, possibly wedge-shaped. Height 31mm. Width 56mm. Thickness 38–43mm. (*7515, unphased*).

51. Block. Part of edge of wedge-shaped block or pedestal. Height 80mm. Width 48mm. Thickness 20–40mm. (*7710, ditch 7710, Phase 3*).

52. Block. Part of top corner of square sectioned block, slightly spatulate face. Height 52mm. Width 56mm. Thickness 36mm. (*7710, ditch 7710, Phase 3*).

53. Block. Fragment of thick round-topped slightly tapering block. Height 67mm. Width 26mm. Thickness 35–44mm. (*7710, ditch 7710, Phase 3*).

54. Block? Part of top of narrow, slightly tapering, roughly spatulate ended block or pedestal. Height 74mm. Width 80mm. Thickness 21–30mm. (*Ditch 759, Phase 4*).

55. Pedestal? Fragment of top of pedestal with troughed top, possibly luting? Height 28mm. Width 53mm. Thickness 24–30mm. (*7710b, ditch 7710, Phase 3*).

56. Pedestal. Fragment of top of narrow pedestal. Height 20mm. Width 42mm. Thickness 19mm. (*Ditch 779, Phase 4*).

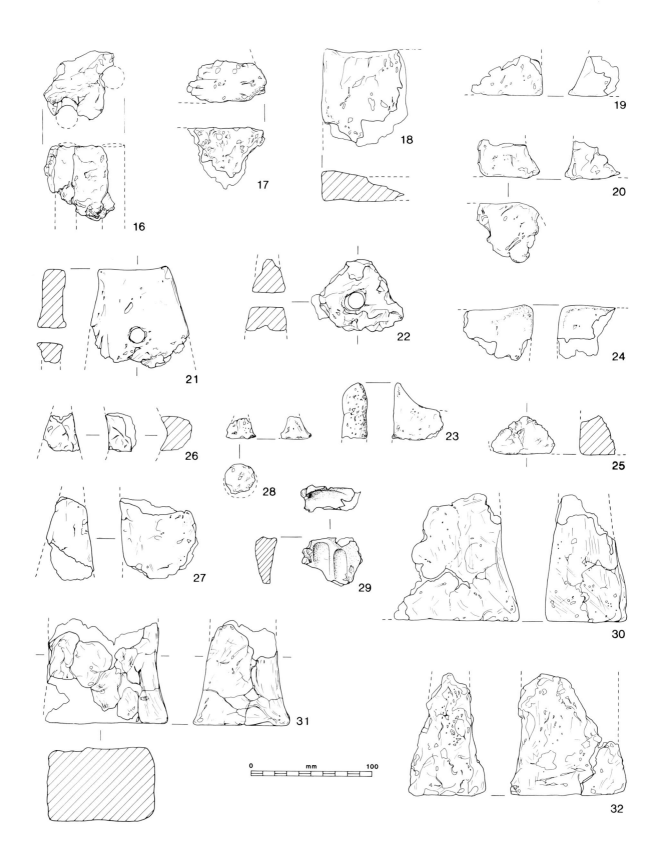

Figure 31 Fired clay: briquetage

57. Pedestal? Fragment of top of pedestal with rounded corner, or possibly block. Height 28mm. Width 56mm. Thickness 25mm. (*7710, ditch 7710, Phase 3*).

58. Pedestal? Fragment of top corner of spatulate or fishtail pedestal, or possibly top of squarish narrow block. Height 34mm. Width 46mm. Thickness 36mm. (*7710b, ditch 7710, Phase 3*).

59. Pedestal? Fragment of top of tapering pedestal or block. Height 22mm. Width 52mm. Thickness 16mm. (*7710b, ditch 7710, Phase 3*).

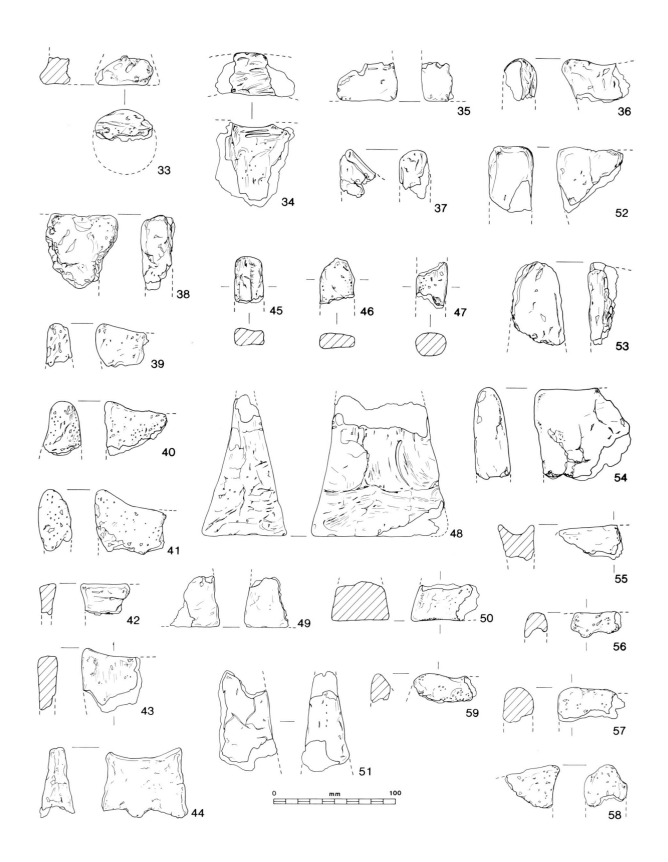

Figure 32 Fired clay: briquetage

Figure 33 Fired clay: briquetage

Fig. 33

60. Block. Small block with parallel faces. Cut away at bottom edge below slight indentation. Both sides missing. Height 64mm. Width 69mm. Thickness 24mm. (*7710, ditch 7710, Phase 3*).

61. Block. Base fragment of squared block. Height 44mm. Width 51mm. Thickness 29mm. (*7710, ditch 7710, Phase 3*).

62. Block. Edge of smallish squared block. Height 51mm. Width 32mm. Thickness 23mm. (*7710b, ditch 7710, Phase 3*).

63. Block. Part of foot of block. Height 34mm. Width 51mm. Thickness 32mm. (*7710b, ditch 7710, Phase 3*).

64. Block. Part of edge of squared block with parallel faces. Height 85mm. Width 64mm. Thickness 32mm. (*Ditch 759, Phase 4*).

65. Block. Part of foot of large block, rectangular at base, front face slopes backwards above. Height 59mm. Width 81mm. Thickness 38mm. (*7710, ditch 7710, Phase 3*).

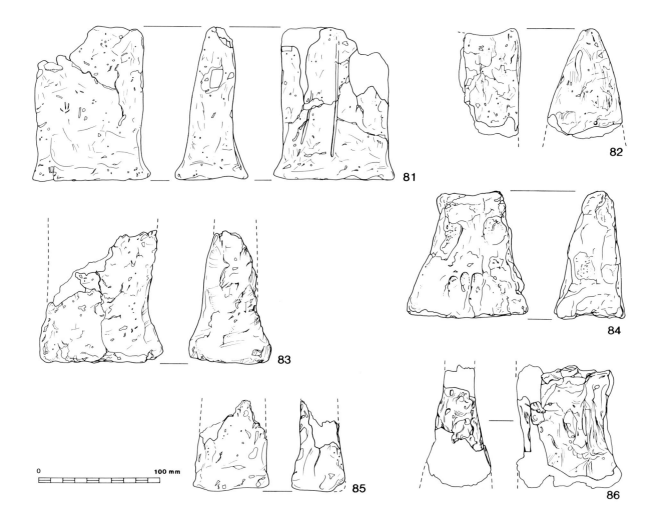

Figure 34 Fired clay: briquetage

66. Pedestal? Base fragment of squarish sectioned pedestal or block. Height 51mm. Width 52mm. Thickness 62mm. (*7710, ditch 7710, Phase 3*).

67. Pedestal? Base fragment of squarish sectioned pedestal or block. Height 29mm. Width 45mm. Thickness 41mm. (*7710b, ditch 7710, Phase 3*).

68. Luting. Incomplete small rod indented by finger, to hold pans together. Height 27mm. Width 21mm. Thickness 11–13mm. (*Ditch 7796, Phase 4*).

69. Pedestal. Fragment of base of round-sectioned pedestal with flared foot; original diameter 80mm. Height 62mm. Width 53mm. Thickness 54mm. (*Feature 7537, unphased*).

70. Pedestal. Fragment of base of oval-sectioned pedestal. Height 47.5mm. Width 68mm. Thickness 45mm. (*7725, unphased*).

71. Pedestal. Part of base of round-sectioned pedestal with flared foot; original diameter 107mm. Height 60mm. Width 93mm. Thickness 74mm. (*771, topsoil*).

72. Pedestal. Section of square-sectioned tapering pedestal. Both ends missing. Height 73mm. Width 33–47mm. Thickness 40mm. (*7720, unphased*).

73. Pedestal. Section of squared tapering pedestal. Both ends missing. Height 101mm. Width 43–73mm. Thickness 53mm. (*78141, ditch 78145, Phase 3*).

74. Small pedestal. Top of small rod, slightly flattened on one face, squarish section. Height 28mm. Width 19mm. Thickness 13mm. (*7728, recent disturbance*).

75. Small pedestal. One end of small rod, flat end, oval in section. Height 41mm. Width 25mm. Thickness 15mm. (*78150, unphased*).

76. Luting. Small lump, finger impressed and pinched into shape. Incomplete. Heavy shell and flint temper. Reddish brown in colour. Height 22.5mm. Width 31mm. Thickness 15mm. Length 29mm. (*7728, recent disturbance*).

77. Luting. Small, finger impressed, complete. Rectangular with two raised edges. Quartzite and grass tempering. Orange in colour. Height 22mm. Width 29mm. Thickness 4–11mm. Length 39mm. (*7728, recent disturbance*).

78. Block. Fragment of foot edge of squared block. Height 41mm. Width 70mm. Thickness 34mm. (*7879, unphased*).

79. Block. Fragment of edge of foot from tapering block, possibly wedge-shaped. Height 34mm. Width 47mm. Thickness 35mm. (*7712, recent disturbance*).

80. Block? Fragment of slightly bulging face, possibly from curved block, or possibly wall of large pedestal. Height 33mm. Width 52mm. Thickness 25mm. (*78299, ditch 78145, Phase 3*).

Fig. 34

81. Block. Almost complete block with squared sides, flared out at foot, tapering in section to top. Height 123mm. Width 89–98mm. Thickness 23–60.5mm. (*7728, recent disturbance*).

82. Block? Fragment of thick, sharply tapering, block with straight edge, slightly dipped top, possibly pedestal? Height 88mm. Width 50mm. Thickness 16–62mm. (*78251, ditch 78145, Phase 3*).

83. Block. Part of squarish block with flared foot, gently tapering in section. Height 106mm. Width 83–102mm. Thickness 39–68mm. (*78415, post-hole 7811, unphased*).

84. Block. Complete wedge-shaped block, rather irregular. Tapers to slightly dipped top. Height 103mm. Width 56–101mm. Thickness 25–59mm. (*78415, post-hole 7811, unphased*).

85. Block. Small squared block base, tapering towards top. Height 71mm. Width 56–63mm. Thickness 30–44mm. (*Post-hole 7847, unphased*).

86. Block. Large fragment of squarish block, tapering in section towards top. Both ends missing. Height 99mm. Width 72–88mm. Thickness 26–54mm. (*Post-hole 7812, unphased*).

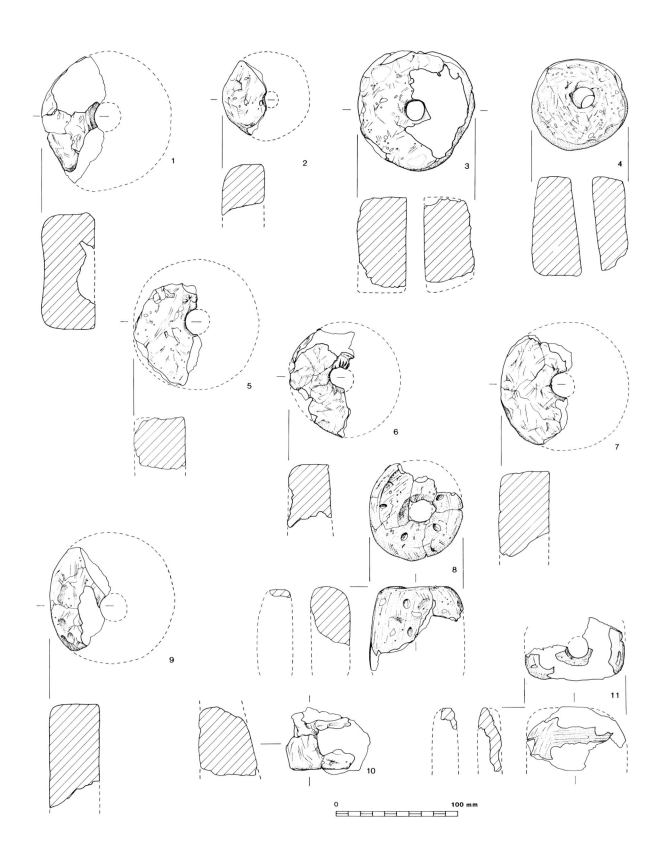

Figure 35 Fired clay: loomweights

IX. Fired Clay
by Joanna K.F. Bacon (1984)

The non-briquetage fired clay objects may be divided into those associated with textile production and those associated with metalworking. The majority of featured pieces are illustrated in Figs 35–36, and described in the Catalogue. Featureless pieces of fired clay are included in the figures in Table 6.

Loomweights

All but one of the twelve identifiable loomweight fragments from Billingborough are of typical Middle Bronze Age bun-shaped or cylindrical form (Fig. 35: 1–11), as found, for example, at Swallow, Lincolnshire (Leahy 1990), Fengate (Pryor 1976), Black Patch (Drewett 1982, 372, fig. 34, nos 1–4), Aldermaston Wharf and Knight's Farm, Burghfield, Berkshire (Bradley *et al.* 1980, 177–217). There are no pyramidal loomweights which at Aldermaston and Pingewood post-date the cylindrical and pre-date the Iron Age triangular loomweights. Gussage All Saints, Dorset (Wainwight 1979) has all three types, whereas Glastonbury, Somerset (Bulleid and Gray 1917) has only pyramidal and triangular. In view of the small number of loomweights from Billingborough the relative numbers of the different types should not be regarded as chronologically significant, although it would appear that weaving was not an important activity on the site after the Middle Bronze Age. Only a single example of a triangular loomweight was found.

Decorated cylindrical examples are rare, and apart from fragments from Fengate with punctate impressions (Pryor 1980, 126, fig.75 no. 4) the example from Billingborough (Fig. 35: 8) seems to be unique. No spindle-whorls were found in the excavations at Billingborough.

The Iron Age triangular loomweight from Billingborough (Fig. 36: 12), from Phase 3 ditch *78135*, is well-fired and neatly made, although smaller than most. A close parallel comes from Verulamium (Wheeler and Wheeler 1936, 178, fig. 25), although that has only a single perforation. Larger triangular loomweights, with generally two or three holes, occur at numerous sites including Willington, Derbyshire (Elsdon 1979), Winklebury, Hampshire (Smith 1977, 113, fig. 40), and Orsett, Essex (Hedges and Buckley 1978).

Mould

Two conjoining fragments of a clay mould (Fig. 36: 13) were recovered from Enclosure 2 ditch *78113* assigned a Phase 3 (later Iron Age) date. The mould was probably for a piece of horse harness, such as a side-ring from a three-link snaffle bit.

Catalogue of fired clay objects

Fig. 35
1. Loomweight. Cylindrical. Height 94mm. Diameter 111mm. Thickness 45mm. (*7710c, ditch 7710, Phase 1*).
2. Loomweight. Cylindrical. Height 40mm. Diameter 74mm. Thickness 37mm. (*77170, unphased*).
3. Loomweight. Cylindrical. Almost complete. Large flint tempering, including piece with possibly retouched edge, and another of 24 × 15mm. Sandy, hard fabric. Blackened. Height 72mm. Diameter 97mm. Thickness 36–38mm. (*7742, Phase 1*).
4. Loomweight. Cylindrical. Complete with askew perforation. Height 80mm. Diameter 74–79mm. Thickness 24–40mm. (*771, topsoil*).
5. Loomweight. Cylindrical. Height 42mm. Diameter 106mm. Thickness 45mm. (*7742, Phase 1*).
6. Loomweight. Cylindrical. Perforation slightly askew. Height 50mm. Diameter 92mm. Thickness 34–40mm. (*78299, ditch 78145, Phase 3*).
7. Loomweight. Cylindrical. Height 70mm. Diameter 105 mm. Thickness 42mm. (*78164, ditch 78145, Phase 1*).
8. Loomweight. Cylindrical. Slightly bulging sides, decorated with fingertip impressions around top and at intervals around body in vertical rows. Height 68 mm. Diameter 78 mm. Thickness 26–34 mm. (*Hollow 772, unphased*).
9. Loomweight. Cylindrical. Height 83mm. Diameter 104mm. Thickness 40–47mm. (*78164, ditch 78145, Phase 1*).
10. Loomweight. Cylindrical. Fragment of side, top and bottom missing, hole askew. Height 55mm. Thickness 40–48mm. (*Gully 78213, unphased*).
11. Loomweight. Cylindrical. Incomplete, worn into oblong shape. Height 52mm. Diameter 82mm. Thickness 18–35mm. (*Hollow 772, unphased*).

Fig. 36
12. Loomweight. Triangular. Single incomplete face of small triangular weight; two definite perforations across corners, possibly a third. Sandy fabric; large flint tempering; some grass impressions. Hard, dark red interior, blackened surface. Height 73mm. Width 64mm. Thickness 25mm. (*7835, ditch 78135, Phase 3*).
13. Mould. Two fragments of an investment mould; ?one in-gate. Probably for casting a ring (*c.* 100mm diameter) from a piece of horse harness. Surface colour varies. (*787, ditch 78113, Phase 3*).

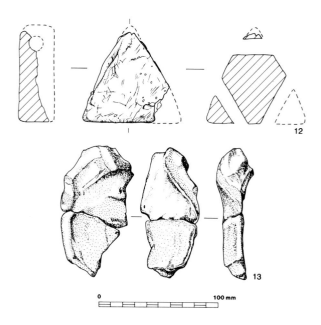

Figure 36 Fired clay: loomweight, mould

X. Worked Bone and Antler
by Joanna K.F. Bacon (1984)

Artefacts of bone and antler were found in both Bronze Age and Iron Age contexts, with a number of others coming from unphased or unstratified contexts. These are illustrated, by phase, in Figures 37–40.

Phase 1: Middle–Late Bronze Age
(Fig. 37: 1–13)
Artefacts of bone and antler found in Phase 1 contexts include bone points (Fig. 37: 1 and 2), pins (Fig. 37: 3 and 4), needles or bodkins (Fig. 37: 5 and 6), a gouge (Fig. 37: 7), an antler pick (Fig. 37: 8) and antler offcuts (Fig. 37: 9–13).

Points
Bone points were in use throughout prehistory. They are likely to have served a multitude of functions; specific uses included, for example, leather working — as pegs used for stretching pelts, and as awls for piercing holes through the skins prior to sewing. There are two examples from Phase 1 contexts Billingborough (Fig. 37: 1 and 2), and other Bronze Age examples have been found at Mildenhall Fen (Clark 1936), at the later Heathery Burn Cave, Co. Durham (Greenwell 1894) and Fyfield Bavant Down, Wiltshire (Clay 1924). The tip of an awl from Black Patch (Drewett 1982, 372 fig. 34, no. 12) is very similar to an example from Billingborough (Fig. 39: 44; from an unphased context).

Pins
Points are often referred to as pins (Clay 1924), causing problems in terminology. Here, the term pin is used for the fine, solid-sectioned, narrow artefacts which could also be tips of needles (Fig. 37: 3 and 4).

Needles
Needles or bodkins (Fig. 37: 5, 6, and 16) do not always survive intact as the eye is more fragile than the tip. Bronze Age examples were found at Mildenhall Fen (Clark 1936).

Socketed Gouges
These were probably used as skinning knives (Wainwright 1979). The Billingborough example (Fig. 37: 7) is a Type B according to the classification of Cunnington (1923).

Antler
One antler pick (Fig. 37: 8) was found. The four sawn-off tines (Fig. 37: 9–12) are probably not roughouts for tools since, in most examples, the pointed end shows signs of abrasion, probably consistent with use as burnishing tools, or for softening leather, as suggested by Smith and Simpson (1966) for the Overton Hill, Wiltshire, barrow finds. Those examples without any abrasion on the tip may represent waste from antler working on the site, evidence for which is provided by one sawn fragment (Figure 37: 13).

Later Phases
Bone points and pins continued in use during the later phases at Billingborough with no changes in style or in their method of manufacture. However, some other types of bone and antler objects were found in assemblages from Phases 2 (Fig. 37: 14–17), 3 (Fig. 38: 18–29) and 4 (Fig. 38: 30–33) which did not occur in Phase 1. Unphased objects are shown in Figure 39.

Many of the unphased objects are likely to be of Iron Age date, particularly where they closely parallel dated pieces from the site or are of a common Iron Age type such as a toggle (Fig. 39: 54). A small quantity of manufacturing waste may also be present (*e.g.* Fig. 38: 27), suggesting that some bones may have been worked on site. In addition, there are four horn cores (Fig. 38: 29; Fig. 40: 61–63) which have cut marks around the base and these provide evidence for horn removal and subsequent working.

The use of many of the bone tools is uncertain and some may have been used in a variety of ways (Sellwood 1984, 387, 392). Even so, the apparent absence, from a comparatively large assemblage, of tools thought to be associated with weaving is noteworthy. Only one piece may be from the handle of a weaving comb (Fig. 38: 26) but the presence of two perforations on such a comb would be rare (*cf* Hodder and Hedges 1977, 18, fig. 1). The notched bone (Fig. 37: 17) made from a horse metatarsal is similar to an example from Danebury from a sheep metatarsal (Sellwood 1984, 392, fig. 7.37; 3.192; 7.38) which was suggested to be a bobbin or perhaps to have been inserted between the warp threads of a loom. Although Billingborough lies at the edge of the presently recorded distribution of weaving combs, the rarity of tools associated with weaving and the discovery of only a single triangular loomweight might suggest that textile working was only a small-scale activity and did not take place on the site after Phase 1.

Catalogue of worked bone and antler

Fig. 37
1. Point. Unidentified bone, possibly sheep metatarsal. Hollowed; sliced to form gently tapering, wide, flat point with a slight kink to one side. Top broken off leaving rough U-shaped section. Signs of wear at point. Length 70mm. Width 2–9mm. Thickness 1–4.5mm. (*7742, no. 258, Phase 1*).
2. Point/needle. Sheep metatarsal, hollowed and sliced to form a wide point. U-shaped section tapering to round-sectioned point, tip missing. Head broken off. Polished surface with some whittling marks visible. Length 43mm. Width 1.5–9mm. Thickness 1.5–5mm. (*Slot 7871, no. 290, Phase 1*).
3. Pin. Sheep or deer ulna whittled to oval-sectioned point. Both ends missing. Length 46mm. Width 1–6mm. Thickness 1.5–2.5mm. (*Slot 7871, no. 267, Phase 1*).
4. Pin. Unidentified bone. Sub-rectangular section thickening slightly to roundish facetted section 15mm from tip then tapering sharply to fine, round-sectioned point. Head missing. Surface polished. Length 37.5mm. Width 0–4mm. Thickness 0–2mm. (*7743d, ditch 7743, no. 242, Phase 1*).
5. Needle. Two conjoining pieces of unidentified sheep bone, oval in section and hollowed. Cut and snapped off at head. Sliced downwards *c.*15mm below head forming wide point tapering towards flat tip. Very smooth surface. Length 43mm. Width 1.5–7mm. Thickness 1–6.5mm. (*7743f, ditch 7743, no. 377, Phase 1*).
6. Needle. Unidentified sheep bone, oval in section and hollowed. Cut and snapped off at head. Smoothed into squarish section and sliced along *c.*10mm below head to form a wide U-sectioned point, tapering suddenly to end with sharp flat tip. Smooth surface with some scratches. Length 42mm. Width 0.5–8.5mm. Thickness 0.5–7mm. (*7743g, ditch 7743, no. 381, Phase 1*).
7. Socketed gouge. Sheep or goat metatarsal, distal end perforated from front and back (diam. 4mm) and cut smooth across top. Shaft hollowed and smoothed into squarish section. Slice cut downwards, 37.5mm from head, with slight dip towards end, forming wide flattish point, tapering from a pronounced U-shaped section to flat, pointed tip. Perforation is at right angles to point. Surface has some polish. Length 78mm. Width 2–18mm. Thickness 0.17mm. (*7742, no. 138, Phase 1*).

68

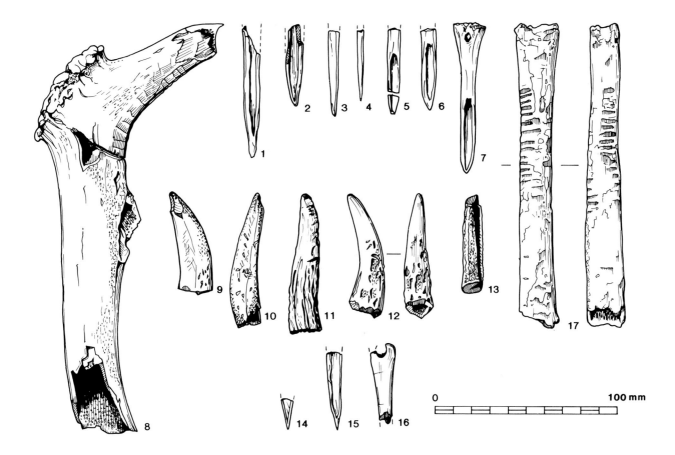

Figure 37 Worked bone and antler (Phases 1 and 2)

8. Antler pick. Base of antler with tine broken off short, possibly through use as a pick. Saw marks across beam below tine. Length 220mm. Width 27–110mm. Thickness *c.* 30–46mm. (*7743d, ditch 7743, no. 90, Phase 1*).

9. Antler tine. Possibly roe deer; smooth surface, tip chipped and broken. Tine snapped off having been weakened by sawing from each side. Length 55mm. Width 19mm. Thickness 18mm. (*78164, ditch 78145, no. 404, Phase 1*).

10. Antler tine. Surface chipped and scored from use. Not possible to tell from base whether sawn or broken off because of damage. Length 72mm. Width 3–18mm. Thickness 3–13mm. (*7742, no. 210, Phase 1*).

11. Antler tine. Partly sawn and partly broken off, with battered tip, possibly from use. Blackened from burning. Length 75mm. Width 4–17mm. Thickness 4–11mm. (*752d, pit 752, no. 40, Phase 1*).

12. Antler tine. Sawn around and snapped off. Shows no sign of wear as on other tines. Length 67mm. Width 2–18mm. Thickness 2–19mm. (*7743b, ditch 7743, no. 367, Phase 1*).

13. Antler tine. Segment of tine, sawn along length and snapped, forming one smooth and one rough edge. Sawn off at top and bottom. Length 52mm. Width 7–15mm. Thickness 8mm. (*78181, pit 78173, no. 280, Phase 1*).

14. Point. Small fragment of unidentified bone, almost flat in section. Neatly squared edges, surface smooth and shiny. Only tip survives. Length 16.5mm. Width 0–5.5mm. Thickness 0–1.5mm. (*77101a, no. 317, Phase 2*).

15. Needle. Sheep/goat metatarsal sawn around and snapped at head. Hollowed; inner division left; sliced down to form long wide flattish point tapering to sharp tip. Length 42mm. Width 0.5–9mm. Thickness 0.5–6mm. (*Hearth 7736, no. 67, Phase 2*).

16. Needle. ?Sheep or goat tibia. Tapering fragment with rounded top and squarish in section. Part of head missing, shaft and tip broken off. Perforated at top (diam. *c.* 5mm). Inside slightly blackened, possibly by burning. Length 43mm. Width 7–14mm. Thickness 3–5mm. (*'Structure' 77101, Phase 2*).

17. Object. Horse metatarsal, both ends broken off; scored marks across all four sides, some less visible due to differential erosion of surface. Length 159mm. Width 19–25mm. Thickness 16.5–22mm. (*Pit 78257, no. 416, Phase 2*).

Fig. 38

18. Point? Part of edge of cow scapula with blade broken off. Thickest part of bone whittled to triangular point with cut marks across it. Surface scratched, especially at flatter end. Length 159.5mm. Width 2–27mm. Thickness 4–12mm. (*787, ditch 78113, no. 330, Phase 3*).

19. Point? Sliver of horse longbone smoothed to a point. Articular end has possible saw marks across it, surface very worn. Length 104mm. Width 1.5–18mm. Thickness 5.5–16mm. (*78134, ditch 78113, no 380, Phase 3*).

20. Pin. Unidentified bone. Flattish, oval in section, tapering gently to squarish sectioned point, tip broken off. Polished surface has slight scratches across shank. Length 35mm. Width 0.5–4mm. Thickness 0.5–3mm. (*7787, ditch 7787, no. 227, Phase 3*).

21. Needle/point. Unidentified bone, possibly deer/sheep tibia. End broken off and hollowed. Sheered down *c.* 20mm from tip to form point. Triangular in section, tapering slightly to more oval section at point. Surface scratched, possibly through whittling or wear. Length 76mm. Width 1–14mm. Thickness 2–12mm. (*77147, ditch 78145, no. 299, Phase 3*).

22. Needle/point. Sheep metatarsal, hollowed and whittled into squarish section. End cut away to form narrow tapering point, squared in section, shorter than most of the other needles. Front part of head broken away. Length 60mm. Width 2.5–8mm. Thickness 1–1.2mm. (*7711, no. 168, land drain*).

23. Pin. Unidentified bone. Oval in section tapering to round-sectioned point. Both ends broken off. Some polish to surface but very abraded towards tip. Length 33mm. Width 2.5–5mm. Thickness 2.5–3mm. (*78225, ditch 78145, no. 307, Phase 3*).

24. Socketed gouge. Sheep metatarsal with hollowed shaft. Pair of perforations (4mm diam.) perpendicular to point, one each side of head. Shaft round in section, tapering naturally to 37mm below head where cut to squarish section, and sliced down forming wide, U-shaped point with flattish tip. Polished surface. Length 99mm. Width 1–17mm. Thickness 1–15mm. (*784, ditch 78145, no. 389, Phase 3*).

25. Needle/point or socketed gouge? Sheep/goat metatarsal, hollowed and sliced down to form flat, wide, slightly tapering shaft. Tip broken off. Head and part of shaft missing. Length 78mm. Width

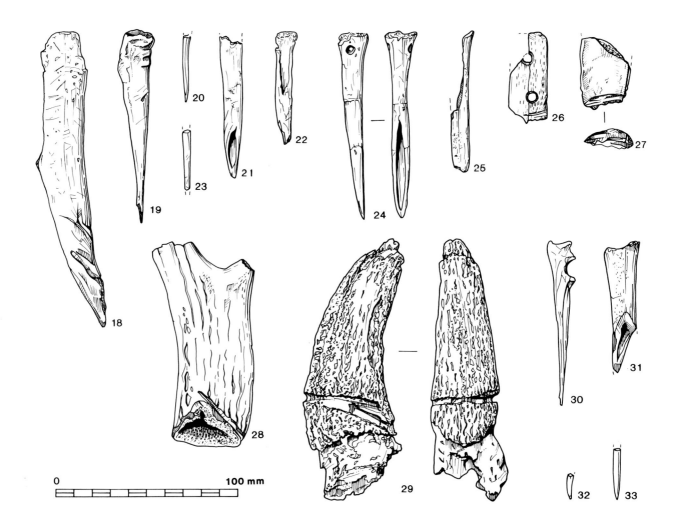

Figure 38 Worked bone and antler (Phases 3 and 4)

c. 9.5mm. Thickness 1.5–10mm. (*78141, ditch 78145, no. 250, Phase 3*).

26. Comb handle? Slice of unidentified bone, possibly rib. Upper surface slightly domed to one side in section, with underside cut flat. Parallel smoothed edges and rounded end with central perforation (5mm diam.) 13mm below top. Second perforation of same size is cut through thickest part and thus askew. Parts of several small, vertical cuts along bottom may be result of cutting teeth. Edge cut at an angle. Several decorative cuts across surface below the perforation, and five thin cuts across top. Length 49mm. Width 20.5mm. Thickness 2.5mm. (*7835, ditch 78135, no. 383 or 385, Phase 3*).

27. Object. ?Bone-working waste. Piece of large unidentified bone with saw marks across one end, other edges all broken off. Length 38mm. Width 28mm. Thickness *c.*8mm. (*787, ditch 78113, no. 166 or 163, Phase 3*).

28. Antler. Section of ?fallow deer antler, both ends sawn and snapped off. Small tine at top broken off, many small scratches below it. Length 104mm. Width 39–57mm. Thickness 17–46mm. (*78123, ditch 78113, no. 207, Phase 3*).

29. Cow horn core. Deep (1–6mm) groove sawn around base. Length 128mm. Width *c.*47mm. Thickness *c.*32mm. (*787, ditch 78113, no. 299, Phase 3*).

30. Point. Fox ulna. Cut/broken to form rough point. Length 88mm. Width 1–17mm. (*Ditch 7797, no. 394 or 395, Phase 4*).

31. Point. End of sheep tibia cut down to form smooth, round-sectioned point. Surface worn, edges chipped and broken. Length 70mm. Width 0.5–17mm. Thickness 0.5–17mm. (*788, ditch 78138, no. 286, Phase 4*).

32. Point/pin. Unidentified bone, sub-rectangular in section, smoothed to round-sectioned point. Both ends broken off. Bone has whitened, possibly due to burning or weathering. Length 13mm. Width 1–3mm. Thickness 1–2mm. (*Ditch 779, no. 271, Phase 4*).

33. Pin. Unidentified bone, possibly bird. Shaft sub-triangular in section, tapering to round-sectioned point 8mm from tip. Most of shaft missing. Smoothed surface. Length 27.5mm. Width 0.5–3mm. Thickness 0.5–2.5mm. (*Ditch 789, no. 412, Phase 4*).

Fig. 39

34. ?Point. Sliver of unidentified bone, whittled to rough point. Length 119mm. (*Post-hole 7751, no. 82, unphased*).

35. Point. Sheep metatarsal, distal end sawn across side 35mm from end and broken off. Smoothed to form wide point roughly U-shaped in section with rounded tip. Surface polished. Length 80mm. Width 3–15mm. Thickness 2–21mm. (*77104, no. 161, unphased*).

36. ?Point. Sliver of cow metatarsal with highly smoothed edges. Head tapers to wide, flattish point, tip missing. Surface scratched, edges nicked in places, battered towards tip. Length 132mm. Width 8–25mm. Thickness 3–18mm. (*7824, no. 23, unphased*).

37. Point. Sheep longbone, sliced downwards, slightly askew, forming long tapering point. Hollowed, U-shaped section, tapering to fine, round-sectioned tip. Surface polished, some scratches. Length 103mm. Width 1–31mm. Thickness 1–15mm. (*781, no. 26, topsoil*).

38. Point. Sheep tibia, distal end. Oval-sectioned shaft, whittled and sliced downwards 19mm from end to form sharp point, squarish in section. Surface polished. Length 118mm. Width 1–23mm. Thickness 1–18mm. (*771, no. 32, topsoil*).

39. Point. Right radius of sheep/deer, both ends missing. Sliced lengthways with U-shaped section tapering to flat, oval-sectioned point. Surface polished. Length 88mm. Width 4–10mm. Thickness 2–6mm. (*771, no. 31, topsoil*).

40. Point. Sheep metatarsal proximal end, sliced lengthways and tapering to flattish point. Part-hollowed forming shallow, U-shaped section, flattening towards point. Tip missing. Whittling marks all over. Length 96mm. Width 5.5–19mm. Thickness 3–10mm. (*771, no. 46, topsoil*).

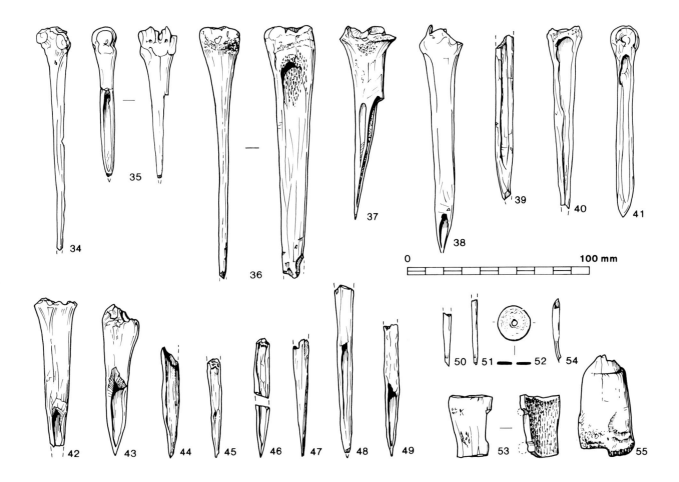

Figure 39 Worked bone and antler (unphased)

41. Point. Sheep metatarsal distal end, broken in half axially where weakened by slicing lengthways to form point. Shaft hollowed and U-shaped in section, tapering to wide, oval-sectioned flat point. Wear across point. Length 102.5mm. Width 1–16mm. Thickness 0.5–12mm. (*771, no. 154, topsoil*).

42. Point. Sheep radius, part hollowed, sliced downwards and slightly askew to form wide, tapering, U-sectioned point, *c.*20mm long. Tip broken off. Surface worn and scratched. Probable whittling marks at point. Length 78mm. Width 8–27mm. Thickness 3–18mm. (*771, topsoil*).

43. Point. Articular end of sheep tibia, part hollowed and sliced downwards at angle to form smooth, tapering point. Length 78mm. Width 1–24mm. Thickness 1–16mm. (*7739, no. 131, medieval plough furrow*).

44. Point. Slice of unidentified, flat bone whittled to long, sharp point: tip missing. Underside hollowed centrally forming slight U-shaped section. One edge and other end missing. Surface polished; scratches and whittling marks around tip. Length 59mm. Width 1–9mm. Thickness 1.5–3mm. (*77170, no. 353, unphased*).

45. Point. Slice of sheep or deer ulna whittled to square-sectioned point. Both ends missing and surface somewhat abraded. Length 52mm. Width 2–7mm. Thickness 2–4mm. (*77168, no. 349, unphased*).

46. Point/needle. Slice of unidentified probable sheep bone. Two adjoining pieces. Hollowed and cut askew. Head broken, tapers to sub-triangular sectioned point. Surface polished, very dark in colour and brittle, possibly burnt. Length 57mm. Width 2–8mm. Thickness 3mm. (*7744, no. 149, medieval plough furrow*).

47. Needle. Unidentified bone, possibly sheep/goat metatarsal. Probably perforated through head. Flattish, U-shaped section tapering to fine, round-sectioned point. Tip missing. Surface polished with some whittling marks visible. Length 62mm. Width 1–9mm. Thickness 1–4.5mm. (*7838, no. 266, unphased*).

48. ?Needle/point or socketed gouge. Sheep metatarsal with end sawn off, and shaft hollowed and smoothed into squarish section. Sliced downwards, *c.*30mm from top to form wide, flat point, tapering gently from almost U-shaped section to flat tip with squared edges. Surface polished, with some scratches; whittling marks visible all over. Length 88mm. Width 1.5–11mm. Thickness 1–11mm. (*751, no. 7, topsoil*).

49. Needle/point. Unidentified bone of sheep/deer. Rounded in section. Top sawn and broken off. Sliced lengthways, *c.*30mm from head to form long, tapering, round-sectioned tip. Surface very abraded. Length 70mm. Width 1–9mm. Thickness 1–9.5mm. (*771, no. 43, topsoil*).

50. Pin. Unidentified bone roughly whittled into squarish sectioned shaft tapering towards point. Both ends missing, possibly unfinished. Length 28mm. Width 2.5–5mm. Thicknes 2–4.5mm. (*77192, no. 361, unphased*).

51. Pin. Unidentified bone. Oval-sectioned, faceted shaft tapers to round-sectioned point. Both ends missing, saw marks around top form slight neck indicative of ornate head, now broken away. Length 35mm. Width 2–3mm. Thickness 2–4mm. (*771, no. 169, topsoil*).

52. Perforated disc. Unidentified bone, possibly sheep scapula. Flat disc, slightly domed upper surface. Cut out from both sides, underside slightly smaller forming lip at top edge. Perforation cut from top, narrows towards bottom. Concentric rings — polishing marks — visible on both faces, which are also marked with parallel saw cuts, covering the base and about one third of upper surface. Diameter 17.5–18mm. Thickness 1–1.5mm. (*771, no. 199, topsoil*).

53. ?Pin Unidentified bone. Roughly fashioned with oval-sectioned, slightly curved, bulbous head, 22mm in length, top missing. Shaft is narrow and squared in section, broken off very short. Length 34mm. Width 2–4.5mm. Thickness 2–3mm. (*771, no. 171, topsoil*).

54. ?Toggle. Unidentified longbone of cow/horse. Slightly tapering segment, smoothed ends hollowed out; large, square perforation cut from one side. Length 32mm. Width 18–24mm. Thickness 3mm. (*771, no. 200, topsoil*).

55. Unidentified object. Metapodial of large size, probably cow/horse. Sliced lengthways and hollowed to form a wide, U-shaped section, gently tapering until 15mm from end where it has been cut into sharp, triangular point. Tip missing. Inner side blackened, possibly through burning. Length 54mm. Width 30mm. Thickness 2–10mm. (*771, no. 243, topsoil*).

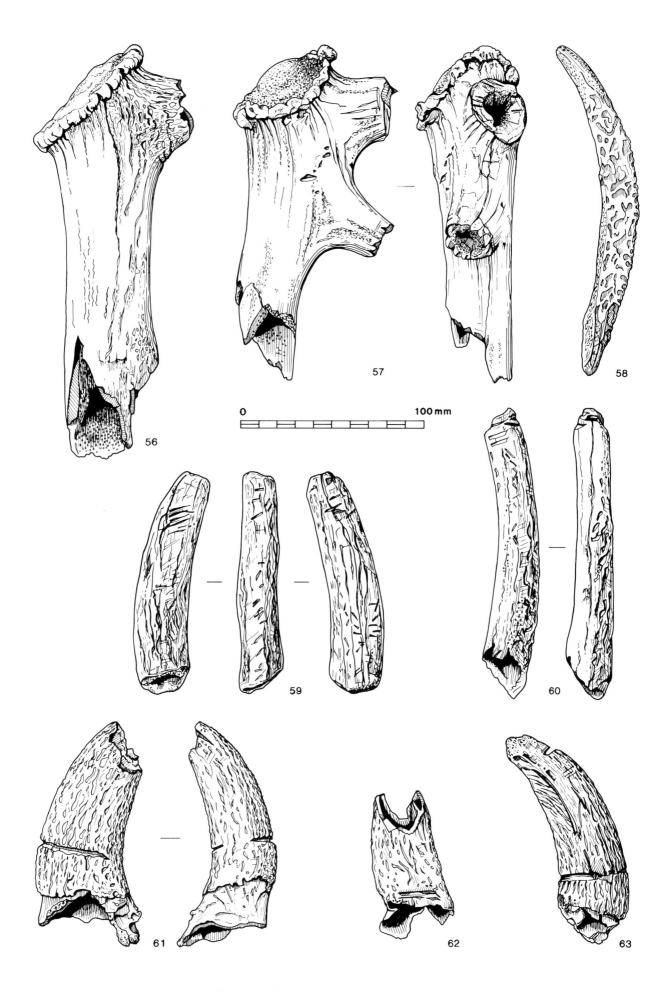

56

57

58

0   100 mm

59

60

61

62

63

Figure 40 Worked bone and antler (unphased)

Fig. 40

56. Antler ?pick. Red deer. Tine broken off, possibly through use. Handle missing; top on opposite side to tine is somewhat battered, possibly through use as a hammer. Length 212mm. Width 47–82mm. Thickness 37–54mm. (*Feature 772, no. 4, unphased*).

57. ?Modified antler pick. Red deer antler base; two tines removed by sawing and snapping off. Each has several saw marks below break. Also saw marks on base; beam broken, not sawn. Length 175mm. Width 33–80mm. Thickness 33–42mm. (*771, no. 34, topsoil*).

58. Antler ?pick. Tine of ?red deer, broken off from antler. Possibly used as pick, the tip being facetted and scratched. Length 176mm. Width 7–21mm. Thickness 7–24mm. (*Post-hole 7748, no. 239, unphased*).

59. Antler tine. Tip sawn off, bottom end partly sawn and partly snapped off. Surface shows many nicks and scratches, some facetting of the smaller end. Length 116mm. Width 16–29mm. Thickness 15–21mm. (*Post-hole 78172, no. 277, unphased*).

60. Antler tine. Long tine roughly sawn and snapped off at both ends. Some scratches on surface below saw marks. Length 152mm. Width 18–26mm. Thickness 18–24mm. (*771, no. 135, topsoil*).

61. Cow horn core. Tip broken off. Base shows signs of being partly sawn before breaking off. Sawn around to depth of 1–3mm near base. Several other saw cuts visible on base. Length 115mm. Width 30–57mm. Thickness 15–30mm. (*771, no. 33, topsoil*).

62. Cow horn core. Top broken off. Base has two parallel saw cuts. Length 75mm. Width 30–41mm. Thickness 25–41mm. (*7819, no. 113, medieval plough furrow*).

63. Cow horn core. Partly sawn, partly broken off from skull. Sawn to depth of 6mm across tip, with shallower cut around base. Length 122mm. Width 7–38mm. Thickness 8.31mm. (*7530, ditch 7530, no. 55, unphased*).

XI. Human Skeletal Material
by Justine Bayley (1996)

Introduction

The excavations produced a small amount of human skeletal material. This comprised two articulated burials (one fairly complete skeleton and one disturbed burial of an individual represented by parts of the torso and upper limbs) and a number of skull fragments, some of which had been deliberately cut and/or polished. The articulated bones were examined, measured where complete bones survived, and the sex and age estimated from the criteria described by Brothwell (1972). The skull fragments, which came from various contexts across the site, are described individually and the occurrence of worked human bone discussed. Further details of these can be found in the archive reports (Bayley 1980; Bayley 1984a).

The Articulated Burials
by Guy Grainger

Grave 78183 (Unphased — ?Early Bronze Age)
(Fig. 4; Pl. II)
The remains are those of an adult female aged over 30 years. Most of the skeleton, except the lower legs, was present but preservation was not very good. Age was assessed from the degree of attrition of the remaining molars, together with the evidence of the mandibular fragment and other loose teeth. Moderate dental hypoplasia and calculus were seen. Very heavy wear was observed on the surviving anterior teeth. Wear on the molars was less severe.

Feature 77119 (Unphased. Probable grave disturbed by medieval plough furrow)
The bones were from an adolescent aged about 18 years. This age was calculated from the degree of fusion of the epiphyses. The bones recovered consisted of the left humerus, radius and ulna, a scapula, a clavicle, ribs,

vertebrae, carpals, and phalanges. The length of the humerus, including the proximal epiphysis, was 315mm which gives a stature estimation of between 164cm and 169cm according to the formulae of Trotter and Gleser (1958).

Catalogue of skull fragments

Twenty-three skull fragments have been recorded (see Fig. 41 for location on skull). Almost all came from Phase 3 (Late Iron Age) or later deposits, except for one fragment (No. 3) from a Phase 1 (Middle Bronze Age) post-hole and another fragment (No. 9) from a Phase 2 (Late Bronze Age/Early Iron Age) context.

1. Major part of the occipital bone from a juvenile. The fracture, near the base, shows two distinct areas of cutting, one in the centre and the other at the right hand side. The cuts are irregular and appear to be made on fresh bone. Their position, low down on the occipital, suggests the removal of the head from the body rather than the separation of the vault from the rest of the skull. (*787, Enclosure 2 ditch 78113, no. 333, Phase 3*).

2. The anterior portion of a frontal (Pl. X). This has been cut from the rest of the frontal about 20mm above the orbits. The cut, a groove 2–3mm wide, has been made from the outside of the skull. In the centre of the bone the cut did not penetrate through the inner table which has broken away leaving a ragged edge. In two areas, at the left side and above the right orbit, short shallow cuts can be seen in the outer table which are false starts or slips made while making the main cut. The alignment of the cut changes slightly on both sides below the temporal crest, coming closer to the orbital margin. (*7723, medieval plough furrow, no. 61*).

3. Another piece similar to No. 2. In this case the cut has been made only 15mm above the orbits where the bone is rather thicker (about 7mm). Again the cut is incomplete in the centre and the inner table has broken. There is no change in the alignment of the cut towards the left end (the right end is missing). (*Post-hole 77106, 4-post structure C, no. 105, Phase 1*).

4. The mastoid process and surrounding areas of the right temporal bone with a small piece of parietal (that in the parietal notch) and an ajoining piece from the right side of the occipital (Pl. XI). A saw cut runs across the top of the pieces on a slightly curved alignment, suggesting it was made in a series of short segments. It goes cleanly through the whole skull thickness (length of cut 85mm). (*Topsoil 771, nos 167 and 172*).

5. Joining fragments of occipital and parietal from the left side of the skull (Pls XII and XIII). The lower edge of the two pieces is sawn and polished, the cut running from asteiron across the lambdoid suture without a break, showing that the occipital and parietal were still joined when this operation was carried out. The cutting was done from the outside of the skull but it was obviously not an easy operation as the line has been changed three times in the 80mm length of the cut (PL. XII). Both inner and outer surfaces and the cut edge of the bone are polished. In addition, two holes of 5–6mm diameter have been drilled through the bone 20mm apart, one 11mm and the other 15mm from the cut edge (Pl. XIII). Both have a slightly 'hour-glass' profile and would therefore seem to have been cut from both sides of the bone. (*Topsoil 771, no. 28; Layer 7797, no. 136, Phase 4; Flood layer 77117, no. 311*).

6. Similar to No. 5; the cut edge is in an equivalent position (Pl. XIV). Fragment from back of left parietal with a small portion of the adjoining occipital (the lambdoid suture is partly fused). Both surfaces are somewhat polished and c. 10mm of the edge of the bone in the parietal notch region is polished flat and smooth. There is a roughly oblong perforation, 12 × 5mm, about 14mm from the cut edge. Its irregular outline suggests that it was probably cut from the outside as two roughly circular adjacent holes. (*787, enclosure ditch 78113, no. 366, Phase 3*).

7. Similar to No. 6. Fragment of parietal and adjoining occipital from left side of skull near asterion. About 20mm of the saw cut is visible on the lower edge of the piece, rather higher up on the skull than the cut on No. 6. It has not gone through the whole thickness of the skull, penetrating only as far as the diploe from the outside. Possible traces of polishing are visible on both surfaces. (*Medieval plough furrow 7744, no. 130*).

8. A piece of frontal from the right side. A portion of the coronal suture from just above pterion survives on one edge. The front edge appears to be cut (in a corresponding position to the cuts on Nos 2

73

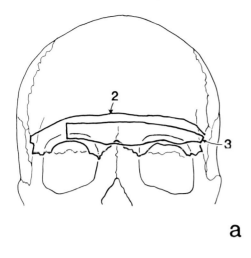

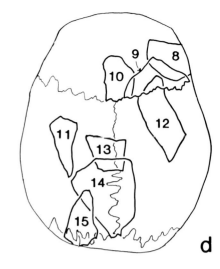

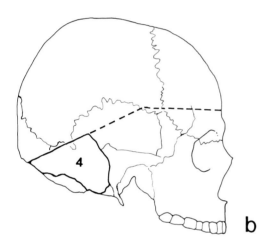

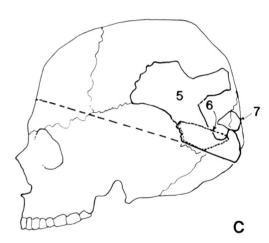

Figure 41 Worked human bone: location on skull of fragment Nos 2–15

and 3) and, approximately perpendicular to this, is a bevelled edge, cut or worn through the whole thickness of the skull; both edges have subsequently been damaged. The outer surface is highly polished, the inner surface and bevelled edge less so. (*7710, enclosure ditch 7710, no. 107, Phase 3*).

9. Triangular fragment of the frontal bone from the right side of the skull; one edge is the coronal suture (Pl. XV). There is an artificial bevel on the slightly curved edge of the fragment running at about 45° to the suture, from the region of bregma forwards and to the right. This cut edge is very well polished as are both the surfaces of the piece. The third edge (running from near pterion to the bevelled edge) has an angled cut line on the inner table though this apparently never penetrated as far as the outer table as this is roughly broken, probably while the bone was fresh. (*7743, enclosure 1 ditch 7743, no. 285, Phase 2*).

10. A frontal fragment with the coronal suture along one edge. It comes from near the mid-line of the skull. Running at a shallow angle to the suture is an abraded and polished zone where the outer table has been removed, tapering away until only the inner table remains on the edge which has subsequently been damaged. (*Topsoil 771, no. 185*).

11. A parietal fragment which, like No. 10, is so abraded and polished that the outer table is completely missing. On one side the diploe has also been removed as the thickness of the fragment tapers to almost nothing. The inner surface is also polished. (*Ditch 779, no. 198, Phase 4*).

12. Parts of frontal and parietal, probably from the right side, with an almost completely obliterated coronal suture. The outer surface is polished. (*78140, enclosure 2 ditch 78113, no. 353, Phase 3*).

13. Portions of both parietals with a partly obliterated sagittal suture. The outer surface is polished. Possibly from the same individual as No. 12. (*787, enclosure 2 ditch 78113, no. 191, Phase 3*).

14. Portions of both parietals (from just in front of lambda) with an almost completely obliterated sagittal suture. The outer surface is polished. Possibly from the same individual as No. 12. (*Ditch 779, no. 216, Phase 4*).

15. Fragment of parietal and occipital, probably from the left side, with an almost completely fused lambdoid suture. The outer surface is rather worn/polished though partly obscured by iron panning. (*Topsoil 781, no. 5*).

16. Fragment of parietal from near saggital suture. (*Ditch 7797, 210, Phase 4*).

17. Three (joining) left parietal fragments with part of the saggital suture. (*Ditch 7797, no. 308, Phase 4*).

18. Parietal fragment from left side near asterion. The outer table appears highly polished but most of it is covered by an iron pan deposit. (*Pit 77106, no. 91, Unphased*).

19. Parietal fragment, highly polished on outside, and infant skull fragment. (*Topsoil 771, no. 179*).

20. Small fragment of occipital with polished inner and outer surfaces. (*Ditch 77107, no. 188, Phase 4*).

74

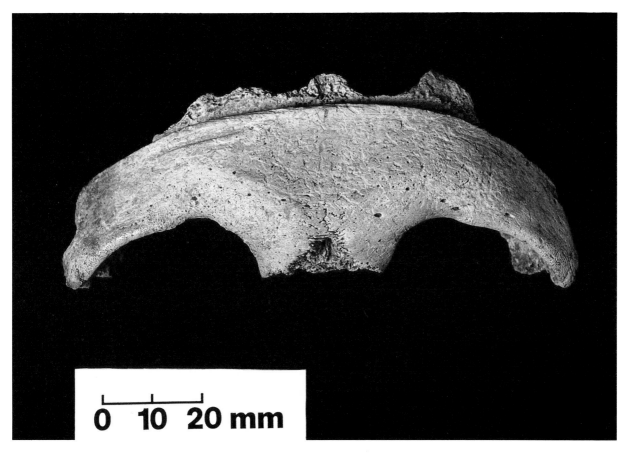

Plate X Worked human bone: No. 2, showing the inner table which was not cut and a shallow second cut over the right orbit. (Scale = 20mm) *Copyright English Heritage*

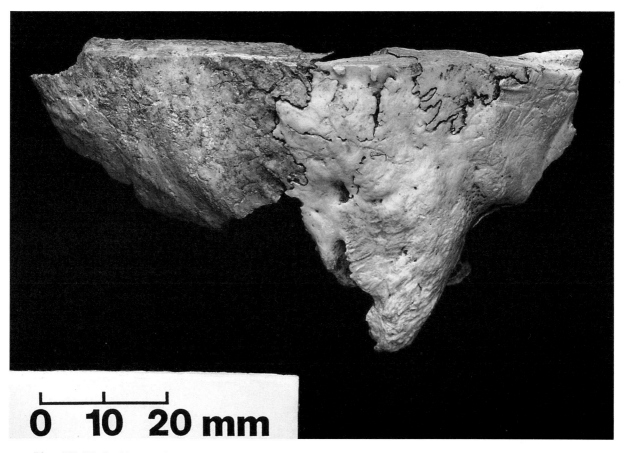

Plate XI Worked human bone: No. 4, showing the change in direction of the cut and a slight mis-cut below. (Scale = 20mm) *Copyright English Heritage*

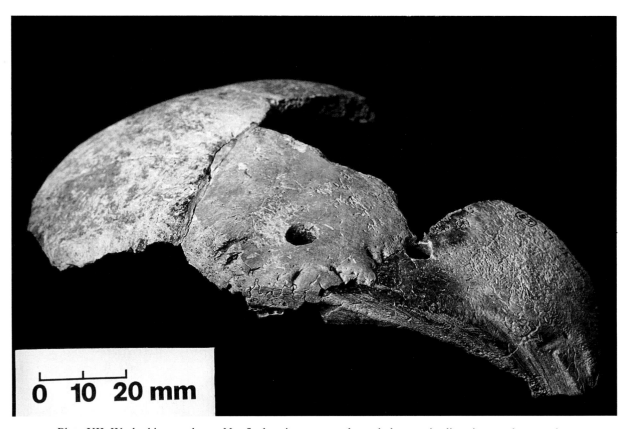

Plate XII Worked human bone: No. 5, showing saw marks and changes in direction on the cut edge.
(Scale = 20mm) *Copyright English Heritage*

Plate XIII Worked human bone: No. 5, showing neatly drilled perforations. (Scale = 20mm) *Copyright English Heritage*

Plate XIV Worked human bone: No. 6, showing the
irregular perforation. (Scale = 20mm)
Copyright English Heritage

Plate XV Worked human bone: No. 9, showing polished
bevel edge. (Scale = 50mm) *Copyright English Heritage*

21. Fragment of right parietal, just anterior to lambda. The inner surface is polished; the outer eroded but possibly originally polished. (*Ditch 779, no. 216, Phase 4*).
22. Fragment of parietal with coronal and saggital sutures, the outer surface polished. (*Topsoil 781, no. 6*).
23. Three joining fragments of left parietal with saggital suture. Two thinner fragments from another individual, the larger piece from a right parietal with part of the lambdoid suture, just medial to asterion. (*Pit 77106, no. 397, Unphased*).

Description of the skull fragments

It is interesting to note that all the stray finds of human bone are fragments of skull, and these are clearly from a considerable number of individuals. Almost all show some signs of post mortem cutting or polishing of the bone. Some joining fragments now appear different colours as they were found in contexts with different soil environments. This suggests either deliberate scattering of the pieces in antiquity or, possibly more likely, accidental dispersal during the time they have been buried.

No. 1 appears to be from a juvenile who was decapitated with a sharp weapon. The polish on the surfaces suggests some post-mortem handling of the defleshed bone.

Nos 2–7 show that the vaults were being cut or sawn from skulls and the rims perforated, presumably so they could be suspended and function as bowls. The cuts crossed the frontal bone just above the orbits, continued across the squamous parts of the temporals to the parietal notches, and then across the occipital, passing close to the external protuberance. Nos 2–4 are unwanted lower parts of the skull, while Nos 5–7 represent the rim portions of the vault. The presence of both shows that the 'bowls' must have been made and used at Billingborough. The rim fragments show abraded and polished surfaces, like those seen on tools and other artefacts made from animal bone and must thus have been polished, or at least handled frequently. Nos 12–23 are further vault fragments which come from higher up on the skull and therefore have no cut edges. They do, however, have the same polished surfaces as Nos 5–7 and are thus probably further parts of skull vault 'bowls'. The coincident locations of Nos 2–3 and Nos 5–7 show that at least three skull vaults are represented. The varying thickness and degree of obliteration of the sutures on other fragments suggests the total number was probably higher, though no accurate estimate of minimum numbers can be made.

The way the bone has broken in Nos 2–3 indicates it was not dry but fairly fresh when cut. There is however nothing to suggest that the individuals were alive when their skulls was cut. The multiple cuts on slightly different alignments and the misplaced cuts visible on Nos 2–7 suggest that the operation was not easy, and that considerable force was necessary; perhaps the saws used were not well-adapted for this type of material. The perforations in No. 5 seem to have been made from both sides, so they must have been made after the vault had been cut from the rest of the skull as access to the inner surface would otherwise have been almost impossible.

Nos 8–11 show more extreme abrasion and polishing than the other pieces and so probably functioned in other ways. Three of the four pieces came from the frontal bone. Nos 8–9 have bevelled edges in positions that do not coincide with the edges of vault 'bowls', while Nos 10–11 have more severely abraded outer surfaces. While it is possible that the bevelled edges functioned as scrapers, the fragments which show these features are small and their position relative to skull sutures means that they would never have been parts of larger pieces that would have been easy to hold. The suggestion therefore seems implausible though no other specific function for these pieces, nor reasons for the evident extreme abrasion they show, can be suggested.

Discussion

Although single fragments of worked bone were found in Phase 1 and Phase 2 contexts, five came from Phase 3 contexts, five from Phase 4 contexts, and nine from later contexts. On this basis, and also on local parallels, an Iron Age date seems most likely for the worked bone. The possibility that some, or all are earlier in date cannot, however, be discounted.

At All Cannings Cross, Cunnington (1927) suggested that the presence of scattered skull fragments was material evidence for the 'head hunting' activities of the inhabitants; the finds from Billingborough could be interpreted in the same way. Four out of thirty-two skull fragments from All Cannings Cross also show signs of post mortem use; one roundel had been perforated near an edge, presumably for use as an amulet, and the other three fragments were worn, apparently from use as scrapers; these could be seen as parallels for Nos 8–9.

More recently Marsh and West (1981) have published a group of skulls from London whose deposition they suggest was non-funerary. They comment on the Celtic practice of 'head-hunting' (Marsh and West 1981, 95) and append a list of Iron Age sites which have produced skulls from non-funerary contexts. None of the material listed by Marsh and West (1981) is similar to the skull 'bowls' from Billingborough, though the perforated skull vault from Hunsbury, Northamptonshire and the similarly perforated fragment from Hillhead broch, Caithness (Parry 1982, 96) may have served similar 'ritual' functions. To these can be added a roundel of occipital, 67–70mm across, with a central perforation of about 10mm diameter from Glastonbury Lake Village (Bulleid and Gray 1917), and an irregular piece of a 'temporal bone, cut and shaped, with a hole through one corner' found at Lidbury Camp, Wiltshire (Cunnington 1917). Cunnington (1927) quotes other reports of worked bone, but on consulting the original references it is not usually clear whether the bone was thought to be human or animal.

Two relatively recent finds from the fen edge can usefully be added to this list of prehistoric worked human bone. There is a skull fragment from Earith, Cambridgeshire, which was both perforated and crudely cut like a comb along one edge (Bayley 1984b), and at Helpringham, Lincolnshire, there is evidence for the production of skull vault 'bowls' like those from Billingborough; an offcut of frontal similar to Nos 2–3 was found (Bayley 1979, Healey 1999).

It is clear that post mortem use of human skulls, or parts of them, was not uncommon in prehistoric Britain. However, functional rather than purely amuletic use seems less common, and to date only Billingborough has provided more than a single fragment of this type of evidence. It may represent a local tradition as Helpringham is less than 10km north of the site.

Chapter 4. Site Economy and Environment

I. Animal bone
by Mary Iles (1992/1999)

Introduction and methods
A total of 10,360 bones was recovered by hand from all phases at Billingborough (Table 10). These were the subject of a preliminary examination by Peter Hayes in 1986, and were studied fully in 1991 when they formed the subject of the writer's undergraduate dissertation at Southampton University (Iles 1992). This report is an edited version of that dissertation which is available in archive.

The animal bones were identified and recorded at the Faunal Remains Unit, Department of Archaeology, University of Southampton. All anatomical elements were recorded to species where possible; where this was not possible the fragments were assigned to either large mammal (cattle-horse size) or small mammal (sheep/goat or pig size) classes.

The following attributes for each identified bone were recorded: anatomy, symmetry, degree of fragmentation, part of the bone surviving, fusion data, the condition of the bone (*i.e.* gnawing and/or weathering), butchery, pathology, and burning.

Measurements were taken following von den Driesch (1976); the wear stages of the lower cheek teeth were recorded following Grant (1982) and epiphyseal fusion followed Getty (1975).

The Minimum Number of Individuals (MNI) was calculated by looking at the most numerous element derived from one side of the body for each species. The calculation was not made for species represented by less than 50 fragments.

Results: general introduction
Of the 10,360 bones, 4468 (43%) were identifiable to species. Although a programme of wet sieving was carried out on site during the excavation, the material recovered was not available for study at the time this report was written. This is likely to be a major reason for the virtual absence of small mammal, amphibian and fish remains, and may also have influenced the presence of smaller elements of the larger species.

Fragmentation
For virtually all phases and species 50% or more of the bone fragments were less than one-third complete (Fig. 42). The major exception to this is Phase 1 cattle, where a third of the bones were complete. However, the degree of fragmentation in an assemblage can have a bearing on the quantification of the group. The calculation of the MNI should reduce any bias introduced by differential fragmentation.

Taphonomy
One other important element that must be considered, is the effect of taphonomic factors such as gnawing and weathering. In Phase 1 *c.* 18% of the bones for cattle,

sheep/goat and horse are gnawed, but the figure is only 5% for pig bones. There is a similar situation in Phase 2 where 16% and 14% of the cattle and sheep/goat bones respectively are gnawed, but only 2% of the pig bones. The situation is slightly different for Phase 3 where almost 10% of the pig bone identified had been gnawed, but this is still less than for cattle and sheep/goat. In Phase 4 pig bone was also found to be less gnawed than other species. Furthermore, in all but Phase 3 pig bone had suffered less from weathering, perhaps indicating that the disposal of pig was somewhat different to that of cattle and sheep/goat.

The total percentage of weathered bone increases from 6% in Phase 1 to 17% in Phase 2, drops marginally to 15% in Phase 3, and rises again in Phase 4 to 18%. Increased weathering in Phases 2–4 may be due to a number of reasons. Changes in the methods of disposing of waste could have been one reason, but a major cause is likely to have been the redeposition of material; it is clear from the study of the pottery that this is an important factor that should be taken into account.

Major domesticates: results by phase

Phase 1

Species representation
Figure 43 shows the relative proportion of the main domestic species calculated using both MNI and NISP (Number of Identified Specimens). On both calculations cattle is the most numerous species, although the calculation of MNI does increase the relative proportion of both sheep and pig, perhaps reflecting the greater fragmentation of the larger cattle bones.

Ageing data
Epiphyseal fusion data for cattle suggests that over 90% of the population survived beyond 10 months of age, but only 50% lived beyond 2 years. Examination of the toothwear on both mandible and loose teeth (Grant 1982) suggests that some cattle survived well into maturity, though the majority did not survive beyond 2 years. This pattern suggests that the cattle were kept predominantly for meat rather than milk as a cull of younger animals would be expected in a dairying economy. A few older animals may have been kept for breeding or possibly for traction.

Epiphyseal fusion data indicate that 91% of sheep/goat survived beyond 10 months, but only 50% beyond 2 years and 25% beyond 2–3 years. Again, the evidence from toothwear extends this picture suggesting a few animals lived well past 3 years. As with cattle, this suggests an emphasis on meat, with perhaps some older animals kept for breeding and for their fleeces.

The small number of pig fragments from Phase 1 means that there are no reliable ageing data.

	Phase 1	% of major domesticates	Phase 2	% of major domesticates	Phase 3	% of major domesticates	Phase 4	% of major domesticates	Site total	% of major domesticates
Cattle	402	55	201	40	964	46	310	46	1877	47
Sheep/goat	232	32	205	41	757	36	279	41	1473	37
Pig	88	12	86	17	102	5	29	4	305	8
Horse	10	1	14	3	252	12	56	8	332	8
Red deer	4				7				11	
Roe deer	6		2		6				14	
Dog	5		41		292		10		348	
Cat					1				1	
Rodent	2		1						3	
Amphibian			3						3	
Bird			4		23		73		100	
Fish					1				1	
Large mammal nfi	454		199		1101		398		2152	
small mammal nfi	449		426		817		423		2115	
unidentified	375		199		764		287		1625	
Total major domesticates	*732*		*506*		*2075*		*674*		*3987*	
Total identified	749	37	557	40	2405	47	757	41	4468	43
Total unidentified	1278	63	824	60	2682	53	1108	59	5892	57
Total	**2027**		**1381**		**5087**		**1865**		**10360**	

nfi — not further identified

Table 10 Animal bone totals by phase

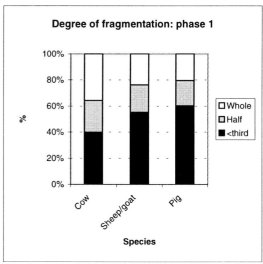

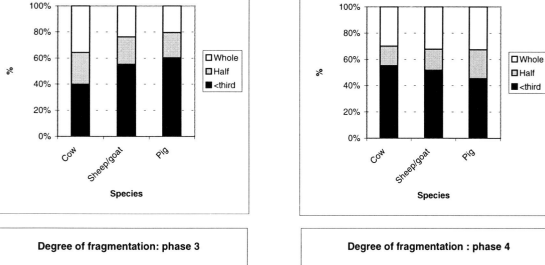

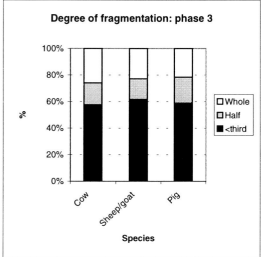

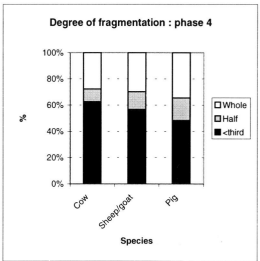

Figure 42 Animal bone: fragmentation by phase

Phase 2

Species representation
This phase yielded a smaller assemblage of animal bone
and the calculation of MNI alters the relative proportion
of species sharply (Fig. 43) suggesting that the pig
assemblage survived relatively intact whilst cattle and
sheep/goat were more prone to fragmentation.

Ageing data
The small number of bones recovered from Phase 2 means
that the ageing data are limited. It would appear that the
majority of the cattle survived past 18 months. Of the
sheep/goat group, epiphyseal fusion indicates that 90% of
the population survived beyond 10 months old, 43%
beyond 2–3 years, and 33% beyond 3 years. The toothwear
data show a preponderance of animals killed at 2 years.
There were very few pig bones which had epiphyseal
fusion data and only five mandibles were suitable for
ageing. From the data available it would be difficult to say
any more than pigs were being killed in their first, second
and third years. In Phase 2, as in Phase 1, it seems that
most of the animals were exploited for their meat.

Phase 3

Species representation
The relative proportion of species alters in Phase 3 with a
marked reduction in the number of pigs represented (Fig.
43) and an increase (by MNI) of the number of sheep/goat.

Ageing data
Epiphyseal fusion data indicates that 94% of cattle
survived beyond 10 months of age, but at around 2–2½
years approximately 50% of the animals were killed. The analysis of
toothwear reflects the picture shown by the epiphyseal fusion data. This
is a very similar pattern to that seen in earlier phases and indicates an
economy biased towards meat.

Epiphyseal fusion data indicates that only 76% of
sheep/goat lived beyond 10 months old. The mandible
data do not appear to conflict with the picture from the
epiphyseal fusion data and both show that there are two
peaks: one is for animals killed in the first year and the
second is for animals of approximately 2–3 years old. This
pattern differs from the earlier phases with fewer older
animals represented and perhaps suggests that the
emphasis was moving more towards meat and away from
fleece.

81

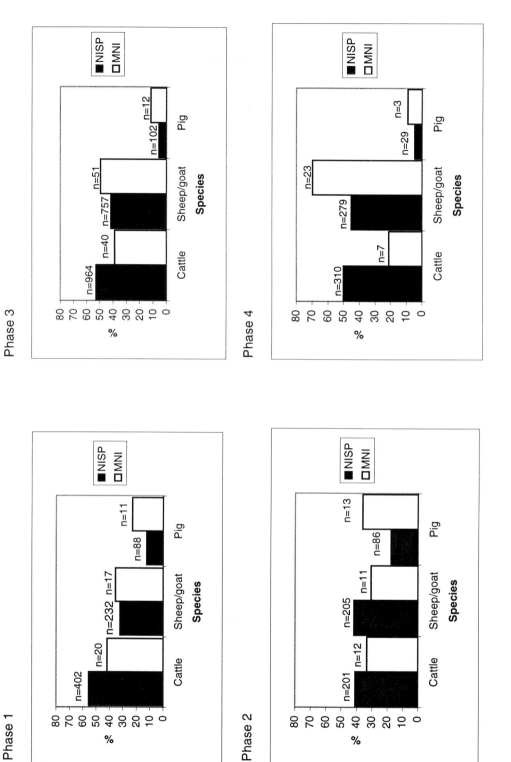

Figure 43 Animal bone:species by phase (NISP = no. of identified specimens; MNI = minimum no. of individuals)

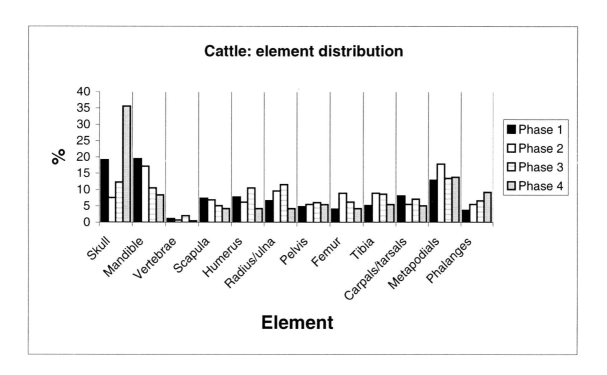

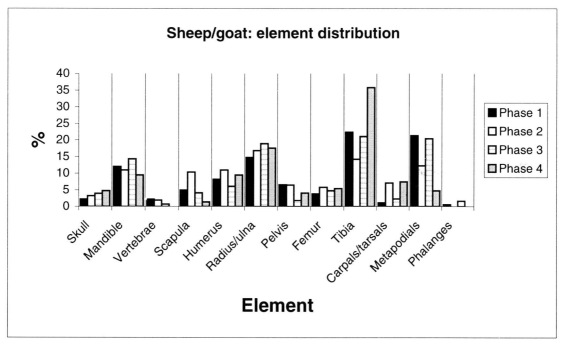

Figure 44 Animal bone: element representation for cattle and sheep/goat

The small amount of pig bone recovered means that there is insufficient data to give a detailed age profile for pig. However, although it is difficult to draw any firm conclusions it would seem that pigs tended to be killed in their second year.

Phase 4

Species representation

The number of bones recovered from Phase 4 is smaller than in Phase 3 (Fig. 43). The pattern seen in Phase 3 continues in Phase 4 with an increase in the relative proportion of sheep and with pig represented by very few fragments. It was decided to calculate the MNI for pig, despite the small number of bones, to enable comparison with other phases.

Ageing data

The small number of bones from this phase means that no assumptions can be made about the age at death of either cattle or pig. For sheep, it is only possible to suggest that some individuals were killed at around 2 years of age.

Element representation for cattle and sheep/goat

All parts of the carcass were represented for both species in all phases (Fig. 44). Some of the smaller sheep/goat elements, for example phalanges, were under-represented and this is probably due to the absence of sieved material. This pattern suggests that the animals were farmed and slaughtered locally, or at the least were imported on the hoof.

Element representation was not studied for other species as the number of fragments was considered too low.

Other species

Horse

Horse is present in all the phases, and tends to increase as a proportion of the assemblage through time. There were two articulated deposits of horse bone in Phase 3, both in the top of enclosure ditch *7710*. One comprised the metacarpal, first phalanx and second phalange; the other included the metacarpal and first phalange. Both were from the right hand side.

Red deer and roe deer

Red deer was identified in Phases 1 and 3, with four fragments from Phase 1 and seven from Phase 3. In these phases deer is represented by bone as well as antler. Roe deer was identified in Phases 1 (six fragments), 2 (two fragments) and 3 (six fragments). There is, in addition to this, a small quantity of worked antler (from red deer) including three possible 'picks' from unphased contexts.

Dog

Dog was present in differing proportions in all phases (Table 7). The number of dog bones in Phases 2 and 3 are distorted by the presence of a partial skeleton, and a near complete skeleton respectively.

The dog skeleton recovered from Phase 2 comprises the axial skeleton; both sides of the pelvis, the axis, cervical vertebrae, thoracic vertebrae, lumber vertebrae, caudal vertebrae, ribs and mandible are present. The absence of long bones may be the result of carnivores scavenging the skeleton. The dog skeleton in Phase 3 came from Enclosure 3 ditch *78135* and is almost complete with only the left hand side humerus, some of the carpal and tarsal bones, and some of the phalanges missing. There were faint cut marks on the top of the skull and on both tibiae, which would indicate that the animal was skinned. The absence of gnawing or weathering on any of the bones suggests that the carcass was rapidly buried.

Bird

There was no bird bone present in Phase 1 but 100 fragments were recovered from the other phases. All bird bone examined is from hand excavation as no material from sieving was available for study.

Only three bird bones were found in Phase 2. These include a scapula from *Anser sp* (Goose); this appears to be a small wild goose similar in size to *Anser brachyrhynchus* (Pink-footed goose), and was the only bird bone from Billingborough that showed evidence of butchery, in the form of a small cut mark. The other bones from Phase 2 are a furcula identified as *Anas sp.* (similar in size to Mallard) and a tibiotarsus unidentifiable to species.

Twenty-two bird bones were found in Phase 3. The largest group was the family *Gruidae* (Crane). Two bones were positively identified as *Corvus corax* (raven), and one other bone is either *C. corone* (crow) or *C. frugilegus* (rook). Two bones were identified as the family Anseriformes. A tibiotarsus has been identified as Anas sp (swan, goose or duck) and is similar in size to mallard, and an ulna has been identified as a small wild goose, similar in size to either *Anser brachyrhynchus* (pink-footed goose) or *Branta bernicla* (Brent goose). Only one bone from a bird of prey was recovered; this was identified as

Buteo sp. It is similar in size to either *Buteo buteo* (Buzzard) or *Buteo lagopus* (rough-legged buzzard).

The number of bird bones recovered from Phase 4 is inflated by the recovery of a complete chicken (*Gallus gallus*) skeleton. Other than the bones from this skeleton there was very little bird bone recovered in Phase 4, and all came from chicken.

Fish

The cleithrum from a haddock was the only fish bone in the assemblage, presumably because it was large enough to be picked up by hand during excavation. It is from the lowest fill (*78116*) of Enclosure ditch 3 (*78135*). It is possible that more fish bone is present in the sieved material, but this was unavailable for study.

Cat

One cat bone was recovered in Phase 3, which was considerably larger than the domestic comparative; this may indicate that the bone came from a wild specimen.

Fox

A fox ulna from Phase 4 had been trimmed to a point.

Butchery patterns

Little evidence of butchery techniques has survived on the bones (Fig. 45). In the earlier phases this may reflect the use of flint tools, although it is suggested that many of the flint tools may be of Neolithic or Early Bronze Age date and thus pre-date Phase 1. Flint leaves very fine cut marks on bone and without detailed microscopic analysis may not be observed. Very few bones had been chopped. A few horse bones bore evidence of butchery, one each from Phase 1 and 2, and eleven from Phase 3.

Discussion and conclusions

Phase 1

The ageing data indicate that cattle in Phase 1 were being killed at an older age than in subsequent phases but unlike the material from Grimes Graves, there is no evidence to suggest that the cattle at Billingborough were part of a dairy herd. Legge (1981) based his conclusion that the cattle at Grimes Graves were from a dairy herd on the high proportions of juvenile animals and adult females killed, suggesting that the adult females would have been those with low milk yield and those that had failed to establish lactation (Legge 1981, 88). Legge also suggests that the dairy economy at Grimes Graves was related to the low fertility and carrying capacity of some of the soils on the Breckland (Legge 1981, 89). By contrast, Billingborough has very few juvenile animals, even allowing for under-representation of bones from younger animals. It is possible that a principal use for cattle in Phase 1 was traction, but there is no evidence from pathology to suggest that this might have been the case. It is most likely, therefore, that cattle were not bred for one, but for a combination of purposes.

At least half of the sheep/goat flock was being killed at 18 months to 2 years. This would be the optimum age at which to kill them for their meat. The older animals indicated by epiphyseal fusion and tooth wear probably relate to those animals kept as breeding stock and those kept for their wool.

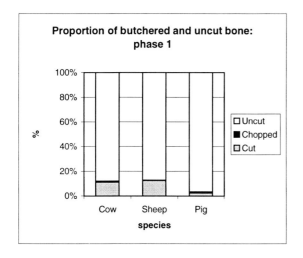

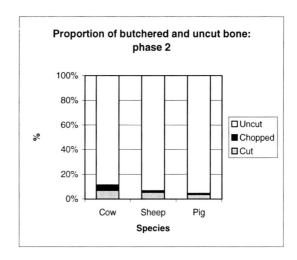

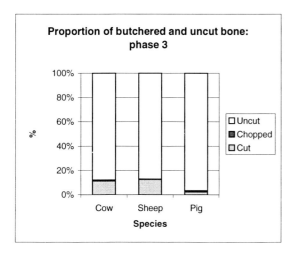

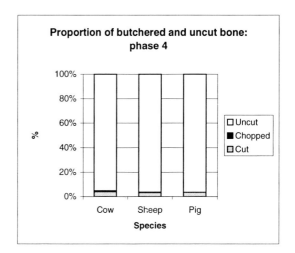

Figure 45 Animal bone: butchery by phase

The proportions of meat bearing animals in Phase 1 at Billingborough are also different to those at Grimes Graves. Cattle and sheep/goat probably represent very similar proportions of the economy at Billingborough, with pig represented by far fewer animals. At Grimes Graves cattle is the dominant species representing 46–63% of the sample, with pig much lower at 5–11%. Legge (1981, 90) has suggested that pig is not as necessary for its fat in a dairy economy and, therefore, would not have been an important part of the economy at Grimes Graves.

The vast majority of the Phase 1 animal bone assemblage came from the ditch of Enclosure 1, and this can also be compared to the assemblage from the three-sided Middle Bronze Age enclosure at Down Farm on the chalk of Cranborne Chase, Dorset. As at Billingborough, sheep/goat are under-represented at Down Farm (Legge 1991). The proportions of sheep/goat and cattle are probably very similar at Billingborough and Down Farm, but pig is uncommon at Down Farm, whatever method is used to calculate the proportions of species present. Approximately half of the sheep/goat at Down Farm were killed by 2 years indicating husbandry

directed towards a meat supply (Legge 1991, 83), as seems to have been the case at Billingborough.

Horse and deer form a very small part of the assemblage from Billingborough, and therefore probably did not contribute much to the meat supply.

Phase 2

Following a period of marine transgression in the first half of the 1st millennium BC one of the principal activities on the site became the production of salt. A relatively small number of bones came from Phase 2 and it is possible, given the absence of evidence for domestic activity in this phase, that much of the material is residual from Phase 1. Cattle and sheep/goat seem to represent similar proportions of the assemblage as in Phase 1, but the differences in preservation between cattle and sheep/goat may mean that sheep/goat are under-represented and were the dominant species present. The salt marsh, which existed to the east of Billingborough at this time, would have been very suitable for the grazing of sheep/goat.

Cattle in Phase 2 were possibly being killed at a younger age than in Phase 1, but again there is no evidence for the deliberate culling of juveniles. The fusion data seem to indicate that about two thirds of the herd were being killed at around 18 months to 2 years which would seem to indicate that their principal use was the production of meat. The majority of sheep/goat seem to have been killed in their second year, again indicating meat production. The proportion of pig in Phase 2 is higher than in Phase 1, and this species began to form a more significant part of the economy in Phase 2. The ageing for pig indicates that they were being killed between their first and second years.

Overall, the evidence suggests that in Phase 2 animals were raised primarily for the production of meat. This may have been salted and perhaps traded with other settlements in the region.

Phase 3

The Phase 2 saltern activity was replaced, perhaps after a lengthy hiatus, in the second half of the 1st millennium BC by a settlement comprising at least two enclosures belonging to a more extensive system of fields and enclosures. The proportions of cattle and sheep/goat present are very similar in Phase 3 to the earlier phases, with sheep/goat the dominant species after calculation of MNI. However, cattle are dominant on fragment counts, probably because of differential preservation. Pig is much less important in this phase. Horse, as in the previous phases, still represents less than 5% of the assemblage.

Ageing data seem to indicate that half of the cattle present were killed at around 2 years of age, with the remainder surviving to well over 4 years of age. The animal husbandry of cattle in Phase 3 seems to be very similar to that of Phase 1, although there is a greater emphasis on the production of meat. It is probable, therefore, that cattle were being used for a number of purposes. This may suggest that traction was also important in Phase 3, as it appears to have been in Phase 1. The ageing data for sheep/goat show a different pattern to that in Phase 1, with fewer of the sheep living beyond 10 months (76% as compared with 90%) suggesting an increase in the slaughter of lambs for meat.

Phase 4

As in the earlier phases, cattle is best represented by the fragment count, but the MNI puts sheep/goat at 70%, representing a much larger proportion of the assemblage than cattle at 21%. No sexing data was available, but the ageing data for cattle indicates that at least some individuals in the herd survived beyond 4 years of age. There is not the high proportion of juveniles that might indicate dairying, but it is possible that the killing of juvenile animals could have taken place outside the area of the excavation.

The available ageing data for sheep/goat in Phase 4 indicates that the majority were killed in their second year, possibly for meat.

Horse fragments become relatively more numerous in this phase and this may reflect its use for transport.

Deer, having more or less constantly declined in importance from Phase 1, is not present at all in Phase 4. Deer does not represent a significant proportion of the assemblage in any of the phases and like the other wild species appears not to have contributed much to the economy at any time.

Conclusion

Much of importance has been learned from this study about the animal economy of Billingborough which remains, despite being excavated more than 20 years ago, the most extensively excavated site of its type on the fen edge in Lincolnshire. The site at Billingborough highlights the changing use of the landscape through time and how the animal economy reflects these changes.

In Phase 1, during the Middle Bronze Age, Billingborough was a dryland site located to use all the available agricultural resources that surrounded it. This is emphasised by the mixed nature of the animal husbandry in this phase. With the deterioration of the climate, and subsequent marine transgression in the Late Bronze Age, the site was abandoned.

There followed in Phase 2, during the Late Bronze Age/Early Iron Age, a period of salt working. If any animal husbandry was taking place in the vicinity at this time it was oriented to meat production, some of which may have been salted and subsequently traded, although it is not possible to prove such an interpretation archaeologically.

As the site dried out during the Iron Age, in Phase 3, settlement was re-established and an extensive system of enclosures and fields laid out. With this change in the type of occupation animal husbandry returned to a mixed approach similar to that seen in Phase 1.

The nature of the occupation may have changed again in Phase 4, and the increase in sheep and horse in this final phase may reflect a less extensive system of fields and perhaps paddocks. The predominance of sheep in Phase 4 is indicative of a 'native' Romano-British site, with the more Romanised towns and villas showing an increased reliance on cattle and pig. King (1978) argues that this change in the Romanised centres reflects the diffusion of Mediterranean cultural tastes. Halstead (1985) suggests that the change in proportion at Romanised sites is due to the more general process of economic intensification in response to the development of urban markets. It would appear that at Billingborough no such intensification took place and that changes in the species exploited probably owes more to local landscape changes than to the impact of the Roman invasion.

II. Molluscs
by C.A.I. French (1978, revised 1988)

Introduction

One series of five contiguous samples was taken from ditch *7710*, the ditch on the north side of Enclosure 1 assigned to Phase 1 (Middle–Late Bronze Age). The sample column was overlain by the fill of a medieval plough furrow (0.23m deep) and topsoil (0.32m deep). The samples were analysed for snails), and the results presented in the form of a relative histogram (Fig. 46).

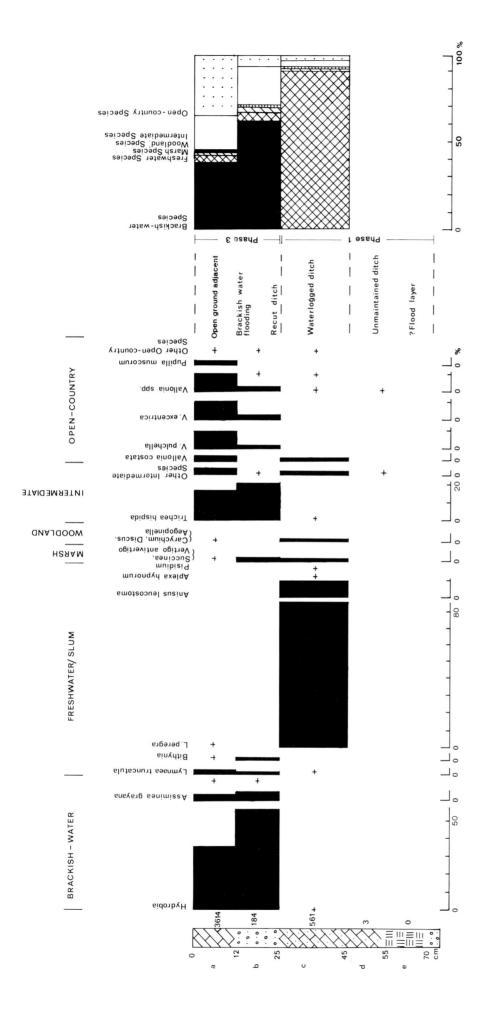

Figure 46 Mollusc sequence in Enclosure 1 ditch 7710

The profile

(see Fig. 5)

Depth (cm)	Layer
0–12	a) Sandy clay loam which is the fill of a later recut of ditch *7710*. 10YR3/3
12–25	b) Loam containing many pebbles and much animal bone which forms the basal fill of the recut of ditch *7710*. 10YR3/3
25–45	c) Silty clay with pebbles. Some weathering of the ditch sides was observed at this level. 10YR3/1
45–55	d) Silty clay with pebbles. 10YR3/1
55–70	e) Clay. 5YR4/1
70+	Gravels

The primary fill (0.55–0.70m) consisted of a dark grey clay (layer *7710e*). However, the layer was devoid of molluscs. The secondary fill (0.25–0.50m) was composed of silty clay with scattered gravel pebbles (layers *7710c* and *7710d*).

The partially infilled ditch was probably subject to standing freshwater conditions and the upper part of the secondary fill then disturbed by an Iron Age (Phase 3) recut (0–0.25m) following approximately the same line as ditch *7710* (layers *7710* and *7710b*). No Phase 2 deposits were present or survived in the section of the ditch sampled.

The basal fill of the Phase 3 recut (0.12–0.25m) contained large quantities of animal bone and medium-sized gravel pebbles, which suggests the recut may have been subject to deliberate back-filling. The upper fill of the recut (0–0.12m) consists of a sandy clay loam. Both these layers are dominated by brackish-water molluscs, which suggest the influence of some kind of seawater 'incursion' in the infilling of ditch recut *7710*, although some of the molluscs may have derived from the backfilled material which possibly incorporated some debris from the Phase 2 salt-working activity.

Results and interpretation

Four major ecological groups of molluscs were found in this series of samples, and these can be equated with fluctuating fresh and brackish-water regimes:

1) Brackish-water snails, such as *Hydrobia ulvae*, *H. ventrosa* and *Assiminea grayana*.

2) Tolerant and freshwater slum snails. There are several species belonging to this group, which are able to withstand fluctuating and poor water conditions in small habitat loci. Species such as *Lymnaea peregra*, *L. truncatula* and *Anisus leucostoma* are the most commonly occurring examples here.

3) Marsh dwellers. There is a very small group of these occurring in very low abundance — *Succinea* and *Vertigo antivertigo*.

4) Terrestrial species, dominated by the intermediate species *Trichia hispida* and a substantial group of open-country species including all three species of *Vallonia* and *Pupilla muscorum*.

The clay primary fill (0.55–0.70m) of ditch *7710* may represent a period of abandonment caused by freshwater flooding, but neither the clay nor the lower secondary fill (0.45–0.55m) provided an environment conducive to the preservation of snails. However, the upper secondary fill (0.25–0.45m) apparently became subject to freshwater waterlogging conditions, and at this time the partly infilled ditch supported more than 90% freshwater/slum species. These suggest variable slowly-flowing to almost stagnant water conditions with an unkempt weedy vegetation of the ditch sides.

The ditch was subsequently recut (0–0.25m) in Phase 3 (Middle–Late Iron Age), and this is reflected by the almost complete break and change in the character of the snails present (Fig. 46), and the substantial lowering of the molluscan abundance which suggests severe disturbance of the habitat. Following the re-cutting of the ditch, it apparently became subject to the influence of brackish water as opposed to fresh water. This is reflected by the dominance of brackish-water dwelling snail species (62% at 0.12–0.25m) (38% at 0–0.12m). Although the terrestrial species also form a substantial component of the assemblage of the recut (31% and 58% respectively), they were probably not living in the ditch. Rather, they have probably been 'collected' from the adjacent area in the brackish water and deposited in the ditch. Nevertheless they are judged to be indicative of open-country conditions in the immediate vicinity of the site.

Discussion

It is clear that the Billingborough site on the edge of the silt fens was subjected to fluctuating fresh and brackish-water regimes. The site was apparently wetter than at Fengate (Cambridgeshire) and subject to much more direct influence of brackish, originally sea-water (French 1980; French 1984). Certainly, the Billingborough Fen is sited on lower ground at 1.6m OD as compared to *c*.4.2m OD at Fengate.

The brackish-water conditions reflected by the snail assemblage in the ditch, and the silt which overlay much of the northern part of the site suggest the influence of some form of marine incursion in the 1st millennium BC. It is impossible to be sure whether a single event or repeated influxes of brackish water are represented. Nevertheless, its effects would have been severe enough to cause considerable disruption to any occupation, if not abandonment, of the Billingborough site. Possible reasons for the inundation range from a generally deteriorating climate in the first half of the 1st millennium BC (Godwin 1966; Piggott 1972) to a rising sea level (Jelgersma 1966; Willis 1961). The silt fen margin area was certainly subject to the influence of salt water in Iron Age and Romano-British times as evidenced by the numerous saltern sites found just to the east of the site, as well as the debris of earlier, Late Bronze Age/Early Iron Age salt making found at Billingborough itself. Also, the deposition of estuarine clay, marine silts and salt-marsh clays resulting from a marine incursion occurring somewhere between *c*.1300 and 300 BC has been suggested (Churchill 1970; Godwin and Vishnu-Mittre 1975) and may have had a bearing on the sequence of activity at Billingborough. The formation of tidal marsh is reflected at Billingborough by the Phase 2 salt-working activity. Thus, it is possible that by the later 1st millennium the area in the vicinity and to the east of the Billingborough site looked something like the present Lincolnshire coast-line around the Wash with tidal marsh, meandering fresh and brackish-water streams, broken silt fen and flat open ground.

Chapter 5. Discussion

by Rosamund M.J. Cleal, A.P. Fitzpatrick and Phil Andrews

I. Pre–Mid 2nd Millennium BC

Although some Neolithic activity might be expected in the Billingborough area, there is only the evidence of a single Peterborough Ware sherd (Fig. 20: 1) to attest activity in this period. It is possible that a very small minority of the struck flint is of Neolithic date, but there are no diagnostic pieces to confirm this.

This single occurrence of a Mortlake or Ebbsfleet Ware sherd is not unusual, as Peterborough Ware often occurs as stray finds (Cleal 1985). The dating of Mortlake Ware is uncertain, but is likely to lie within the late 4th to early 3rd millennium BC. Some intermittent and small scale use at this time of the area would not be inconsistent with the dry land conditions which existed prior to the marine transgressions of the mid 2nd millennium BC, and the results from the Fenland Project (Hayes and Lane 1992, 205) go some way to confirming this although only sparse scatters of worked flint were found.

There is more evidence for use of the site during the Early Bronze Age period than in the Neolithic, but it consists only of stray finds, mainly redeposited. A single feature, grave *78183*, which contained a severely disturbed inhumation, may belong to this period. The feature contained a single sherd of Phase 1 (Middle Bronze Age) pottery, but the grave was so disturbed and shallow that it seems highly likely that the pottery is intrusive. The grave alone would not be convincing enough evidence for activity in the Early Bronze Age were it not for the presence of other stray finds of this date on the site. The barbed and tanged arrowhead (Fig. 16: 11), one of four from the site, the axe-hammer fragment (Fig. 19: 3), the fragment of jet spacer bead (Fig. 18: 1) and the small number of sherds of Food Vessel (Fig. 20: 3) and possibly Collared Urn (Fig 20: 2) are all likely to be Early Bronze Age. Much of the worked flint is also likely to be of this date. The blade illustrated in Fig. 13: 10 may also be of Early rather than Middle Bronze Age date, although it is so badly damaged that its form is uncertain. Of the Early Bronze Age finds only the blade was recovered from close to the grave, but if the grave was disturbed during the Phase 1 occupation of the site any artefacts might well have become widely dispersed. It seems unlikely, however, that all the Early Bronze Age finds were originally in one grave, and it would seem that some other transient activity or activities took place at the site during this period.

Other finds of probable Early Bronze Age date from the parish of Billingborough include a perforated mace head recovered approximately 300m to the east of the site and an unprovenanced stone hammer head (Trust for Lincolnshire Archaeology Sites and Monuments Record). It may also be relevant to note that there is a concentration of at least seven probable round barrows at Hoe Hills, Dowsby, less than 4km to the south of the site at Billingborough (May 1976, 72). Although unexcavated, a Late Neolithic–Early Bronze Age date is considered likely for this group of monuments (Hayes and Lane 1992, 206, fig. 122).

II. Phase 1: Middle–Late Bronze Age (Mid to Late 2nd Millennium BC)
(Fig. 47)

It is not possible to be specific about either the absolute date of the inception of the first enclosure (Enclosure 1) at Billingborough, or its duration of use. However, a span of possibly 500 years or more is indicated by two radiocarbon dates from the lower and upper fills of the enclosure ditch which gave dates of 1530–1260 cal BC (BM-1410, 3148 ± 57 BP) and 800–370 cal BC (HAR-2523, 2410 ± 80 BP) respectively. On the grounds of the pottery it would also seem reasonable to place the beginnings of the Phase 1 settlement in the second half of the 2nd millennium BC, while the appearance of some angled vessel forms in the upper ditch filling of the Enclosure 1 ditch hints at the enclosure having continued in use into the later stages of the Bronze Age, perhaps around the turn of the millennium or in the very early 1st millennium BC. The occurrence of these forms in the upper ditch filling also suggest that in its later stages at least the enclosure ditch was not regularly cleaned out, and that settlement continued within the area enclosed by the ditch, although that was largely silted up. This hint that the nature of the enclosure may have changed during its life cannot be pursued because of the paucity of material from the Enclosure 1 ditch. There is little ceramic material from the lower ditch fillings, even on the eastern side which was the most prolific generally, and the upper fillings were removed by later disturbance on the northern and western sides. It is also unfortunate that the only molluscan section studied was in the northern ditch, in which the Phase 1 filling was truncated by the Iron Age recut. Even if this information had been available, however, and it had proved possible to identify some change through time in the eastern ditch, it is likely that it would not have been possible to link this to internal features, and the nature of settlement within the enclosure would have remained largely obscure.

The Phase 1 settlement has therefore, to be largely regarded as a single-phase phenomenon, with the proviso that there may have been changes within the enclosure concomitant with the minor changes in the ceramics in the upper ditch filling, which it is simply impossible to recognise. With this allowance made, it is possible to draw some conclusions about the nature of the settlement, with some confidence.

The environment during Phase 1
Although there is no environmental evidence from Billingborough at this stage, as the lower filling of the Enclosure 1 ditch did not produce any molluscan evidence, some information about the contemporary environment in the area may be extrapolated from the sections exposed during dyke survey in Horbling and

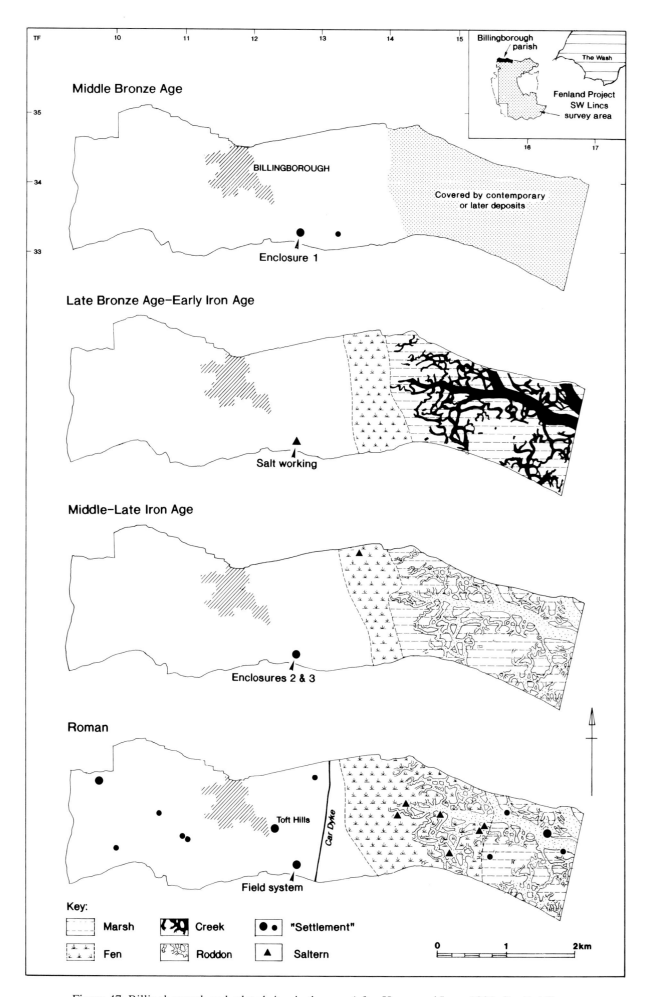

Figure 47 Billingborough and related sites in the area (after Hayes and Lane 1992, figs 7–10)

Hacconby Fens (Chowne 1980, 295–6). At Horbling Fen, some 2km to the north-east of Billingborough, the sequence showed a thick layer of till with a weathered upper surface containing pockets of charcoal, overlain by a band of peat which produced a radiocarbon date of 1430–1030 cal BC (HAR-1749, 3010 ± 70 BP). This may indicate climatic deterioration late in the 2nd millennium cal BC (Chowne 1980, 295), with freshwater flooding causing peat to form on the fen edge. The exact conditions in the immediate vicinity of Billingborough during the life of the Phase 1 settlement remain uncertain, but it would seem that the site lay on dry land a kilometre or so to the east of the fen edge. Hayes (1985, 245–61) has suggested that the freshwater flooding led to the development of a fen wood or alder carr environment.

The nature of the settlement
As a result of the post-Bronze Age activity in the area, and, in particular, the extensive damage caused by the medieval plough furrows, it is not possible to draw many conclusions about the internal organisation of the settlement. With the exception of the possible fence line and the four-post structures it is virtually impossible to identify with confidence any larger structures. That such structures existed, however, is strongly suggested by the number of surviving post-holes, many of which contain only Phase 1 pottery and may therefore be assigned with some confidence to this phase (see Fig. 4). Enclosures of this date, with internal sub-divisions and structures, are known from other parts of the country, and indeed there are also close parallels for the three-sided ditch. The well-known Deverel-Rimbury associated enclosures of Wessex include several examples in which the ditches do not form a complete circuit, such as those at Ogbourne Maizey Down, Wiltshire (Piggott 1942), and Angle Ditch, Dorset (Pitt Rivers 1898). One excavated example, at Down Farm (Barrett et al. 1991, figs 5.27, 5.28) shows a form strikingly similar to that of Billingborough. At Down Farm a fence line enclosed the settlement area within the ditch. The size of these enclosures varies considerably, from, for instance, approximately 0.1 hectares at Down Farm, including the area enclosed by the fence at that site, to 0.81 hectares at Martin Down, which is larger than the majority of these enclosures (Barrett et al. 1991, 219). At Billingborough the area enclosed by the ditch, if a straight line is drawn between its terminals, is approximately 0.23 hectares. It has been suggested above that the distribution of post-holes might indicate the existence of some form of barrier, possibly a hedge, between the two ditch terminals. No evidence for a barrier was found during the excavation, but aerial photographs show a fairly clear 'boundary feature' on the fourth (south) side of the enclosure (see Fig. 2), perhaps supporting the suggestion that a bank or hedge rather than a ditch may have defined this boundary.

Comparison with these other enclosures would suggest the likelihood of two or three roundhouses or similar structures having been present, and this is not unlikely considering the number of post-holes likely to belong to this phase. However, as noted above, later damage to the site caused by ridge-and-furrow cultivation has made the recognition of any such structures impossible. The occurrence of daub in unphased post-holes can only suggest that some buildings probably did exist. Similarly, the disturbance to and recutting of the enclosure ditch along the north and west sides in Phase 3

has removed the majority of material likely to have been contemporary with the later Phase 1 use of the enclosure or the area formerly occupied by it. It is not possible, therefore, to consider spatial variation in the ditch filling, except for the lower layers. However, in these, there is a marked concentration of material in the eastern length of ditch. As a crude measure of this the mean sherd weight per metre length of ditch excavated may be considered. In the western ditch layer 78164 produced only 28g of pottery per metre; in the northern ditch, layers 7710c and 7710d produced 16g per metre; but in the eastern length the mean in layers 7743 e, f, g, h, j, and k is 335g per metre. This is obviously only a crude measure, as it takes no account of the irregular form of the ditch, but it can be seen from the illustrated sections (Fig. 5) that the lower layers were not markedly deeper in the eastern arm than in the northern and western arms. Even if the lower fillings were to be slightly deeper in the eastern ditch, this would seem unlikely to account for the whole of the variation. Nor would it account for the occurrence of at least one largely reconstructable vessel from the primary filling (Fig. 23: 40), from layer 7743h. The occurrence of complete pots placed in ditches is a recurrent feature on other sites of this date (Barrett et al. 1991, 200)

Although it has proved impossible to recognise house structures, six four-post structures have been identified with some confidence. The surviving four-post structures all lie in the eastern half of the enclosure, and it is possible that this is a reflection of the original layout of the settlement with any roundhouses lying in the western half. In particular there appears to be a line of four-post structures running parallel to the eastern arm of the ditch and located approximately 6m back from it. The gap between structures and ditch would seem likely to reflect the former presence of an internal bank, the presence of which is also hinted at by the disposition and nature of some of the ditch fillings (e.g. layer 78147). This type of peripheral location for four-posters is not unusual, and can be paralleled both on Bronze Age and later sites. Four-post structures are normally interpreted as granaries, although other functions such as excarnation towers have been suggested (e.g. Ellison and Drewett 1971, 183–94). No carbonised plant remains are recorded from any of the post-holes at Billingborough, and thus there is no archaeobotanical evidence which might support their interpretation as granaries on this site.

Other hints of internal spatial organisation are given by the line of post-holes running across the centre of the site which has been interpreted as a fence line. This does not align with the putative line of the fourth (south) side of Enclosure 1 and may not, therefore, have been contemporary. However, similar features have been recorded within Bronze Age enclosures elsewhere. For example, an enclosure within a Late Bronze Age settlement at Lofts Farm, Essex contained a row of nine post-holes, 16.5m long, which ran east–west across the site and may have continued into an unexcavated area. It was suggested that these post-holes supported a screen which may have divided the enclosure in two (Brown 1988, 260, fig. 4; 8). The circular Late Bronze Age enclosure at Mucking, North Ring, also in Essex, had a row of 18 post-holes some 15m long running north–south which has been interpreted as a fence (Bond 1988, 13, fig. 3, feature 1739). As at Billingborough the size and depth of the post-holes varied and some had been recut. At North

Ring another fence and a gully, both running east–west, were interpreted as belonging to a later phase, but they could have been contemporary and formed a cruciform division of the enclosure (*cf* Parker-Pearson 1990; Parker-Pearson 1996). Although the suggested alignment at Billingborough is neither proven nor dated, the similarities with these examples suggest that it may represent a fence or facade which served to structure space and activity within the Bronze Age enclosure.

In view of the difficulties encountered in identifying the structural elements of some Bronze Age settlements, even where there has been little or no later damage, such as at Thorny Down, Wiltshire (Stone 1941; Ellison 1987) it is perhaps not surprising that so little can be reconstructed at Billingborough. But even with relatively few structures identifiable, it is possible to reach some conclusions about the nature and range of activities carried out at the Phase 1 settlement.

There appears to be no doubt that Enclosure 1 was used for settlement; the quantity of finds, particularly the pottery, animal bone, worked bone and antler, and loomweights attributed to Phase 1 provide strong evidence for this although no house structures were identified. A mixed economy is indicated by several factors, in particular the animal bone. Analysis of the animal bone indicates that cattle were being used principally for meat and traction, with sheep/goats and to a lesser extent pigs being raised for meat. The number of loomweights (but no surviving spindle-whorls) would suggest that at least some sheep were being kept for their wool, and the presence of certain worked bone objects such as points and pins would indicate that some leather working took place on the site. Wild species, principally deer, formed only a very small part of the assemblage, as they did in all phases. Evidence for cereal production is circumstantial, as no samples were taken for botanical remains, and is dependent on the interpretation of the four-post structures as granaries and the identification of some of the larger pottery vessels as storage jars for grain. If the vessels with cut surfaces are correctly associated with salt production it may be that salt was produced nearby. The cut grog-tempered vessels present in some Phase 1 contexts (*e.g.* Fig. 28: 51–54) may represent an early form of briquetage container and thus evidence for the development of salt making in the Middle Bronze Age, but the dating available is not precise enough to be certain of this.

Billingborough, as a dryland site, would have been able to utilise all the agricultural and pastoral resources that surrounded it, whereas contemporary but more marginal sites on the fen edge such as at Fengate, near Peterborough (Pryor 1980) may have had an economy based more on pastoralism, with cattle being raised principally for milk for dairy produce. At present, Billingborough represents the only Middle Bronze Age site excavated in the area although a second site approximately 500m to the east is recorded with similar pottery on the surface (Hayes and Lane 1992, 17, fig. 7), and several other pottery scatters are recorded along the fen edge to the south (Hayes and Lane 1992, fig. 123).

III. Phase 2: Late Bronze Age–Early Iron Age (Early–Mid 1st Millennium BC)
(Fig. 47)

During the early 1st millennium BC widespread marine inundation occurred following a period of freshwater flooding along the fen edge. This would have caused widespread disruption if not abandonment of sites and this may also have been true for the settlement at Billingborough. The flood deposit present along the northern edge of the site was almost certainly a result of this marine transgression, but the nature and chronology of the disruption to the settlement is less clear. Enclosure 1 was abandoned and was succeeded, possibly after a hiatus of several centuries by a phase of salt-working activity. A radiocarbon date of 840–390 cal BC (HAR-3101, 2500±100 BP) from pit *78256* containing some briquetage makes Billingborough one of the earliest salt-making sites known in the country. Two similar dates were obtained from features which appear to have been broadly contemporary: a date of 780–370 cal BC (HAR-2483, 2390±70 BP) from post-hole *7898*; and one of 800–370 cal BC (HAR-2523, 2410±80 BP) from the upper fill of Enclosure 1 ditch *7743* which also contained a considerable quantity of briquetage.

Despite the relatively large quantities of briquetage recovered, the *in situ* evidence for salt production was comparatively slight — though perhaps not unexpected given the damage caused by medieval ploughing. Two or three hearths (*7511*, *7512* and *7736*) presumably used for boiling provide the most tangible evidence, with gullies *77102*, *78174* and *78175* perhaps representing the vestigial traces of structures, possibly temporary shelters or windbreaks. The location of the hearths (and two other, unphased examples, *7816* and *7817* which may have been associated with this activity) along the northern edge of the site may not have been fortuitous as they may have lain close to an inland part of a tidal creek, suggested by the flood deposit to the north, where the salt water or muds could most easily have been controlled and extracted. The Billingborough Lode, *c.* 100m to the south of the site, may be a canalised version of an early creek which may also have provided a source of saline water and mud. The available evidence suggests that in the Iron Age salt production would have been a three-stage process. Initially, the water was left to evaporate naturally in basins, then the highly saline water heated in vessels until the salt crystallised, and finally the salt was rinsed in freshwater and the drying process repeated. Peat and wood for fuel would have been readily available locally at Billingborough, as would clay for manufacturing briquetage containers and the range of associated props, bars and so on that were required.

It has been remarked (Hayes and Lane 1992, 20) that the (Phase 2) shell-tempered briquetage from Billingborough resembles that associated with Middle Iron Age (450–100 BC) pottery further to the south at Bourne, but this need not be surprising for, as shown at Billingborough and elsewhere, there seems generally to have been little change in the range of briquetage in the fenland area throughout the Iron Age, and the change in principal inclusion type, from shell to chopped vegetation, sand and/or silt appears to have taken place in the Roman period (Hayes and Lane 1992, 219–21). It seems unlikely, however, that salt making continued on the site into the Middle Iron Age.

It is unclear whether the salt-making activity at Billingborough represented a seasonal activity. The archaeological features do not suggest that there was permanent occupation on the site at this time, but settlement may have lain close-by, perhaps on the higher ground to the west around the present village of Billingborough. The Fenland Project has revealed no evidence for this, although the existence of settlement was not always reflected in the presence of pottery on the surface (Hayes and Lane 1992, 20).

It has proved difficult due to problems of residuality and later disturbance to clearly establish which finds derived from Phase 2. However, the animal bone assemblage from contexts assigned to this phase suggests that the main emphasis of animal husbandry at this time was towards raising cattle, sheep and pigs for meat. The development of the salt marsh to the east would have provided ideal grazing for sheep in particular. It might be concluded from this that meat from these animals was being salted on or near the site for consumption locally, and perhaps also for trade with other communities along with salt itself. Little can be suggested concerning any arable cultivation except that the damper, brackish conditions would have restricted the range of crops that could have been grown.

The site excavated at Billingborough remains the earliest salt-making site in the area, though possibly contemporary sites have subsequently been recognised at Tetney and near Bourne (Palmer-Brown 1993), and what may have been a slightly later, Middle Iron Age site was found during the Fenland Project approximately 1.5km to the north-east of Billingborough close to the edge of the marsh (Hayes and Lane 1992, 20, fig. 9). No later Iron Age or Roman salterns were located near Billingborough, and these seem generally to have been concentrated further to the south, especially around Bourne, along the edge of the salt marsh which in this area had become more stable by the later 1st millennium BC (Hayes and Lane 1992, 210, figs 125 and 126). To the north, around Billingborough, tidal marshes continued to deposit sediments, and it has been suggested that the general absence of later salterns in this area might have been due to the formation of peat having been slower in this more gently sloping area (Hayes and Lane 1992, 209), and thus there may have been a dearth of fuel for boiling the salt water.

IV. Phase 3: Middle–Late Iron Age (Later 1st Millennium BC)
(Fig. 47)

The landscape
The salt-working activity of Phase 2 was succeeded, probably a century or more later, by the establishment of a new series of enclosures (Enclosures 2 and 3). The evidence from the aerial photographs shows that they belong to a wider pattern of enclosures and field systems, suggesting the increasing drainage and physical organisation of the fen edge. The limited palaeo-environmental evidence from the recut of Enclosure 1 ditch *7710* suggests, however, that at least one seawater 'incursion' occurred during this phase, and it seems likely that a narrow band of fenland, perhaps only 2km wide, is likely to have separated the site from tidal

salt marshes to the east. The dating evidence suggests that the reoccupation of the fen edge at Billingborough may have been as early as the 3rd century BC, with the enclosures passing out of use by the second half of the 1st century BC. The layout of Enclosures 2 and 3 suggests that they were broadly contemporary, but in the absence of any stratigraphic links and more refined dating of the finds this cannot be proven.

The extensive cropmark evidence in the area (see Fig. 2) shows Enclosures 2 and 3 to lie towards the east end of a line of enclosures, approximately 1km in length, aligned east–west and apparently based on a linear ditch (perhaps bounding a droveway). These enclosures are also considered likely to be of Iron Age rather than Romano-British date and extend, on the evidence of air-photographs, from the slightly higher ground to the west of Billingborough village down towards the fen edge in the east, with Enclosure 3 appearing to lie at the extremity of this system. A system of enclosures apparently based on a linear east–west ditch is also recorded approximately a kilometre to the north of Billingborough (Hayes and Lane 1992, 20). This suggests the sustained drainage, and perhaps recolonisation, of the fen edge.

The enclosures
The relative sequence of the two enclosures could not be established with certainty but Enclosure 2 may just pre-date Enclosure 3. It is uncertain whether both had similar purposes. Only a single post-hole within Enclosure 2 could certainly be assigned an Iron Age date, but it remains possible that some of the undated post-holes in this area which have been ascribed to Phase 1 did belong to Iron Age structures for which no building plans can be recognised due to plough damage. Certainly, more post-holes are found within 3m of the Phase 1 enclosure ditch, an area perhaps occupied by an accompanying internal bank, than elsewhere on the site. (It is also interesting to note that the cropmark evidence (see Fig. 2) shows some linear features within and possibly contemporary with Enclosure 2 which were not apparent during the excavation). However, several features did survive within the small area of Enclosure 3 exposed, and the possibility that the apparent lack of features within Enclosure 2 is a real one cannot be discounted. With the exception of the number of finds from the upper fill (*784*) of the Phase 1 enclosure ditch (*78145*) where it was incorporated within Enclosure 2, few finds were recovered from Enclosure 2. The finds from layer *784* could be accounted for by the deliberate infilling of the depression using occupation debris deriving from Enclosure 3. The profile of ditch *78113* of Enclosure 3 suggests that it was cleaned out at least once (see Fig. 10).

Despite the lack of features and finds, which could suggest that Enclosure 2 was not for settlement but instead for stock or other uses, a number of features around the entrance find parallels on settlement sites. Although the stratigraphical relationship of the three gullies (all numbered *78233*) near the entrance of Enclosure 2 could not be established, related ditches or trenches have been found near the entrances at a number of later Iron Age enclosures in Northamptonshire. At these sites the ditches were generally much larger, up to 4m wide and over 2.4m deep, and the trenches lay behind the rampart or bank. They are suggested to have supported timber revetments around the end of the bank (Dix and Jackson 1989). At Billingborough, however, the shallow central gully appears to block the entrance.

Although enclosures with these entrance arrangements were considered to be restricted to Northamptonshire by Dix and Jackson (1989), another example, and one which is very similar to Billingborough in that the trenches lie between the ditch and any bank, is known at Weelsby Avenue, Grimsby, South Humberside (Sills and Kingsley 1990; J. Sills pers. comm.). At Weelsby Avenue, and also at Weekley enclosure C (Dix and Jackson 1989, 163), the gate is between the ditch ends and so forward of the rampart. If post-hole *78263* belonged to a gateway at Billingborough then it could suggest that the gate also stood in advance of any bank.

Weelsby Avenue and Weekley enclosure C are both settlements datable to the 1st centuries BC and AD. Although trenches *78233* are shallow, it may be suggested that Enclosure 2 at Billingborough falls within this loosely defined group of enclosures with banks or ramparts enhanced by revetments or palisades and perhaps with a gateway in advance of the ditch. Whether it was a settlement or for other purposes cannot be determined.

The ditch (*78135*) defining Enclosure 3 was shallower than that around Enclosure 2 but there is more convincing evidence for settlement within it. Only the eastern edge of Enclosure 3 was exposed in the excavation, but air-photographic evidence shows it to have been sub-rectangular and of similar size of slightly larger than Enclosure 2. A circular cropmark approximately 10m in diameter lies in the centre of Enclosure 3. The most economical interpretation of the circular cropmark is that it represents the 'eaves drip' gully of a roundhouse. It is clear from the small area of Enclosure 3 exposed that it is likely to have contained more features than Enclosure 2. Post-hole *7885* was possibly part of a gateway and a more sophisticated entrance or internal divisions is suggested by gullies *78103* and *78129* which appear to lead in from the gateway and may have held a fence or palisade. There was also a hearth (*7894*) which, it is suggested, lay in the lee of an internal bank.

As the enclosures appear to be broadly contemporary and likely to be associated with the same settlement, the finds from them and associated field ditches (*7710*), may be considered together.

The increasing proportion of residual material amongst the animal bones recovered from Phase 3 contexts makes changes from the preceding phase difficult to detect. The evidence hints that cattle were being raised for both meat and traction, with sheep being kept for both meat and wool, and a stock-based agriculture is likely to have predominated in this area. Although the evidence is ambiguous, there appears to have been a decline in the importance of pigs and this may be obscured by the quantity of redeposited material. At least some of the Iron Age enclosures are likely to have been directly related to stock-rearing and used as either pens or paddocks during the winter months, with ditched droveways allowing the herding of animals between them. Summer grazing may well have been on the fens. Other enclosures may have been fields for arable but in the absence of archaeobotanical data this cannot be proven. Otherwise there is no direct evidence for cultivation other than two unstratified fragments of rotary quern which can only be said to be Iron Age or later in date.

Cat, red and roe deer may have been hunted as much for their fur or skin, teeth or antler, as for their meat. Evidence for fowling, presumably near to extensive wetlands either within the area of peat or the tidal salt marsh, comes from the bones of crane, duck and goose and it is likely that eggs were collected. The single fish bone, of haddock, is from a deep-sea fish but due to the methods of recovery, such remains are certainly under-represented.

The artefacts provide further evidence for craft activities alongside or in the immediate vicinity of the enclosures. A small quantity of iron slag, probably derived from smithing, and the smith's 'poker' (Fig. 14: 1) indicate small-scale iron working. The clay mould (Fig. 36: 13) provides some, albeit slight, evidence for the casting of copper alloy (possibly horse furniture) — perhaps associated with the iron-working activity. The contemporary occurrence of these metalworking activities has been noted at other Iron Age enclosures most notably Gussage All Saints, Dorset (Wainwright 1979; Fell 1988) but comparable evidence also comes from the region at Weelsby Avenue, Humberside (Sills and Kingsley 1990; J. Sills pers. comm.). The range of worked bone and antler objects attest to leather, horn and textile working, although only a single loomweight, of triangular form, has been assigned to this phase and no certain examples of antler or bone weaving combs were found. However, as only a small and perhaps peripheral part of what appears to have been an extensive area of Iron Age activity was investigated, and other crafts could have taken place elsewhere in the vicinity.

There is some evidence for continued salt making in the vicinity from a saltern site identified during the Fenland Project (Hayes and Lane 1992, 20). This was associated with Middle Iron Age pottery and lay approximately 1.5km to the north-north-east of the site at Billingborough, presumably on the edge of the tidal marsh.

A considerable number of human skull fragments, virtually all having been worked, were found and bear directly on the rituals enacted at and around the settlement. All but three of the worked fragments came from Phase 3, Phase 4 and later contexts in the north-east half of the site. The greatest concentration within any feature was four fragments in the top of Phase 3 Enclosure 2 ditch *78113*.

The working of human bone might be thought more characteristic of the later Bronze Age/Early Iron Age (Wilson 1981, 129–30, 152; Wait 1985, 88, 118) and it is possible that all the later material should be regarded as having been redeposited. There is one fragment of human bone from post-hole *77106* assigned to Phase 1 four-post structure C. However, as the best parallel for the working of the skull comes from nearby Helpringham (Bayley 1979; Healey 1999) and is of Middle Iron Age date, it may be that they represent a localised ritual. Although only a small part of the settlement at Billingborough was excavated, the location of the skulls in boundary context contrasts with contemporary finds elsewhere which are frequently in the interior of settlements (Wait 1985, 98–108). The worked bone entirely comprises fragments of skull, some of which have been cut to form 'bowls'. The evidence from the offcuts of human bone suggests this was carried out on site.

Other evidence for explicitly ritual activity is likely to include the burial of a dog in the Enclosure 3 ditch, while a number of the bones of one of the cranes, found close together, recalled the decapitated but otherwise complete crane buried in the enclosure ditch of the Iron Age settlement at Haddenham V, Cambridgeshire (Evans and Serjeantson 1988, 368).

These deposits of people and animals are complemented by the formal, votive deposition of the iron metalworking 'poker' within a shallow recut or pit in the top of the Bronze Age Enclosure 1 ditch (*7710*) which is in keeping with the widespread practice of burying Iron Age metalwork in boundary contexts or liminal contexts (Hingley 1990).

As marshland gradually developed, stabilised and matured along the fen edge during the Iron Age it would have provided an extensive zone of rich grazing potential. In the absence of palaeo-botanical data it is impossible to determine if this was the agricultural basis of the settlement or whether mixed farming was practised, with the fen, wetlands, and, perhaps, the open sea, also being exploited.

If the ascription of the enclosure systems known from air photography to the Iron Age is correct, the comparative lack of late prehistoric pottery from field walking carried out by the Fenland Project (with virtually none from the vicinity of Enclosures 2 and 3 at Billingborough (Hayes and Lane 1992, 233)), may mask what was a both a more intensive and extensive period of renewed settlement along the fen edge than before. The seasonal use of the fens is likely to have increased also. This renewed activity on the fen edge appears to precede the appearance of much more extensive settlements further inland on higher gound, including nearby sites such as Ancaster Gap and Old Sleaford. Old Sleaford is, at present, the most southerly example of such sites (May 1984) and some of the materials found in them such as rouletted pottery and coins are also rare in the south Lincolnshire Fenland. The rarity of Late Iron Age pottery found in the Fenland Survey might indicate a decline in the settlement of the fen edge at this time, but it could also hint that as with much of Late Iron Age Norfolk and Suffolk, the region simply all but stopped making pottery; or at least pottery which survives in the plough soil. By that time, however, Enclosures 2 and 3 at Billingborough appear to have been abandoned. There is no evidence at Billingborough at least to support the suggestion (Lane 1988, 320) of an extended chronology for the Middle Iron Age pottery. Whatever the relationships between inland and fenland Lincolnshire, their histories appear to have diverged quite markedly in the Late Iron Age.

V. Phase 4: Early Romano-British (1st Century AD)
(Fig. 47)

The Iron Age system of enclosures appears to have been succeeded by a field system in the early Roman period. There was little evidence for activity later than the 1st century AD on the site. Apart from a copper alloy bracelet likely to be late Roman, a few stray coin and pottery finds of 3rd/4th-century AD date are recorded from unstratified contexts.

Cropmark evidence (see Fig. 2) suggests that the field system at Billingborough extended further to the west and on a slightly differing alignment to the Phase 3 enclosures, with field boundaries extending out towards the fen edge. This probably reflects a continuing stabilisation of the marsh and development of peat, with subsequent expansion of farming activity onto this newly available area. As in Phase 3, the available evidence would suggest that these fields were for livestock rather than arable use, with sheep perhaps being the major species present which, along with cattle, were raised principally for meat.

The Fenland Project has recorded evidence for three substantial Romano-British settlements in the parish of Billingborough (Hayes and Lane 1992, 20, fig. 10). One lay on the upland in the west of the parish, one at 'Toft Hills' approximately 600m to the north-west of the site at Billingborough, and one on the main roddon (silt-filled former channel) in the fen. Similar distributions of Romano-British sites in these different zones have been recorded in other parishes along the fen edge (*e.g.* Hayes and Lane 1992, fig. 25), with a large number of saltern sites on the boundary of the fen and marsh in areas which were still tidal.

The Roman site at 'Toft Hills' has produced numerous finds including building material, and represents the only putative 'villa' site for at least 10km to the south and east of the area surveyed during the Fenland Project. The field system excavated at Billingborough may have been broadly contemporary and perhaps associated with this site, whatever its status, and perhaps represents part of a general period of expansion and settlement on the fen edge and associated marshland at this time. The Car Dyke, a major, but enigmatic, Roman monument whose function remains uncertain, crosses the area just 300m to the east of the site at Billingborough, with a 27m wide causeway just to the north (Simmons 1979). It seems not to have been dug for drainage nor apparently as a flood defence, in this area at least, but it clearly represents a substantial undertaking in the management of the developing area along the fen edge.

(Written in 1991/1996)

Bibliography

Abbott, Wyman G., 1910 'The discovery of prehistoric pits at Peterborough', *Archaeologia* 62, 333–9

Allen, C.S.M., 1988 *Bronze Age Pottery of the Second Millennium bc in the East Midlands of England*, (Unpubl. PhD thesis, Univ. Nottingham)

Allen, C.S.M., 1991 'Thin sections of Bronze Age pottery from the East Midlands of England' in Middleton, A. and Freestone, I. (eds), *Recent Developments in Ceramic Petrology*, Brit. Museum Occ. Paper 81, 1–15

Allen, C.S.M., Harman, M. and Wheeler, H., 1987 'Bronze Age cremation cemeteries in the East Midlands', *Proc. Prehist. Soc.* 53, 187–221

Annable, F.K. and Simpson, D.D.A., 1964 *Guide Catalogue of the Neolithic and Bronze Age Collections in Devizes Museum*, (Devizes)

Baker, F.T., 1975 'Salt making sites on the Lincolnshire coast before the Romans', in de Brisay, K.W. and Evans, K.A., 1975, 31–2

Barrett, J.C., 1980 'The pottery of the Later Bronze Age in lowland England', *Proc. Prehist. Soc.* 46, 297–319

Barrett, J.C., Bradley, R. and Green, M., 1991 *Landscape, Monuments and Society: The Prehistory of Cranborne Chase*, (Cambridge)

Bayley, J., 1979 *A Skull Fragment from Helpringham*, Ancient Monuments Laboratory Rep. 2847, (London)

Bayley, J., 1980 *Billingborough: Report on the Human Skeletal Material*, Ancient Monuments Laboratory Rep. 3021, (London)

Bayley, J., 1984a *Some Skull Fragments from Billingborough, S. Lincolnshire*, addition to Ancient Monuments Laboratory Rep. 3021 (1980), (London)

Bayley, J., 1984b *A Worked Fragment of Human Skull from Earith, Cambridgeshire*, Ancient Monuments Laboratory Rep. 4260, (London)

Bond, D., 1988 *Excavation at the North Ring, Mucking, Essex*, E. Anglian Archaeol. 43

Bowman, S.G.E., Ambers, J.C. and Leese, M.N. 1990 'Re-evaluation of British Museum radiocarbon dates issued between 1980 and 1984', *Radiocarbon* 32, 59–79

Bradley, R.J., 1975 'Salt and settlement in the Hampshire Sussex borderland' in de Brisay, K.W. and Evans, K.A. 1975, 20–5

Bradley, R.J., Lobb, S., Richards, J. and Robinson, M., 1980 'Two Late Bronze Age settlements on the Kennet gravels: excavations at Aldermaston Wharf and Knight's Farm, Burghfield, Berkshire', *Proc. Prehist. Soc.* 46, 217–96

Brailsford, J., 1949 'Excavations at Little Woodbury: parts IV and V', *Proc. Prehist. Soc.* 15, 156–68

Brewster, T.C.M., 1980 *The Excavation of Garton and Wetwang Slacks*, Nat. Monuments Rec./ E. Riding Archaeol. Res. Comm. Prehist. Excav. Rep.2 [Microfiche only], (London)

Brothwell, D.R., 1972 *Digging up Bones*, (London)

Brown, N., 1988 'A late Bronze Age enclosure at Lofts Farm, Essex', *Proc. Prehist. Soc.* 54, 249–302

Bulleid, A. and Gray, H. St. G., 1917 *The Glastonbury Lake Village, Vol. 2*, (Glastonbury)

Calkin, J.B., 1948 'The Isle of Purbeck in the Iron Age', *Proc. Dorset Natur. Hist. Archaeol. Soc.* 70, 1948 (1949), 29–59

Chowne, P., 1978 'Billingborough Bronze Age settlement: an interim note', *Lincolnshire Hist. Archaeol.* 13, 15–21

Chowne, P., 1980 'Bronze Age settlement in south Lincolnshire' in Barrett, J. and Bradley, R. (eds), *Settlement and Society in the British Later Bronze Age*, Brit. Archaeol. Rep. Brit. Ser. 83, 295–305, (Oxford)

Chowne, P., 1988 *Aspects of Late Prehistoric Settlement in Lincolnshire: A Study of the Western Fen-margin and Bain Valley*, (Unpubl. PhD thesis, Univ. Nottingham)

Chowne, P., 1993 'A note on the pottery dating' in Lane, T.W., *The Fenland Project, No. 8: Lincolnshire Survey, the Northern Fen-Edge*, E. Anglian Archaeol. 66, 97

Chowne, P. and Lane, T., 1987 'Excavations of Bronze Age cremation cemeteries at Old Somerby and Ropsley and Humby, Lincolnshire', *Lincolnshire Hist. Archaeol.* 22, 35–40

Churchill, D.M., 1970 'Post-Neolithic to Romano-British sedimentation in the southern Fenlands of Cambridgeshire and Norfolk' in Phillips, C.W. (ed.), *The Fenland in Roman Times*, Roy. Geog. Soc. Res. Ser. 5, 132–46, (London)

Clark, J.G.D., 1934 'Derivative forms of the petit tranchet in Britain', *Archaeol. J.* 91, 32–58

Clark, J.G.D., 1936 'Report on a Late Bronze Age site in Mildenhall Fen, west Suffolk', *Antiq. J.* 16, 29–50

Clark, J.G.D., Higgs, E.S. and Longworth, I.H., 1960 'Excavations at the Neolithic site at Hurst Fen, Mildenhall, Suffolk (1954, 1957 and 1958)', *Proc. Prehist. Soc.* 26, 202–45

Clay, R.C.C., 1924 'An Early Iron Age site on Fyfield Bavant Down', *Wiltshire Archaeol. Natur. Hist. Mag.* 42, 457–96

Cleal, R.M.J., 1984 'The Late Neolithic in Eastern England' in Bradley, R. and Gardiner, J. (eds), *Neolithic Studies, a Review of some Current Research*, Brit. Archaeol. Rep. Brit. Ser. 133, 135–58, (Oxford)

Cleal, R.M.J., 1985 *The Late Neolithic in Eastern England*, (Unpubl. PhD thesis, Univ. Reading)

Cleal, R.M.J., 1991 'Briquetage' in Cox, P.W. and Hearne, C.M., *Redeemed from the Heath. The Archaeology of the Wytch Farm Oilfield (1987–90)*, Dorset Natur. Hist. Archaeol. Soc. Monog. 9, 143–9, (Dorchester)

Clough, T.H.McK. and Cummins, W.A., 1988 'The petrological identification of stone implements from the East Midlands: third report' in Clough, T.H.McK. and Cummins, W.A. (eds), *Stone Axe Studies: Vol. II*, Counc. Brit. Archaeol. Res. Rep. 67, 45–8, (London)

Clough, T.H.McK. and Green, B., 1972 'The petrological identification of stone implements from East Anglia', *Proc. Prehist. Soc.* 38, 108–55

Coles, J.M., 1987 *Meare Village East: the Excavations of Arthur Bulleid and H. St George Gray 1932–1956*, Somerset Levels Pap. 13, (Exeter)

Coles, J.M., Orme, B.J., May, J. and Moore, C.N., 1979 'Excavations of Late Bronze Age or Iron Age date at Washingborough Fen', *Lincolnshire Hist. Archaeol.* 14, 5–10

Crummy, N., 1983 *The Roman Small Finds from Excavations in Colchester 1971–9*, Colchester Archaeol. Rep. 2, (Colchester)

Cunliffe, B., 1983 *The Publication of Archaeological Excavations. The report of a joint working party of the CBA and the DOE*, (London)

Cunnington, M.E., 1917 'Lidbury Camp', *Wiltshire Archaeol. Natur. Hist. Magazine* 40, 12–36

Cunnington, M.E., 1927 *The Early Iron Age Inhabited site at All Cannings Cross Farm, Wiltshire*, (Devizes)

Curwen, E.C., 1934 'A Late Bronze Age farm and Neolithic pit dwelling at New Barn Down, Clapham, near Worthing', *Sussex Archaeol. Collect.* 74, 153–7

Dacre, M. and Ellison, A., 1981 'A Bronze Age cemetery at Kimpton, Hampshire', *Proc. Prehist. Soc.* 47, 147–203

Davey, P.J., 1973 'Bronze Age metalwork from Lincolnshire', *Archaeologia*, 104, 51–127

de Brisay, K.W., 1975 'The Red Hills of Essex' in de Brisay, K.W. and Evans, K.A. 1975, 1–19

de Brisay, K.W. and Evans, K.A. (eds), 1975 *Salt – The Study of an Ancient Industry*, (Colchester)

Dix, B. and Jackson, D., 1989 'Some Late Iron Age defended enclosures in Northamptonshire' in Gibson, A. (ed.), *Midlands Prehistory*, Brit. Archaeol. Rep. Brit. Ser. 204, 158–79, (Oxford)

Drewett, P., 1982 Late Bronze Age downland economy and excavations at Black Patch, East Sussex', *Proc. Prehist. Soc.* 48, 321–400

Dunning, G.C., 1934 'The swan's neck and ring-headed pin of the Early Iron Age in Britain', *Archaeol. J.* 91, 269–95

Ellison, A.B., 1975 *Pottery and Settlement of the Late Bronze Age in Southern England*, (Unpubl. PhD thesis, Univ. Cambridge)

Ellison, A.B., 1987 'The Bronze Age settlement at Thorny Down: pots, post-holes and patterning', *Proc. Prehist. Soc.* 53, 385–92

Ellison, A.B. and Drewett, P., 1971 'Pits and post-holes in the British Early Iron Age: some alternative explanations', *Proc. Prehist. Soc*, 37, 183–94

Elsdon, S.M., 1979 'Baked clay objects: Iron Age' in Wheeler, H., 'Excavation at Willington, Derbyshire, 1970–1972', *Derbyshire Archaeol. J.* 99, 58–220

Elsdon, S.M., 1982 *A Skeleton Guide to Late Iron Age Pottery in Lincolnshire*, (Nottingham, privately circulated)

Elsdon, S. and May, J., 1987 *The Iron Age Pottery from Dragonby: A Draft Report*, (Univ. Nottingham)

Evans, C. and Serjeantson, D., 1988 'The backwater economy of a fen-edge community in the Iron Age: the Upper Delphs, Haddenham', *Antiquity* 62, 360–70

Farrar, R.A.H., 1975 'Prehistoric and Roman saltworks in Dorset' in de Brisay, K.W. and Evans, K.A. 1975, 14–20

Fell, V., 1988 'Iron Age metalworking tools from Gussage All Saints, Dorset', *Proc. Dorset Natur. Hist. Archaeol. Soc.* 10, 73–6

Feugère, M., 1985, *Les Fibules en Gaule Méridionale de la Conquête à la Fin du Cinquième Siècle après J.-C.,* Revue Archéologique de Narbonnaise Supplément 12, (Paris)

Flügel, E., 1982 *Microfacies Analysis of Limestones*, (Berlin)

Ford, S., Bradley, R., Hawkes, J. and Fisher, P., 1984 'Flint-working in the metal age', *Oxford J. Archaeol.* 31, 157–73

Fowler, P.J., 1960 'Excavations at Madmarston Camp, Swalcliffe, 1957–8', *Oxoniensia* 23, 3–48

French, C.A.I., 1980 'An analysis of molluscs from two second millennium ditches at the Newark Road Subsite, Fengate, Peterborough' in Pryor, F.M.M., *Excavations at Fengate, Peterborough, England: The Third Report*, Northamptonshire Archaeol. Soc. Monog. 1/Roy. Ontario Mus. Archaeol. Monog. 6, 204–212, (Toronto and Northampton)

French. C.A.I., 1984 'An analysis of molluscs from two Iron Age ditches at the Catswater Site, Fengate' in Pryor, F.M.M., *Excavations at Fengate, Peterborough, England: The Fourth Report*, Northamptonshire Archaeol. Soc. Monog. 2/ Roy. Ontario Mus. Archaeol. Monog. 7, Appendix 2, (Toronto and Northampton)

Frere, S., 1975 *Principles of Publication in Rescue Archaeology*, (London)

Getty, R., 1975 *Sisson and Grossman's The Anatomy of the Domestic Animals*, (Philadelphia)

Godwin, H., 1966 'Introductory address', in Sawyer, J.S. (ed.), *Proceedings of the International Symposium on World Climate, 8,000 to O BC*, 3–14, (London)

Godwin, H. and Vishnu-Mittre, 1975 'Flandrian deposits of the Fenland margin at Holme Fen and Whittlesey Mere, Hunts', *Phil. Trans. Roy. Soc. London, B*, 270, 561–608

Goodall, I.H., 1987 'Objects of iron' in Beresford, G., *Goltho: the Development of an Early Medieval Manor c. 850–1150*, Engl. Heritage Archaeol. Rep. 4, 177–87, (London)

Gouletquer, P.L., 1974 'The development of salt making in prehistoric Europe', *Essex J.* 8, 2–14

Grant, A., 1982 'The use of tooth wear as a guide to the age of domestic ungulates' in Wilson, B., Grigson, C. and Payne, S. (eds), *Ageing and Sexing Animal Bones from Archaeological Sites*, Brit. Archaeol. Rep. Brit. Ser. 109, 91–108, (Oxford)

Green, H.S., 1980 *The Flint Arrowheads of the British Isles*, Brit. Archaeol. Rep. Brit. Ser. 33, (Oxford)

Greenwell, W., 1894 'Antiquities of the Bronze Age found in the Heathery Burn Cave, near Stanhope, County Durham', *Archaeologia* 54, 87–114

Gurney, D.A., 1980 'Evidence of Bronze Age salt-production at Northey, Peterborough', *Northamptonshire Archaeol.* 15, 1–11

Halstead, P., 1985 'A study of mandibular teeth from Romano-British sites' in Pryor, F. and French, C.A.I., *The Fenland Project No. 1: Archaeology and Environment in the Lower Welland Valley, Volume 1*, E. Anglian Archaeol. 27, 219–24

Hampton, J.N., 1983 'Some aspects of interpretation and mapping of archaeological evidence from air photography' in Maxwell, G.A. (ed.), *The Impact of Aerial Reconnaissance on Archaeology,* Counc. Brit. Archaeol. Res. Rep. 49, 109–23 (London)

Harding, D,W., 1975 'The pottery' in Jackson, D.A. 1975, 69–94

Hawkes, C.F.C. and Hull, M.R., 1987 *Corpus of Ancient Brooches in Britain. Pre-Roman Bow brooches,* Brit. Archaeol. Rep. Brit. Scr. 168, (Oxford)

Hayes, P.P., 1985 'Relating Fen Edge Sediments, stratigraphy and archaeology near Billingborough, south Lincolnshire' in Fieller, N.R.J., Gilbertson, D.D. and Ralph, N.G.A. (eds), *Palaeoenvironmental Investigations: Research Design, Methods and Data Analysis,* Brit. Archaeol. Rep. Int. Ser. 258, 245–69, (Oxford)

Hayes, P.P. and Lane, T.W., 1992 *The Fenland Project No. 5: Lincolnshire Survey, the South-West Fens,* E. Anglian Archaeol. 55

Healey, R.H., 1969 'Bourne Ware' in Whitwell, J.B. and Wilson, C.M. (eds), 'Archaeological notes 1968', *Lincolnshire Hist. Archaeol.* 4, 108–9

Healey, R.H., 1999 'An Iron Age salt-making site at Helpringham Fen, Lincolnshire (excavations by the Car Dyke Research Group 1972–7)' in Bell, A., Gurney, D.A. and Healey, R.H., *Lincolnshire Salterns: Excavations at Helpringham Fen, Holbeach St John and Bicker Haven,* E. Anglian Archaeol. 89

Healy, F., 1988 *The Anglo-Saxon Cemetery at Spong Hill, North Elmham, Norfolk, Part VI: Occupation During the 7th–2nd Millennia BC,* E. Anglian Archaeol. 39

Healy, F., 1996 *The Fenland Project No. 11: The Wissey Embayment: Evidence of Pre-Iron Age Occupation Accumulated Prior to The Fenland Project,* E. Anglian Archaeol. 78

Hedges, J. and Buckley, D., 1978 'Excavations at a Neolithic causewayed enclosure, Orsett, Essex, 1975', *Proc. Prehist. Soc.* 44, 219–308

Hillam, J., 1989 'Dendrochronology in England: the dating of a wooden causeway from Lincolnshire and a logboat from Humberside' in *Actes du XIIIe Colloque de l'A.F.E.A.F. Le Berry et le Limousin à l'Age du Fér: Artisanat du bois et des matières organiques,* Association pour la Recherche Archaeólogique en Limousin, 137–40, (Guerat)

Hingley, R., 1990, 'Iron Age "currency bars": the social and archaeological context', *Archaeol. J.* 147, 91–117

Hodder, I. and Hedges, J.W., 1977 '"Weaving combs": their typology and distribution with some introductory remarks on date and function' in Collis J.R., (ed.), *The Iron Age in Britain — A Review,* 17–28, (Sheffield)

Holden, E.W., 1972 'A Bronze Age cemetery-barrow on Itford Hill, Beddingham, Sussex', *Sussex Archaeol. Collect.* 110, 70–117

Iles, M., 1992 *A Discussion of the Animal Economy of the Bronze Age to Iron Age site of Billingborough, Lincolnshire,* (Unpubl. undergraduate dissertation, Univ. Southampton)

Jackson, D.A., 1975 'An Iron Age site at Twywell, Northamptonshire', *Northamptonshire Archaeol.* 10, 31–93

Jackson, D.A., 1983 'The excavation of an Iron Age settlement at Brigstock, Northants, 1979–81', *Northamptonshire Archaeol.* 18, 7–32

Jackson, D.A. and Ambrose, T.M., 1978 'Excavations at Wakerley, Northamptonshire', *Britannia* 9, 115–242

Jackson, D.A. and Dix, B., 1986–7 'Late Iron Age and Roman settlement at Weekley, Northamptonshire', *Northamptonshire Archaeol.* 21, 41–93

Jackson, D.A. and Knight, D. 1985 'An Early Iron Age and Beaker site near Gretton, Northamptonshire', *Northamptonshire Archaeol.* 20, 67–86

Jacobi, G., 1974 *Werkzeug und Gerät aus dem Oppidum von Manching,* Die Ausgrabungen in Manching 5, (Weisbaden)

Jelgersma, S., 1966 'Sea level changes during the last 10,000 years' in Sawyer, J.S. (ed.), *Proceedings of the International Symposium on World Climate from 8000 to 0 BC,* 54–71, (London)

Jones, M.U., 1977 'Prehistoric salt equipment from a pit at Mucking, Essex', *Antiq. J.* 57, 317–9

Kent, P.E. and Gaunt, G.D., 1980 *British Regional Geology: Eastern England from the Tees to the Wash,* (London)

King, A., 1978 'A comparative study of bone assemblages from Roman sites in Britain', *Univ. London Inst. Archaeol. Bull.* 15, 207–32

Knight, D., 1984 *Late Bronze Age and Iron Age Settlement in the Nene and Great Ouse Basins,* Brit. Archaeol. Rep. Brit. Ser. 130, (Oxford)

Lane, T.W., 1988 'Pre-Roman origins for settlement on the Fens of south Lincolnshire', *Antiquity* 62, 314–21

Lane, T.W., 1993 *The Fenland Project, No. 8: Lincolnshire Survey, the Northern Fen-Edge,* E. Anglian Archaeol. 66

Lawson, A.J., 1980 'The evidence for Late Bronze Age settlement and burial in Norfolk' in Barrett, J. and Bradley, R. (eds), *Settlement and Society in the British Later Bronze Age,* Brit. Archaeol. Rep. Brit. Ser. 83, 271–94, (Oxford)

Lawson, A.J., 1983 *The Archaeology of Witton, near North Walsham, Norfolk,* E. Anglian Archaeol. 18

Leahy, K., 1986 'A dated stone axe-hammer from Cleethorpes, South Humberside', *Proc. Prehist. Soc.* 52, 143–52

Leahy, K., 1990 'Finds of Bronze Age loomweights and pottery from Swallow', *Lincolnshire Hist. Archaeol.* 25, 48–9

Legge, A.J., 1981 in Mercer, R.J. (ed.), *The Agricultural Economy in Grimes Graves, Norfolk. Excavations 1971–1972, Vol. 1,* Dept. Environ. Archaeol. Rep. 11, (London)

Legge, A.J., 1991 'The animal remains from six sites at Down Farm, Woodcuts' in Barrett, J., Bradley, R. and Hall, M. (eds), *Papers on the Prehistoric Archaeology of Cranborne Chase,* Oxbow Monog. 11, 54–100, (Oxford)

Longley, D., 1980 *Runnymede Bridge 1976: Excavations on the site of a Late Bronze Age Settlement,* Surrey Archaeol. Soc. Res. Vol. 6, (Guildford)

Longworth, I.H., 1981 'Neolithic and Bronze Age Pottery' in Mercer, R.J., *Grimes Graves, Norfolk: Excavations 1971–72: Vol. I,* Dept. Environ. Archaeol. Rep. 11, 39–59, (London)

Longworth, I.H., Ellison, A. and Rigby, V., 1988   *Excavations at Grimes Graves, Norfolk, 1972–1976, Fasicule 2. The Neolithic, Bronze Age and Later Pottery*, (London)

Mackreth, D.F., 1987   'Brooches of bronze and iron' in Cunliffe, B., 1987, *Hengistbury Head, Dorset, Vol. 1. The prehistoric and Roman Settlement 3500 BC–AD 500*, Oxford Univ. Comm. Archaeol. Monog. 13, 142–51, (Oxford)

Mackreth, D.F., 1988   'Excavation of an Iron Age and Roman enclosure at Werrington, Cambridgeshire', *Britannia* 19, 59–151

Manby, T.G., 1980   'Bronze Age settlement in eastern Yorkshire' in Barrett, J. and Bradley, R. (eds), *Settlement and Society in the British Later Bronze Age*, Brit. Archaeol. Rep. Brit. Ser. 83, 307–70, (Oxford)

Marsh, G. and West, B., 1981   'Skullduggery in Roman London?', *Trans. London Middlesex Archaeol. Soc.* 32, 86–102

Matthias, W., 1976   'Die Salzproduktion — ein bedeutender Faktor in der Wirtschaft der frühbronzezeitlichen Bevölkerung an der mittleren Saale', *Jahresschr. Mitteldt. Vorgesch.* 60, 373–94

May, J., 1976   *Prehistoric Lincolnshire*, Hist. Lincolshire 1, (Lincoln)

May, J., 1981   'Report on pottery' in Simpson, W.G., 'Excavations in field OS 124, Maxey, Cambridgeshire', *Northamptonshire Archaeol.* 16, 34–64

May, J., 1984   'The major settlements of the later Iron Age in Lincolnshire' in Field, F.N. and White, A.J. (eds), *A Prospect of Lincolnshire*, 18–22, (Lincoln)

Megaw, J.V.S., Thomas, A.C. and Wailes, B., 1961   'The Bronze Age Settlement at Gwithian, Cornwall', *Proc. West Cornwall Field Club* II, No. 5, 200–15

Miron, A., 1991   'Die späte Eisenzeit im Hunsrück-Nahe-Raum. Mittel-und spätlatènezeitliche Gräberfelder' in Haffner, A. and Miron, A. (eds), *Studien zur Eisenzeit im Hunsrück-Nahe-Raum. Symposium Birkenfeld 1987*, Trierer Zeitschrift Beiheft 13, 151–69, (Trier)

Mook, W.G., 1986   'Business meeting: recommendations/resolutions adopted by the Twelfth International Radiocarbon Conference', *Radiocarbon* 28, 799

Moore, A.W.G. and Williams, J.H. with Boddington, A., 1975   'A later Neolithic site at Ecton, Northamptonshire', *Northamptonshire Archaeol.* 10, 3–30

Muckelroy, K., 1981   'Middle Bronze Age trade between Britain and Europe: a maritime prospective', *Proc. Prehist. Soc.* 47, 275–98

Nan Kivell, R. de C., 1925   'Objects found during excavations on the Romano-British site at Cold Kitchen Hill, Brixton Deverill, 1924', *Wiltshire Archaeol. Natur. Hist. Mag.* 43, 180–91

Ozanne, P.C. and Ozanne, A., 1960   'The pre-barrow occupation' in Alexander, J., Ozanne, P.C. and Ozanne, A., 'Report on the investigation of a round barrow on Arreton Down, Isle of Wight', *Proc. Prehist. Soc.* 26, 276–96

Palmer-Brown, C., 1993   'Bronze Age salt production at Tetney', *Curr. Archaeol.* 136, Vol. 12(4), 143–5

Parker Pearson, M., 1990   'Review of Bond 1988', *Essex Archaeol. Hist.* 21, 156

Parker Pearson, M., 1996   'Food, fertility and front doors in the first millennium BC' in Champion, T.C. and Collis, J.R. (eds), *The Iron Age in Britain and Ireland: Recent Trends*, 117–132, (Sheffield)

Parry, T.W., 1982   'Holes in the skulls of prehistoric man and their significance', *Archaeol. J.* 85, 91–102

Phillips, C.W.B., 1933   'The present state of archaeology in Lincolnshire, part 1', *Archaeol. J.* 90, 106–49

Phillips, C.W.B., 1935   'Neolithic 'A' bowl from near Grantham', *Antiq. J.* 15, 347–8

Piggott, C.M., 1942   'Five Late Bronze Age enclosures in north Wiltshire', *Proc. Prehist. Soc.* 8, 48–61

Piggott, C.M., 1946   'The Late Bronze Age razors of the British Isles', *Proc. Prehist. Soc.* 12, 121–41

Piggott, S., 1972   'A note on climatic deterioration in the first millennium BC in Britain', *Scott. Archaeol. Forum* 4, 109–13

Pitt-Rivers, A.L.F., 1898   *Excavations in Cranborne Chase, Vol. IV*, (privately printed)

Pitts, M.W., 1978   'Towards an understanding of flint industries in post-glacial England', *Univ. London Inst. Archaeol. Bull.* 15, 179–97

Poole, C., 1984   'Briquetage containers' in Cunliffe, B., *Danebury: An Iron Age Hillfort in Hampshire, II, the Excavations 1969–1978: The Finds*, Counc. Brit. Archaeol. Res. Rep. 52, 426–30, (London)

Poole, C., 1987   'Salt working' in Cunliffe, B., *Hengistbury Head, Dorset. Vol. 1: The Prehistoric and Roman Settlement, 3500 BC–AD500*, Oxford Univ. Comm. Archaeol. Monog. 13, 178–80, (Oxford)

Pryor, F.M.M., 1974   *Excavation at Fengate, Peterborough, England: the First Report*, Roy. Ontario Mus. Archaeol. Monog. 3, (Toronto)

Pryor, F.M.M., 1976   'Fen edge land management in the Bronze Age: an interim report on excavations at Fengate, Peterborough 1971–75' in Burgess, C.B. and Miket, R. (eds), *Settlement and Economy in the Third and Second Millennia BC*, Brit. Archaeol. Rep. Brit. Ser. 33, 29–49, (Oxford)

Pryor, F.M.M., 1980   *Excavation at Fengate, Peterborough, England: the Third Report*, Northamptonshire Archaeol. Soc. Monog. 1/Roy. Ontario Mus. Archaeol. Monog. 6, (Northampton and Toronto)

Rice, P.M., 1987   *Pottery Analysis. A Sourcebook*, (Chicago and London)

Riehm, K., 1954   'Vorgeschichtliche Salzgewinnung an Saale und Seille', *Jahresschr. Mitteldt. Vorgesch.* 38, 112–56

Riehm, K., 1960   'Die Formsalzproduktion der vorgeschichtlichen Salzsiedestätten Europas', *Jahresschr. Mitteldt. Vorgesch.* 44, 180–217

Rodwell, W., 1976   'Iron pokers of La Tène II–III', *Archaeol. J.* 133, 43–9

Roe, F., 1966   'The battle-axe series in Britain' *Proc. Prehist. Soc.* 32, 199–245

Roe, F., 1969   *A Study of the Battle-axes, Axe-hammers and Mace-heads from England, Scotland and Wales*, (Unpubl. M.Litt dissertation, Univ. Cambridge)

Roe, F., 1979   'Typology of stone implements with shaft holes' in Clough, T.H.McK. and Cummins, W.A. (eds), *Stone Axe Studies*, Counc. Brit. Archaeol. Res. Rep. 23, 23–48 (London)

Rollo, L., 1988 'The shell-gritted wares' in Mackreth, D., 'Excavation of an Iron Age and Roman enclosure at Werrington, Cambridgeshire', *Britannia*, 19, 107–20

Rye, O.S., 1981 *Pottery Technology. Principles and Reconstruction*, (Washington)

Saunders, C., 1977 'The Iron firedog from Welwyn, Hertfordshire, reconsidered', *Hertfordshire Archaeol.* 5, 13–21

Sellwood, L., 1984 'Objects of bone and antler' in Cunliffe, B., *Danebury: An Iron Age Hillfort in Hampshire, II, the Excavations 1969–1978: The Finds*, Counc. Brit. Archaeol. Res. Rep. 52, 371–95, (London)

Sills, J. and Kingsley, G., 1990 'An Iron Age bronze foundry at Weelsby Avenue, Grimsby', *Lincolnshire Archaeol. Hist.* 25, 49–50

Simmons, B.B., 1979 'The Lincolnshire Car Dyke: navigation or drainage?', *Britannia* 10, 183–96

Smith, I.F., 1965 *Windmill Hill and Avebury: Excavations by Alexander Keiller, 1925–39*, (Oxford)

Smith, I.F., 1974 'The Neolithic' in Renfrew, C. (ed.), *British Prehistory: a New Outline*, 100–36, (London)

Smith, I.F. and Simpson, D.D.A., 1966 'Excavation of a round barrow on Overton Hill, north Wiltshire', *Proc. Prehist. Soc.* 32, 122–55

Smith, K., 1977 'The Excavation of Winklebury Camp, Basingstoke, Hampshire', *Proc. Prehist. Soc.* 43, 31–129

Spratling, M.G., 1979 'The debris of metal working' in Wainwright, G.J., *Gussage All Saints. An Iron Age Settlement in Dorset*, Dept. Environ. Archaeol. Rep. 10, 125–49, (London)

Stead, I.M., 1976 'The earliest burials of the Aylesford culture' in Sieveking, G. de G., Longworth, I.H. and Wilson, K.E. (eds), *Problems in Social and Economic Archaeology*, 401–16, (London)

Stead, I.M., 1979 *The Arras Culture*, (York)

Stead, I.M., 1991 *Iron Age Cemeteries in East Yorkshire: Excavations at Burton Fleming, Rudston, Garton-on-the-Wolds and Kirkburn*, Engl. Heritage Archaeol. Rep. 22, (London)

Stevens, F., 1937 'A horse trapping from Old Sarum near Salisbury', *Antiq. J.* 17, 438–40

Stone, J.F.S., 1936 'An enclosure on Boscombe Down East', *Wiltshire Archaeol. Natur. Hist. Mag.* 47, 466–89

Stone, J.F.S., 1941 'The Deverel-Rimbury settlement on Thorny Down, Winterbourne Gunner, south Wiltshire', *Proc. Prehist. Soc.* 7, 114–33

Stuiver, M. and Pearson, G.W., 1986 'High-precision calibration of the radiocarbon time scale, AD 1950–500 BC', *Radiocarbon* 28, 805–38

Stuiver, M. and Reimer, P.J., 1986 'A computer programme for radiocarbon age calculation', *Radiocarbon* 28, 1022–30.

Swinnerton, H.H., 1932 'The prehistoric pottery sites of the Lincolnshire Coast', *Antiq. J.* 12, 239–53

Swinnerton, H.H. and Kent, P.E., 1976 *The Geology of Lincolnshire from the Humber to the Wash,* 2nd ed., (Lincoln)

Taylor, R.J. and Brailsford, J.W., 1985 'British Iron Age strap-unions', *Proc. Prehist. Soc.* 51, 247–72

Tite, M.S., Bowman, S.G.E., Ambers, J.C. and Matthews, K.J., 1987 'Preliminary statement on an error in British Museum radiocarbon dates (BM–1700 to BM–2315)', *Antiquity* 61, 168

Tomalin, D.J., 1983 *British Biconical Urns: Their Character and Chronology and their Relationship with Indigenous Early Bronze Age Ceramics*, (Unpubl. PhD thesis, Univ. Southampton)

Tomalin, D.J., 1988 'Armorican vases à anses and their occurrence in southern Britain', *Proc. Prehist. Soc.* 54, 203–21

Trotter, M. and Gleser, G.C., 1958 'A re-evaluation of estimation of stature based on measurements of stature taken during life and long-bones after death', *Amer. J. Phys. Anthrop.* 16, 79–123

von den Driesch, A., 1976 *A Guide to the Measurement of Animal Bones from Archaeological Sites*, Peabody Museum Bulletin 1, (Cambridge, Mass.)

Wainwright, G.J., 1979 *Gussage All Saints. An Iron Age Settlement in Dorset*, Dept. Environ. Archaeol. Rep. 10 (London)

Wait, G.A., 1985 *Ritual Religion in Iron Age Britain*, Brit. Archaeol. Rep. Brit. Ser. 149, (Oxford)

Wheeler, R.E.M., 1943 *Maiden Castle, Dorset*, Rep. Res. Comm. Soc. Antiq. London 12, (London)

Wheeler, R.E.M. and Wheeler, T.V., 1936 *Verulamium. A Belgic and Two Roman Cities*, Rep. Res. Comm. Soc. Antiq. London 11, (London)

Willis, E.H., 1961 'Marine transgression sequences in the English Fenland', *Ann. New York Acad. Sci.* 95, 368–76

Wilson, C.E., 1981 'Burials within settlements in southern Britain during the pre-Roman Iron Age', *Univ. London Inst. Archaeol. Bull.* 18, 127–69

Index

Illustrations are denoted by page numbers in *italics*

agriculture
  Phase 1, 92
  Phase 2, 93
  Phase 3, 94
  Phase 4, 95
  see also animal bone
Ancaster Gap (Lincs), 95
animal bone
  analysis, methods of, 79
  butchery, 84, 85
  by phase
    Phase 1, 79-80, 82, 84-5
    Phase 2, 80, 81, 82, 85-6
    Phase 3, 80, 81-3, 86
    Phase 4, 80, 82, 83, 86
  by species
    bird, 84
    cat, 84
    cattle, 83
    deer, 84
    dog, 84
    fish, 84
    fox, 84
    horse, 84
    sheep/goat, 83
antler, worked, 68, *69-70, 72*, 73
archive, 1
arrowheads, flint, 27, *28*, 89
ash deposits
  Phase 1, 12, 14
  Phase 2, 14
awls
  copper alloy, 21, *22*, 23
  iron, *24*
axe-hammer, stone, 29, *30*, 89

banks
  Enclosure 1, 9, 91
  Enclosure 2, 17, 93
beads, jet, 29, *30*, 89
bobbin?, bone, 68, *69*
bodkins *see* needles/bodkins
bone, worked, 68, *69-72*, 73; *see also* animal bone; human bone
bone working waste, 68, *70*
Bourne (Lincs), 92, 93
bowls, human bone, 77, 78, 94
bracelet, copper alloy, 21, *22*, 23, 95
briquetage
  function, 56-7
  by type
    containers
      analysis, methods of, 57; catalogue, 58, *59;* fabric, 57; forms, 57-8
    non-container
      catalogue, 60, *61-5;* categories, 59-60
Bronze Age period
  discussion, 89-92
  excavation, 7-16
brooches
  copper alloy, 21, *22*, 23
  iron, *24*
burial, dog, 95; *see also* inhumations

Car Dyke (Lincs), 1, 95
clay structure, 14
coins, Roman, 23, 95
comb *see* weaving comb handle
copper alloy objects, 21, *22*, 23
copper alloy working, 23, 26, 94
cropmarks, 1, *4*

dagger/dirk, copper alloy, *22*, 23
dating, 5

daub, 25, 91
dirk *see* dagger/dirk
disc, bone, *71*
ditches
  Phase 1, 7, *8*, 9, *10*, 91
  Phase 3
    Enclosure 1, recut, 20
    Enclosures 2 & 3, *17-18*, 19, 93, 94
    field system, *16-17*, 19, 93
  Phase 4, *20*
  see also gullies
droplet, copper alloy, 23, 26
droveways, 93, 94

Earith (Cambs), 78
economy *see* agriculture
enclosures
  Enclosure 1
    discussion, 89-92
    excavation, 7, *8*, 9, *10-11*, 12, *13*, 14
  Enclosure 2
    discussion, 93-4, 95
    excavation, *16-17*, 19
  Enclosure 3
    discussion, 93-4, 95
    excavation, *16-18*, 19
English Heritage, 1
environmental evidence, summarised
  Phase 1, 89-91
  Phase 2, 92
  Phase 3, 93
  see also molluscan analysis
excavation, strategy and methods, 2, *4*

fence lines
  Phase 1, 11, 12, *13*, 91-2
  Phase 3, 94
field systems
  Iron Age, 16, 19, 93
  Romano-British, 20, 95
finger ring, copper alloy, *22*, 23
fired clay, 25-6; *see also* briquetage; clay structure; loomweights; mould; pottery
fitting, copper alloy, *22*, 23
flint, 26-7, *28*, 29
flooding, 88, 91, 92, 93
four-post structures, *11*, 12, *13*, 91
fowling, 94
fuel, 92, 93
funding, 1

geology, 1-2
gouges *see* socketed gouges
Grimsby (S Humb), Weelsby Avenue, 94
gullies
  Phase 1, 12
  Phase 2, 14, *15*, 16, 92
  Phase 3, *16, 17*, 19, 93-4
  Phase 4, 20
see also ditches

Hacconby Fen (Lincs), 91
Haddenham (Cambs), 95
hammer head, stone, 89
harness equipment?, copper alloy, *22*, 23; *see also* mould
head-hunting, 78
hearths
  Phase 2, 14, *15*, 92
  Phase 3, 19, 94
hedges, 7, 91
Helpringham (Lincs), 78, 94
Hoe Hills (Lincs), 89
Horbling Fen (Lincs), 89, 91
horn cores, 68, *70, 72*, 73, 94
human bone

inhumations, 73
skull fragments
    catalogue, 73, *74-7*
    description, 77
    discussion, 78, 94
hunting, 94

inhumations, *7*, 73, 89
Iron Age period
    discussion, 92-5
    excavation, 14-20
iron objects, 23, *24*
iron working, 25, 94
ironstone, 25

jet objects, 29, *30*

leather working, 68, 92, 94
location, *3*
loomweights, *66-7*, 92, 94

mace head, 89
metatarsal, notched, 68, *69*
molluscan analysis, 86-8
mould, clay, 26, *67*, 94

needles/bodkins, bone, 68, *69-71*
Neolithic period, 7, 89

Old Sleaford (Lincs), 95
oven flooring, 60, *62*

phasing, 5
picks, antler, 68, *69*, *72*, 73
pins, bone, 68, *69-71*
pits
    Phase 1, 12, 14
    Phase 2, 14, 92
plough damage, 5, 16, 91
points, bone, 68, *69-71*
poker, iron, 23, *24-5*, 94, 95
post-excavation analysis, 1
post-holes
    Phase 1, 11, *12*, 91-2
    Phase 2, 16
    Phase 3, 17, 19, 93, 94
pottery
    fabric analysis, 45-7
    methods, 31
    quantification, 31
    residues, 37
    by period
        Neolithic, 31, *47*
        Early Bronze Age, 31-2, *47*
        Middle Bronze Age

catalogue, 47, *48-50*, 51, *52*; description, 32-8; discussion, 38-40
Late Bronze Age/Early Iron Age
    catalogue, 51, *52;*description, 40; discussion, 40-2
Middle–Late Iron Age
    catalogue, 51-2, *53-5*, 56; description, 42; discussion, 42-5
Romano-British, 45, 56
medieval, 56
post-medieval, 56
see also briquetage
projectile point, iron, *24*

quarry, flint, 14, 26
quern fragments, 30, 94

radiocarbon dates, 5
razor/knife, copper alloy, 21, *22*, 23
recording, 2
ridge-and-furrow, medieval, 5; *see also* plough damage
rod, copper alloy, 21, *22*, 23
Romano-British period, 20, 95
round barrows, 89
roundhouse, 19, 94
rubber, 30

salt production, 14, 56-7, 92-3, 94
sampling, 2, 86
seasonality, 93, 95
sheet, copper alloy, 26
Simmons, B.B., 1
slag, 25, 94
socketed gouges, bone, 68, *69-71*
spear, iron, *24*
structures
    Phase 1, *8*, 9, *11*, 12, *13*, 14, 91-2
    Phase 2, *15*, 16, 92
    see also clay structure; four-post structures; roundhouse
sunken feature, 12, *13*

Tetney (Lincs), 93
textile working, 68, 92, 94; *see also* loomweights
Toft Hills (Lincs), 95
toggle, bone, 68, *71*
topography, 1-2
tree-hole, 12
tuyère hole, 25

villa, Romano-British, 95
votive deposits, 20, 24, *25*, 95

weaving comb handle?, 68, *70*
Weekley (Northants), 94

X-ray fluorescence analyis, 26